PRAISE FOR *SYNC*

"Awaken your innate and ancient abilit[y] [pat]terns in your life and surroundings and u[... ...] Kirby Surprise. The author lucidly explains how our brains are, in fact, predicated on this ability to detect patterns out of the morass of sensory stimuli we take in at any given moment. Not only can we detect these synchronistic events around us, but we should. Even more, we can directly participate in the manifestation of synchronistic phenomena through vigilance and focused attention. The author beckons us to change our reality by changing our relationship to synchronicity and offers practical guidelines—and even a set of seven games—to put synchronicity to work in your life. You'll find this an entertaining, edifying, and engaging read. Read on!"

—Dale Harrison, PhD, Elon University, member of the 2010 Yale University Synchronicity Summit

"A true thriller from cover to cover—Kirby Surprise proves that there really is nothing more fascinating and mysterious than the human mind."

—Linda Watanabe McFerrin, author of *The Hand of Buddha* and *Dead Love*

"Dr. Surprise is at once psychologist, bard, modern shaman, and cartographer, offering anyone who reads this book an empowering new perspective on our own awesome power of creation."

—Lori A Jespersen, PsyD, author of *From This Day On*

"Once the butt of jokes and derision, the concept of synchronicity is now a topic that is being taken seriously. Quantum physics, chaos and complexity theory, and on-local phenomena have found this arcane perspective to be a surprising contemporary framework from which to understand many puzzles of the cosmos and of humanity's place in it. Kirby Surprise has provided his readers with an original revision of synchronicity that may well take his readers by surprise!"

—Stanley Krippner, PhD, professor of Psychology, Saybrook University, and coauthor of *Personal Mythology*

Synchronicity

The Art of Coincidence, Choice, and Unlocking Your Mind

By
Dr. Kirby Surprise

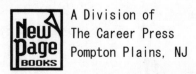

A Division of
The Career Press
Pompton Plains, NJ

SYNCHRONICITY
EDITED AND TYPESET BY NICOLE DeFELICE
Cover design by Lucia Rossman, Digi Dog Design
Printed in the U.S.A.

To order this title, please call toll-free 1-800-CAREER-1 (NJ and Canada: 201-848-0310) to order using VISA or MasterCard, or for further information on books from Career Press.

The Career Press, Inc.
220 West Parkway, Unit 12
Pompton Plains, NJ 07444
www.careerpress.com
www.newpagebooks.com

Library of Congress Cataloging-in-Publication Data
Surprise, Kirby.
  Synchronicity : the art of coincidence, choice, and unlocking your mind / Kirby Surprise ; [foreword by] Allan Combs. --
1
        p. cm.
  Summary: "Synchronicity examines the evidence for the human influence on the meaningfulness of events, and the way
the modern computational model of the mind predicts how we create meaning. It demonstrates that these events, based
on the activity of the mind, are caused by the person who perceives them"-- Provided by publisher.
  Includes bibliographical references and index.
  ISBN 978-1-60163-183-1 (pbk.) -- ISBN 978-1-60163-643-0 (ebook) 1. Coincidence. 2. Coincidence--Psychic aspects. I.
Title.

  BF175.5.C65S87 2011
  153.4--dc23

                                                                                2011037687

Dedication

This book is dedicated to Allan Combs. Allan is that rare person who makes his students reach for what is possible. An extraordinary educator, he also demonstrated a deep humanity, sincerity, and kindness in his willingness to help bring this book into reality. Above all, his encouragement and generosity of spirit have been a guiding light during the creation of this work.

I would also like to thank Linda Watanabe McFerrin, writing teacher extraordinaire. Her wisdom as a writing coach made this book possible. She possesses the rare gift of understanding how to foster a writer's talents, while gently explaining with razor wit what he needs to do to create marketable work. Her patience, skill, and understanding of the art of writing and business of publishing were invaluable.

Contents

Foreword

Synchronicity refers to those random yet seemingly meaningful coincidences that enrich our lives, sometimes to our amazement, sometimes to our distress, and sometimes to our delight. At such times, it seems that the cosmos has orchestrated this or that event just for our own private viewing. In that moment, we seem irrevocably embraced by a universe much larger than ourselves. Whether this synchronistic event is trivial or profound, it is in this instant personal, enigmatically meaningful, and cosmic.

Perhaps it is not surprising that people have been searching for the deeper meaning of their relationship to the world around them since the beginnings of time. Among the most ancient relics of ancient Chinese civilization, dating back more than 5,000 years, are the bones of sheep, boar, deer, as well as the shells of tortoises, fired

9

to create seemingly random patterns of cracks in their surfaces thought to augur the shapes of future events. Much later, Chinese Taoists would create a simple and profound method of sensing this larger shape of reality through the tossing of a set of small yarrow sticks and, using the book of interpretations titled *The I Ching* or *Book of Changes*, interpreting the patterns in which they fall. The idea here is that each event that surrounds us, especially those that might seem random, reflect the greater reality in which we live.

One is reminded of the Taoist story of the rainmaker, brought to a village in hopes of ending a serious drought. To the amazement of the local people he did nothing at all except move into his new home and begin to live quietly there. Eventually, though, it began to rain! When folks asked the rainmaker his method, he said that when he arrived at the village he immediately sensed a lack of harmony, so he settled in and began to live a peaceful and balanced life. Eventually his own harmony began to spread, and since rain is part of the natural harmonious order of things it soon began to rain.

The West has few traditions as unitive as Taoism, but many people have sensed this greater oneness and become aware of its presence. The use of the Tarot deck reflects this awareness. It is a counterpart of the Eastern yarrow sticks.

Long before the *I Ching* or the Tarot deck, however, the mythologies of virtually all primary cultures included figures who toy mischievously with the stings of human fate. Some of these are well developed into complex characters who play their roles in equally complex mythic systems, while others are simple and straightforward. Some are friendly and some are not. Examples include the Native American coyote, Anansi the West African and Caribbean trickster spider, Japanese fox spirit tricksters, and Br'er Rabbit from the southern United States. All of them are troublemakers! But in the larger picture, they also benefit their cultures by stirring things up and forcing people to seek new and creative ways of coping with them.[1]

One of the most highly developed tricksters in the West was the Greek god Hermes, said to be the friendliest of gods to men. Honored as an Olympian, he played many roles. He was the messenger of Zeus, and lord of transitions of all kinds. For example, he appears in the *Iliad* to guide unseen the old king Priam through the battle lines to retrieve the corpse of his dead son, Hector. In the *Odyssey*, he helps Odysseus (Ulysses) make his way safely cross the island of Aeaea to rescue this crew, all changed to pigs by the witch Circe. In similar fashion he plays the role of psychopomp, a guide to dying souls to their destination in the underworld.

It was not until modern times that systematic efforts were made to understand coincidences from objective and even scientific perspectives. Some of the most thorough of such investigations were carried out nearly a century ago by the brilliant and eccentric Austrian biologist, Paul Kammerer. His formulation of *The Law of Seriality* dealt with repetitions in time and space of events, facts, numbers, and names. In pursuit of such sequences, he spent hours in public places watching people pass by, noting the incidences of particular hats, articles of clothing, parcels, and so on. He analyzed these in detail, categorizing them into first, second, third, and higher order series. Additionally, he developed a complex classification system that emphasized structural relationships in each coincidence: homologous, analogous, and so on. In 1971, the brilliant European author, Arthur Koestler,[2] recounted one of his stories, still not translated directly into English.

A certain M. Deschamps, when a little boy in Orléans, was given by M. de Fortgibu, a visitor to his parents, a piece of plum pudding which made an unforgettable impression on him. As a young man, years later, dining in a Paris restaurant, he saw plum pudding written on the menu and promptly ordered it. But it was too late, the last portion had just been consumed by a gentleman whom the waiter discretely pointed out—M. de Fortgibu, whom Descamps had never seen again since that first meeting. More years passed and M. Deschamps was invited to a dinner party where the hostess had promised to prepare that rare dessert, a plum pudding. At the dinner table M. Deschamps told his little story, remarking, 'All we need now for perfect contentment is M. de Fortgibu'. At that moment the door opened and a very old, frail and distraught

gentlemen entered, bursting into bewildered apologies: M. de
Fortgibu had been invited to another dinner party and came
to the wrong address.[3]

Carl Jung was the first modern theorist to explore the meaning of
coincidences in terms of the inner psychological lives of the persons who
experience them. He officially introduced the term *synchronicity* in 1952
through a small book titled *Synchronicity: An Acausal Connecting Principle*,[4] though he had introduced the term earlier in his Introduction to
Richard Wilhelm's translation of the *I Ching*. Jung felt that the fall of
the yarrow sticks, and thus the reading given by the *I Ching*, is an example of synchronicity itself, and reflects the relationship of the larger field
of action in which the reader finds him- or herself to the inner dynamics
of their own deeply unconscious processes. His ideas were developed, in
part, through his friendship with the quantum physicist Wolfgang Pauli,
whose own life was a veritable torrent of uncanny coincidences.[5]

Modern interpreters of synchronicity often take their cue from
Jung's classic work, but do not restricted themselves to his theory of the
unconscious. Others have taken metaphysical or even spiritual views of
synchronicity, a few even claiming that you can control or even create
the seemingly coincidental events of day-to-day reality by making the
correct mental adjustments. Most readers who come to this book will
have already given some thought to such ideas.

I will say no more here, but if you are looking for answers to the
profound enigma of the meaning and nature of meaningful coincidences
in your own life, answers that bring psychological insight and spiritual
understanding, then you have come to the right place. Professor Surprise
has given us the finest book of its kind: a clear and delightfully readable
account of the nature of chance in the lives of ordinary people; and he
has flavored his offering with a perfect sauce of delicious examples.

—Allan Combs, coauthor with Mark Holland of *Synchronicity:
Though the Eyes of Science, Myth, and the Trickster*

One

You Have an Amazing Ability

"Nothing determines who we will become so much as those things we choose to ignore." —Sandor McNab

Synchronistic Event

One cool autumn day I was sitting in my car waiting to pick up a friend. I was listening to the radio to pass the time. During a commercial break an ad for the movie *Carrie* was played. The movie is about a teenager who discovers she has the ability to move objects at a distance. I started having fantasies about what it would actually be like to experience moving an object this way. I had seen the film; during its climax, Carrie uses her power to crush her family's home. I looked across the street and saw an old cottage. Focusing on the house, I fantasized about what being able to move an object that large would be like. I was remembering a *National Inquirer* headline about a house that supposedly was turned over on its side by some psychic force. I was wondering what effect such a power would have on a person, how it might feel to move a house. As I stared at the house the entire cottage shuddered violently. The house started to move. It rolled over onto its side. The roof was now facing me. I was astonished and felt panicky. I stared at the overturned house and wondered, could I have really done this? I wondered if this was just a vivid dream. I decided I was awake and the event was real.

"OK," I said to myself. "If I just did that, then I want to see the house crushed like in the movie."

As I stared, awestruck, the house again began to shudder. The roof started to collapse inward as if the center of the house were slowly imploding. Beams burst through walls and windows shattered as the house began to tear itself apart. A moment later, I saw a flash of yellow paint above the house, then the largest bulldozer I'd ever seen climbed lazily over the center of the house, crushing the structure into rubble in a few moments. It then started to load the debris into waiting dump trucks. The house had obscured the demolition equipment from sight. With the radio on and windows up, I couldn't hear the tractor engine. My fantasy had come to pass, my wish fulfilled through a series of synchronistic events.

You already have the ability to create SE

You have an amazing ability. Your thoughts and feelings, your memories and experiences, are reproduced in the events around you as coincidences. It's not only you with this ability, its everyone. We all live in a reality in which our thoughts and emotions are mirrored back to us as synchronistic events.

This is not some world of science fiction or fantasy, its the real world around you, at this very moment. This seemingly magical ability goes largely unnoticed, unexplained, and misunderstood. This ability is real. Its not magic, but is the core of most myths about magic. This book is about getting oriented to powers you already use.

Synchronistic events (SEs for short), happen when your inner and outer worlds seem to mirror each other. When I first began seeing SEs in the world around me, I wondered if they were real. I had no frame of reference for suddenly being in the midst of daily SEs that centered around my own thoughts and experiences. As a child, I had heard of a few historical SEs such as those surrounding the Lincoln and Kennedy assassinations. One had been shot in a theatre and the assassin caught in a warehouse. The other shot from a warehouse and the assassin caught in a theatre. Lincoln had a secretary named Kennedy. Kennedy had a secretary named Lincoln. Occasionally other urban legends of coincidence would make the rounds. I heard various conspiracy theories, some about secret societies such as the Masons or the Illuminati, or secret government agencies. Some were good science fiction. Some were just paranoid. But these SEs were about the larger society in general. There was never mention of the possibility that events could seem to center around anyone we knew, no less us personally. Certainly, as children, we were never told that our own thoughts could cause events in the world—or were we?

Break a mirror and get seven years bad luck. Step on a crack, break your mother's back. Don't open an umbrella in the house. Its bad luck to walk under a ladder. Wish on the first star you see in the evening. Throw salt over your shoulder to prevent bad luck. We have all heard a host of superstitions passed from generation to generation by fairy tale and oral history. Every culture has its own do's and don'ts that may bring good or bad luck. Aren't these messages that our thoughts and actions have an effect on events in the environment? By the time I was five or so, my parents were dutifully trying to help me grow past magical thinking. The school system was teaching us the science. I was told these beliefs were just superstitions based on ignorance and fear, in this material world all things had causes and effects. Magic and superstition were the foolishness of the ignorant. Then on Sundays we went to church. I watched priests perform rituals that somehow influenced supernatural forces, causing them to intercede on behalf of parishioners. I heard miraculous stories about how prayers changed the events of people's lives. It was a confusing time to be a child. We were told that miracles can happen, small ones at least. It was just that we personally were not allowed to perform them. The nagging feeling persists for many of us that there is some way, spiritual, perhaps magical, to have events shift the odds in our favor. The odds can be shifted in our favor, and the ability is innate to each one of us. This ability to create SEs is built into our nature. It's not a supernatural, but completely natural ability. There is no religion to buy into. No teacher to follow. No training to endure. You're doing it right now. This book is just a user's manual, and hopefully a good story.

SE tends to defy the way we usually think about cause and effect. In the SE of the moving house, there was a connection between the observer and the event, but finding the cause seems impossible. The house moved, but there was no physical force exerted by the observer. Radio commercials, memories, and patterns of thought and physical events became coordinated, but there was no obvious force doing so. Yet there is a pattern evident in the events. People have always reported seeing SEs. They are the basis for many superstitions and religious beliefs. Let's take an imaginary journey to explore why SEs are an innate part of human experience.

SE EVOLVED AS A NATURAL ABILITY

Imagine you are one of our ancient ancestors. You are standing on the edge of the African savanna 50,000 years ago. You are physically a modern human. By this time, our ancestors had stopped evolving, having perfected their particular survival strategy. Physically, we were weak creatures; under five feet tall, about 100 pounds, no claws, teeth practically useless as weapons. We are almost blind in the dark, with a poor sense of smell. We do one thing better than any other creature. We recognize patterns. We sacrificed much to support a larger brain. Neural tissue is expensive. It consumes up to four times the glucose and oxygen of muscle, and needs complex specialized biological systems to be maintained. Our brains need a lot of protein, making hunting a requirement. Our young have to be born underdeveloped so the birth canal can accommodate our head size. If we had a body that matched the relative brain size of other mammals, we would tip the scales at around 2,000 pounds. This increased brain size allows us to process information faster and with more flexability. This has allowed us to become so adaptable that further physical evolution became unnecessary perhaps as long as 20,000 years ago. We evolved a superb ability to not only remember vast amounts of information, but to process and match patterns in a complex, changing, and uncertain environment.

So, there you are, a relatively small mammal standing in the savanna with the grass up to your waist. The grass waves in windblown patterns as patches of clouds pass across it. In places, the grass is lit by bright sunlight, in others, it is covered in shadow. A plush carpet of moving patterns and shapes spreads out before you to the distant horizon. You are naked. You have a stick topped with a razor-sharp flint spearhead, and you're hungry. You know that somewhere out in the grass are animals that will provide you and yours with the necessities of survival. Also hidden in the grass are predators that would be happy to feed you to their families. Both predator and prey here have adaptations that allow them to hide and hunt in the grass. Even if you can clearly see an antelope in the distance, getting to it is dangerous. There are other predators around the herds stalking the same prey. Your task, using that costly brain, is to look for patterns in the motion, texture, and contrasts of the grasslands around you. You must match from memory and experience which patterns mean food, and which mean death. Is that a line of motion that could mean a lion parting the grass as it stalks? Is it the wind moving the grass near a stream hidden by the ground cover? Is that dark spot on the brown color of the grass there because there is more water there, or is there a deer lying down in the grass? How is one to decide?

The computational model of the mind

Computer science calls these kinds of pattern-matching problems exercises in fuzzy logic. The problems our hunting ancestor faced in pattern-matching are unsolvable with modern computers. The amount of information is too large. The problems too complex for computers to make such decisions. These real-life problems are too complex for even our superbly evolved brains to solve with certainty. By the time our on-board bio-computer could be sure about the patterns we are looking at, the food would have moved on, or we would be lunch. Computers have a hard time dealing with maybe. Evolution came up with an answer for this problem; it developed a highly specialized area of the brain whose job is to "guess." That area, about the size of a walnut, on the frontal lobe of the brain, is you. It is the area that can refer to "me" and "I." It can place itself in a mental model of the world around it. Your senses, memory, emotions, and motor control systems are all processed by other areas of the brain. The information is piped forward on massive bundles of data-conducting neurons, to you. You live in a universe your brain creates for you. You are the self-aware decision-making area. You are the executive ego.

Here is your situation: Imagine you are sitting on top of a wall. In front of you is the savanna, the outside world you need to survive in. This outer world stretches far beyond any of your senses. Even what your senses report is far too complex to experience in its entirety. In back of the wall, behind you, is your personal inner world. This is the brain and the mind that arises from it. Your inner world also stretches far beyond your ability to perceive. It is also too complex to understand in its entirety. Your job is to listen to the demands of the inner world, take all the information it gives you, and use it to get what you need from the outside world. You, the executive ego, are the part that decides when the patterns in the grass look enough like a deer to warrant taking the chance of running up to it and throwing your spear. Or when the pattern means it might be a lion and it's time to hunt somewhere else.

You are the part that decides what the patterns mean. In every task of life, we take our best guess with incomplete information. You match the experiences in your memory with the patterns of the outside world. You assign a meaning to those patterns and gamble that your guess is correct. You look for patterns and decide what they mean to you and your needs. Guess correctly enough of the time, and you get the chance to pass your genes on to the next generation.

Your mind does more than match patterns and assign meaning. It looks for the way patterns behave over time. Your mind plans and imagines what it wants to find in the future, decides what patterns it wants to look for. It looks for patterns that allow it to predict future events. As our ancestral hunter, you would have studied the pattern of the seasons. You would know the patterns of migration the other animals used throughout the year. This allowed you to predict where game would be during what season, or time of day. You would have learned their patterns of escape and evasion, then predict what hunting pattern would most likely end in success. There are some problems inherent in assigning meanings to patterns of events. We are always working with incomplete information. In the mental shorthand we experience much is deleted or lost in translation. Much is added from memory to make up for information that is unavailable. Many of our experiences are ignored because they are too cumbersome to process. There will be more on these additions and subtractions in later chapters. We rarely understand the ultimate causes of the events we are trying to out-guess. Philosophy is a luxury if you're hungry.

SE AS A NATURAL ADVANTAGE

There is an old joke about two vultures sitting in a tree. One turns to the other and says, "To hell with patience, I'm going to kill something!" Our ancestral hunter had the same basic brain and processing power we do. I imagine they got tired of trying to figure out how the environment was going to behave. Our ancestral gamblers would have had a strong desire to "stack the deck" in their favor with any possible advantage.

In the caves of Les Trois Freres, France, are some of the world's oldest cave paintings. One of the images is a shaman wearing a stag mask. This is probably a depiction of a magical rite. The tribe hoped the shaman could, by his imitation of the prey, make the stag appear during the hunt. These people were probably as intelligent as we are. They lived and died by their wits. So why were they dancing around with animal masks? Because they had noticed a connection between the events of the hunt and their internal experiences. They were aware of SE, and like a gambler trying to better his odds, tried to exploit the patterns they saw as best they could.

When a group of stag turned into the hunter's path each time the shaman danced like one, it was an SE. They wanted to make it happen on purpose. Superstition is sometimes created when people try to capitalize on SE. The shaman saw the stags show up when he danced like one of them, so he hopes that they will do it every time. The problem is the stags don't always show up no matter what the dancer does. Many a hapless shaman has been done in by his fellow tribesmen when the promised game did not appear. Having the game appear out of the complex patterns of events is a hit and miss proposition at best. As we shall see in the next chapter, the human effect on events can be scientifically measured. It is usually a few percentage points.

We influence reality, we don't create it

If we did, nobody would be poor, sick, or have to pay taxes. Yet, every culture has its magical thinking around hunting, weather, and fertility. Why then, if the human influence can only tip the scales a few percentage points by changing SE, does so much of "primitive" culture center around SEs? The answer lies in evolution.

Darwin and evolution have stood the test of time. Evolution works. Evolution shows that even a slight advantage over the course of generations means the difference between who passes their traits on to the next generations and who's genetic patterns wind up in the dust-bin of evolutionary history. We have developed the way we think and match patterns because it gives us an evolutionary edge. We use SE the same way.

Your natural adaptive specialty is to look for any pattern that gives you an advantage. You are looking for information. You are looking for meaning. We perform dizzying feats of mental computation when we do something as simple as recognize an object as separate from its background.

We can name it, apply classifications to it, and consider not only what it can be used for, but what it means that the object is where it is, when it is. We can give both objects and events context that can be used to predict other events. Just looking around a room, or across a savanna, we perform calculations computer theorists currently consider impossible. Yet we find doing relatively simple tasks like adding eight 10-digit numbers in our heads impossible. Why? Evolution doesn't keep what it doesn't use. There was no survival advantage for our hunting ancestors to be able to add 10-digit numbers, or rarely even count to 10. The problem never needed to be solved, so the brain did not develop that specialization. Your brain can do the staggering math needed to chase an antelope across the plain, estimating the animal's own mental processes, predict its actions, and coordinate hundreds of muscles at once to throw a spear and hit a moving target. Its not magic, its processing power. Every function is needed. None are extra.

MAGIC IS NOT MAGICAL

SEs are not just accidents of interpretation. We evolved to perceive SEs because there are advantages to being able to match patterns in this way. Let's consider the "magical" viewpoint. Our ancestral hunters manipulated their internal experiences through rituals and symbols, like dancing in a stag mask. The inner world influences the events of the outer world. Our hunting ancestors tried to use SE to increase their chances of survival. They tried to forge a cause and effect relationship between their own inner states and what they wanted from the outside world. The hope was "If I dance like this, think these thoughts, feel these feelings, game will appear." This was a straight-forward attempt to change events in the environment in their favor. Our hunter was probably carrying charms, magical decorations, even scarifications and body modifications as reminders of his intent. These were sophisticated adults. They knew no magic yields a certainty of desired outcome. They were looking for those few percentage points that would tip the odds in their favor. If influencing events were possible, even if the effect were slight, it would give an evolutionary advantage to those creatures who used it as part of their strategy. If it is possible to influence events by modifying internal states, you can bet that some organisms would evolve ways to do it. I believe that is exactly what we did. We used a slight advantage over thousands of generations and developed a natural ability to discern and create SEs.

Almost as valuable as making game appear during a hunt, would be knowing ahead of time where they would show up. Knowing the future is almost as profitable as creating it. "Primitive" cultures are superstitious. They look for signs and portents of the future in the events around them. Every culture has developed systems of divination that are used to predict and advise on future events. We are pattern-matchers, and that is what divination does. It looks for SE in the patterns of entrails, tea leaves, and the cracks in tortoise shells. More sophisticated systems have complete lexicons of symbolic meanings. These include Tarot cards, astrological systems, runes, and the patterns in passages of poetry selected by coin and stick tosses, such as those in the *I Ching*. Our ancestral hunter probably did not have much in the way of set symbolic metaphors by which to predict events, but they did have their experience of the world itself. Consider our small, pattern-matching ancestors on the edge of the grasslands again. Their brains have the same processing power our modern minds have, so what are they doing with all that miraculous brain power? It is easy to imagine them looking for learned patterns of color and motion to make their best guess about what lives in the grass. It's easy to imagine they see patterns and read meanings we would not because we lack their experience. If you read accounts of "primitive" indigenous hunters who have not had the advantage of being westernized, you find another layer of pattern-matching. They are reading all the events in their environment, looking for meanings conveyed by the metaphoric or symbolic content of the events. They look for images in the clouds, pictures in the patterns of the moving grass. The appearance of a particular bird, at a particular moment while they were having a particular thought, can constitute a message about where the game is, or what path they should take. The spirits, whichever spirits they believe in, speak to them through the events around them. They read the meanings of SE in the world as a source of nuanced information, not certainty, but another pattern to be matched and probability to be considered. Rather than being child-like, magical thinkers, they were processing complex metaphors and correlations of meaning to derive relevant survival information.

BRINGING SE BACK INTO THE MODERN WORLD

Synchronistic Event

A man wakes up on the morning of his 55th birthday. He notices it is 5:55. He takes 55 minutes to eat and dress, then turns on the T.V. and finds it on channel five. The date is May 5th. He leaves his fifth floor apartment, gets on the number five bus, and travels five miles to work. He takes the fifth elevator to the fifth floor of his office at 555 Fifth Street. He notices there are five people on the elevator with him. He gets off and goes to the fifth door on the left to his office. Being a bright person, he notices all the co-incidental events involving the number five. He starts to wonder how he might take advantage of them. On his desk he finds a racing form someone has left. He turns to the fifth page, and finds that the fifth horse in the fifth race is named "Your Lucky Fives." He figures this must be a message, a sure fire way to make some money, so he calls the local bookie and places $5,000 on the race. He calls back at 5 p.m., and asks how his horse did. The bookie replies, "He came in fifth!"

Our gambler saw a real pattern of SE, but he mistook the pattern of *meaning* for a pattern of *causation*. Let's look at the SE of this story with the synchronicity as mirror idea in mind. The protagonist had his 55th birthday on his mind. It was a concern, and for a short time the events around him patterned off that concern. Possibly he was feeling he had not accomplished enough in the world and was seeking a way to feel more secure and validated, looking for a chance to feel special and empowered. The sequence of SE provided all of this, as well as the opportunity to consciously experience the disappointment he was feeling about his current life situation. The SEs mirrored his internal processes, and caused him to re-experience his internal world in the context of the outer world.

Houses roll for people all the time. Events reflect the patterns of our processing. It is our modern gambler who thought of the events in a simplistic and naive way. Had he been our primitive hunter, he would have taken the events under advisement. SE would have been one more pattern to add to the calculations he was making, instead of taking them as hard facts to be acted on. After all, that would be thinking and acting like a child.

Sometimes we create patterns of SE that are passed down through generations. Say an owl, normally nocturnal, gets chased out of its nest in the daytime by some other animal. The confused bird then happens to fly through a nearby village. Several locals see this unusual behavior. Shortly after this, someone suffers some misfortune. Presto, a superstition is born as the villagers start to expect misfortune to happen every time an owl is seen in daylight from then on. The original meaning of the omen is created by the initial observers, then passed on as myth to others, who in turn create more SEs with that pattern through their expectations. The synchronistic event occurs, but its meaning is created by the people who participate in it.

Some SEs and some superstitions, no doubt are created when the patterns of two events become randomly associated. The Greeks believed it was possible to produce rain by beating special rocks with wet tree branches. This actually works. If you beat a rock with a wet tree branch long enough, it will rain. It may take days, weeks, or even months, but eventually it will rain. When the rain comes, it may have synchronistic meaning, but the meaning lies in the person's inner experience. Beating the rock did not magically make it rain. It is unfortunate that the focus of attention on SEs is usually on the external events, rather than on the personal meaning of the experiencer. Its like looking for the cause of the reflection in a mirror by examining the mirror. I believe that such seemingly superstitious behaviors deserve our respect. Even if somewhat misdirected, these represent the earliest attempts to figure out how the universe worked. People back then did what scientists do now: look for insights into the patterns of nature in the hopes of improving the quality of life. Such were the beginnings of experimental science, and people who attempted to use SE were working within the limits of their understanding of the universe. Physicists 1,000 years from now will probably see us in much the same way; we did our best considering the limitations of what we had to work with. The science of today will likely become the superstition and mythology of the future.

EVIDENCE AND EXISTENTIAL ANXIETY

We have no lack of SEs in our modern era. We do have considerably more anxiety about them than in times past. Our modern mythologies lend little comfort to those confronted by acausal events. I have asked many people about their experiences with meaningful coincidences. I have never met someone who has never experienced an SE of some kind. Defaulting to an explanation of mere coincidence is common. It is my impression that when a person attempts to explain away SE as "mere coincidence," it is often a way of defending against the existential anxiety such events can produce. We need there to be explanations for the things around us. Mentally, we are still on the savanna trying to determine which patterns mean survival or danger. The final position for some people becomes "such events don't exist because they are just not possible." The problem with this position is there is no reason why SE is not possible. In physics, any event not ruled out by the known laws is considered possible. SEs violate no laws of physics. They often beat the odds of probability, but they don't violate causal laws. In fact, the research done in related areas has tended to confirm not only the existence of SEs, but show them to be responsive to the psychological states of the observer as well.

When I was being educated in the scientific method, I became interested in an often misunderstood fact of experimental design. The best experiments are those where the subjects have been randomly selected, the subjects don't know what the experiment is actually about, and the person performing the experiment does not know what the expected outcome of the experiment is. This is called a double-blind experiment. The reasoning is if the researcher carrying out the experiment knows what results he is looking for, he will alter the outcome of the experiment. The data will move in the direction he had expected. There are schools of scientific philosophy around this problem, and different names for the various ways this happens. Some changes in outcome are caused by judgment calls of the researchers. Some data is changed by the way it is analyzed. But the core problem the method is meant to help eliminate is a basic, hard-to-swallow, scientific fact: the expectations of the researcher change the outcome of the events in the experiment just by the act of observation and expectation. Howls of protest can no doubt be heard in the minds of many well-educated researchers, declaring this as a misinterpretation of the scientific method, but it is the reason the method exists. The participants expecting a known outcome produces the same effect. The placebo effect accounts for as much as 30 percent of any therapeutic effect in an experiment. Many herbal remedies that people have relied on for centuries are now being subject to double-blind experiments. Some do work. Some are being found to have no effect at all, but people still report getting better because they believe in them. They expect, and the mirror reflects, the expectation.

INVITATION FROM AN AMUSED OBSERVER

You are personally responsible for at least some of the SE that you experience. With some attention and imagination, you can learn to use this ability creatively. You can "tweak" reality a few percentage points in the direction of your attention. The model of synchronicity presented here was created to fill the gap between the reality of SE, and the lack of reasoned explanation about how it works and what to do with it. We will look at what has been said about synchronicity by the creator of the term, Carl Jung, and then reviews the findings of the research on the subject. When I started doing this research, I expected to find articles, research findings, or dissertations that attempted to disprove the existence of SE. I thought this was going to be a controversial book. I found a huge body of literature verifying the existence of SE. I found nothing that made a case against SE being real. I did find that one of the most vexing problems of scientific experimentation is finding a truly random event of any kind. Even truly random numbers, needed for various kinds of statistical analysis, are notoriously hard to generate. Unnoticed patterns pervade everything.

For readers who are already aware of SE, I offer this model as the personal mythology of another amazed and amused observer. To the reader who is just becoming interested in SE, I offer a paradox and word of caution. SEs are a mirror held up to the mind of the observer. If you are not aware of, or choose not to believe in SE, your mind will reflect this by not presenting you with these patterns. I see no problem with this; awareness of SEs is not a critical skill for survival. They may even become an unwelcome distraction. If, however, you choose to become aware of the SEs that surround you, you will have to live with that knowledge, and SEs, most probably for the rest of your life. Such knowledge becomes part of who you are and is not easily forgotten or ignored. Once you know the earth isn't flat, its hard to go back. So, if you're looking for a nice piece of purely intellectual entertainment, this model is not for you. If you would rather not spend time staring into the funhouse mirror of your own mind, you might want to turn your attention elsewhere. If you would like to take the chance of embarking on an adventure of exploration through SE, and don't mind that certainty is nowhere to be found, read on.

Two

Don't
Believe
Everything
You Think

THE REAL MATRIX

You are performing computational tasks no conceivable computer system ever will. You are that mind, that brain, that miracle. Your brain takes billions of separate sensory inputs, and constructs the version of reality you experience. Even more amazingly, you recognize what that massive pattern of information means. The brain constructs your reality. You carry your "Matrix" computer around with you in your skull. Your bio-computer filters and changes the data you experience automatically. Your brain tries to give you only the information you actually need to survive. The brain "edits" reality. Most of what your senses report gets deleted. Much of what you think you experience in the world right now isn't really there. It's information constructed in an area of your brain's

29

working memory. The $64,000 question is if you are locked into this bone-box, how is it you are able to change the order of events around you? You're going to learn how you do this, and why it is partially under your control.

I am a fair typist at best. My lack of speed at a keyboard is based on how I learned. I was offered the usual typing courses in high school. My teachers tried to show me how to use home finger positions and to learn typing without looking at my hands. I went ahead and did it my way. I did not build on the foundations I was being taught. I learned the wrong motor patterns, and found that later, I can't achieve the useful skill of fast and flawless typing. I based my initial learning on the wrong patterns. The higher skill levels then became difficult to achieve. There is a science to learning to type, or play music, or create SEs. It all depends on the patterns you start with, and how early you are willing to change mistaken habits. I sometimes treat clients who have delusions about the causes of SEs. Some start having conversations with TV and radio broadcasts. Others see these coincidences everywhere, and are driven to distraction by the stories they tell. These people never learned the first lesson; SEs are a mirror. Take a breath. Imagine the first typing lesson; put your fingers on the home position keys. The first, most basic foundational position; you are looking into a mirror of your complete being. Synchronicity is you.

JUNG AND SE

Carl Jung was one of the great minds of the 20th century. His model of synchronicity was the first. It is still the most popular. And it is wrong. His model, like a bad first typing habit, has deprived readers of their personal power and set them on a path to poor understanding. He did not believe we are the cause of these events. But Jung did know we are somehow connected to them:

> Synchronicity designated the parallelism of time and meaning between psychic and psychophysical events, which scientific knowledge has thus far been unable to reduce to a common principal. The term explains nothing, it simply formulates the

occurrence of meaningful coincidences which, in themselves, are chance happenings, but are so improbable that we must assume them to be based on some kind of principal, or on some property of the empirical world...from this it follows either that the psyche cannot be localized in space, or that space is relative to the psyche.

Simple translation: Science doesn't know what's going on here. Something real is happening. Either part of us exists beyond the limits of time and space, or time and space are being changed by some part of us. Jung was right on both counts. He was not willing to concede we personally create SEs. Without a model to explain how we create SEs, such a statement would have been a career-ender. Hopefully times have changed. Carl Jung created the term *synchronicity* to describe what he called an "acausal connecting principal." At an early age, he noticed that some events were tied together in mysterious ways to form incredible coincidences. These events often seemed to carry meanings and follow patterns. It is common in older cultures to look for signs in the events around them to predict the future, or to use for decision-making. Jung realized that these reports of SEs were more than superstitious beliefs or misinterpreting reality. The coincidences were objectively real, and connected with the observer. He describes two of his own experiences with synchronicity in the following two incidents:

Synchronistic Event

I am faced with the fact that my tram ticket bears the same number as the theater ticket which I buy immediately afterwards, and I receive that same evening a telephone call during which the same number is mentioned again as a telephone number...

Synchronistic Event

My example concerns a young woman patient who, in spite of efforts made on both sides, proved to be psychologically inaccessible. The difficulty lay in the fact that she always knew better about everything. Her excellent education had provided her with a weapon ideally suited to this purpose, namely a highly polished Cartesian rationalism with an impeccably "geometrical" idea of reality. After several fruitless attempts to sweeten her rationalism with a somewhat more human understanding, I had to confine myself to the hope that something unexpected and irrational would turn up, something that would burst the intellectual retort into which she had sealed herself. Well, I was sitting opposite her one day, with my back to the window, listening to her flow of rhetoric. She had had an impressive dream the night before, in which someone had given her a golden scarab, a costly piece of jewelry. While she was still telling me this dream, I heard something behind me gently tapping on the window. I turned around and saw that it was a fairly large flying insect that was knocking against the window-pane from outside in the obvious effort to get into the dark room. This seemed to me very strange. I opened the window immediately and caught the insect in the air as it flew in. It was a scarabaeid beetle, or common rose-chafer (Cetonia aurata), whose gold-green color most nearly resembles that of a golden scarab. I handed the beetle to my patient with the words, "Here is your scarab." This experience punctured the desired hole in her rationalism and broke the ice of her intellectual resistance. The treatment could now be continued with satisfactory results.

Jung's formal writing about SE started with his interest in the ancient Chinese book of changes called the *I Ching*. It has 72 passages that describe different images and actions. Each passage is assigned a six-bar hexagram. Each bar is either a broken or unbroken line. The 72 hexagrams are all the possible combinations of these lines. Coins or sticks are thrown and values assigned to them are read. These values are then converted into the lines of the hexagram. The passage indicated is then read as if it were a commentary on whatever current situation the thrower was asking about.

Jung became fascinated by the apparent accuracy of the *I Ching*. Out of random events the oracle was producing meaningful information. He assumed that the symbols in the book's passages described common primordial patterns of human thought. Jung believed they were a part of a common unconscious language. In attempting to explain how the work produced meaning from random chance, he reasoned that the images it contained somehow transcended human experience, and connected with the source of nature itself. This was the beginning of the theory of archetypes, and his explanation of the cause of SEs.

An archetype is a pattern of force that causes external and internal events to constellate around it in specific patterns of meaning. It is a "something" that changes both the pattern of events and your thoughts. The result is your thoughts and the events around you mirror each other. Jung believed there are four levels of consciousness. The first is ego consciousness. This is approximately what you consider your conscious self. Ego consciousness arises out of the next deepest level, the personal unconscious. This is made of personal experiences and memories. This developed out of a vast area called the collective unconscious. It connects all of us the way the sea floor connects all the continents and islands that rise from it. It is the common ground. Below even this is the psychoid level. At this level subjective and objective are mixed and merged without clear boundaries. There is no clear internal or external reality. The inner and outer worlds are actually fused at this primitive level, consciousness is just emerging from the background of the infinity of timeless and spaceless consciousness. During Jung's lifetime, the idea of existence beyond time and space was ridiculed by most scientists. These were concepts left to the mystics, the philosophers, and the delusional. In your lifetime, science has reversed this position. We now have the unified model of everything: String Theory, which confirms dimensions outside of our time and space. Reality, as we shall see in later chapters, is much stranger than we ever imagined.

The archetypes are found at the psychoid level. They are the patterns of creation. They are not thought of as causes in and of themselves, they are patterns that events and perceptions follow as they emerge from the collective consciousness. It is as if events and experiences orbit around them. Jung said SEs occur when internal and external events become constellated by an archetype into the archetype's pattern. What happens then is called a co-occurrence event. The person's psychological state and the external events of the environment seem to mirror each other. This produces the experience of meaning in the SE. In Jung's model, the archetype has brought both the psychological state of the person and the events into a synchronous relationship.

Jung believed the archetypes existed in a continuum outside of time and space, in an eternal present moment that encompassed all of the past, present, and future. He believed synchronicity produces its effects because its force is exerted across all of time in an eternal moment that encompass the entire universe. According to Jung, this continuum would have to encompass characteristics of both a physical and psychic space. He thought such a space was beyond our ability to understand. He called the possibility of knowing the way synchronicity operated from it "unthinkable." Perhaps he should have said "I don't know."

Jung described the working of the *I Ching* by speculating the person doing the reading must concentrate in a hopeful and expectant way. This focus withdraws their psychic energy from parts of their psychological structures. This creates a condition of instability. The focus on structure sinks to deeper areas of consciousness. This causes impressions from psychoid levels to rise to awareness. The patterns these impressions raise is caused by the constellating effects of the archetypes, the person's mind reorganized from the bottom up, until the impressions reached conscious awareness as thoughts and feelings during the reading. The same archetypes that create the SE produce the particular hexagrams which will match the person's psychological processes. Synchronicity operates across time; it determines both the internal conditions which led the person to consult the oracle, and the answer it gives.

SE BEYOND JUNGIAN THINKING

This is where the major errors of Jung's model start, along with the mental patterns that build bad cognitive habits later, and prevent you from understanding your own abilities. Jung was grasping at straws. He did not want to publicly say people can affect the world around them. He knew most of his peers would consider this, well, nuts. The explanation he came up with is unlikely. There are no archetypes. There is no energy conveyor belt pulling psychic energy out of people and shuffling it to the archetypes. Nobody has ever seen an archetype; you might as well say SEs are being made by aliens, angels, or the spirit of Walt Disney. Get rid of the concept of archetypes—it's not needed and has no functional use. When you start creating your own SE, the idea of archetypes will just get in your way, like a bad typing habit. Of course, if you look for them, you will find them. SEs are a mirror, make any face in it you like.

According to Jung, it was not possible for a person to intentionally create SEs. They affect us; we do not influence them. He did believe that a person could be made more sensitive to the occurrence of these events by altering their consciousness in certain ways. He said paying attention could make a person sensitive to the constellating effects of the archetypes. The person, in effect, can choose to come within the influence of an archetype. Jung said that the influence of an archetype could produce profound psychological and spiritual changes in a person. These changes could be for good or ill. Several others have taken up the question of the influence of synchronicity on the personality, and its possible usefulness as a diagnostic tool. Studies of the *I Ching* (Rosengarten, 1985) show SEs in an *I Ching* reading can be an accurate tool for predicting personality traits as compared to standardized personality tests. The same study also found SEs produced by the Tarot were reliable enough to be used as a diagnostic tool. Other systems of divination also produce equally meaningful events, but are based on different patterns and symbols.

The symbol of water in a Tarot reading doesn't mean the same thing as it does in an *I Ching* reading. Each system is looking for different patterns. If archetypes were universal, you would expect to find they mean the same things across cultures. This problem has been addressed (VonFronz, 1975) (Bash, 1976) by attempting to reduce archetypes to numbers. This leads into the murky waters of numerology. This effort fails as well. Different cultures assign different meanings to numbers, and many don't even have the concept of 0 at all.

My father used to tell us bar jokes. "A guy walks into a bar..." kind of jokes. Here's one: A guy is walking down the street one dark night and passes in front of a bar. Under the street light in front of the bar is a drunken man crawling around looking for something. "Lose something?" The first man asks.

"My car keys." The drunk replies.

"Where did you last see them?"

The drunken man points to a dark alleyway down the block.

"If you lost them over there, why are you searching for them over here?" The first man asks.

"Because this is where the light is!"

Explanations for synchronicity are often based on what the person already believes, not on actual evidence. Jung looked for an explanation for SE in his model of archetypes because that's where his light happened to be.

It is possible to associate any system of thought or experience with synchronicity, and make subjective connections that may have only personal meaning. In the following example, Jung describes a pattern of SE which he believed to be the results of the "fish" archetype:

Synchronistic Event

I noted the following on April 1, 1949: Today is Friday. We have fish for lunch. Somebody happens to mention the custom of making an "April fish" of someone. That same morning I made a note of an inscription

which read: "Est homo totus medius piscis ab imo." In the afternoon a former patient of mine, whom I had not seen for months, showed me some extremely impressive pictures of fish which she had painted in the meantime. In the evening I was shown a piece of embroidery with fish-like sea monsters in it. On the morning of April 2 another patient, whom I had not seen for many years, told me a dream in which she stood on the shore of a lake and saw a large fish that swam straight towards her and landed at her feet. Only one of the persons mentioned here knew anything about it.

In his fish example, Jung would say both he and the events he reported had come under the influence of the fish archetype. Instead of the power of an archetype causing these events, I propose that it was the focus of Jung's attention on the image of the fish that was the source of the events he noted. Is it possible that people themselves are the source of SE? The idea scares some people. It can cause fear of regression to the renunciation of faith in order wrought by empirical science. At least it used to be that way in Jung's day. Modern physics is much less fearful about alternative realities than it used to be. Jung's model offered a way to make the concept of personal influence over some aspects of SEs somewhat tolerable, and a little less threatening. The causal linear time we depend on and the acausal time SEs operate on are not contradictory. SEs exist as patterns of relationships between causal events, the synchronistic aspects of an event exist as meanings we perceive rather than physical forces that move events. No physical energy is needed; synchronicity is a range of consciousness. Your being able to alter the sequence of events around you on a truly universal scale is not a fantasy, nor is it an unlimited "God-like" power. SEs are not physically based, and in no way conflict with physical laws. Your being able to influence patterns of synchronicity likewise violates no physical laws. There is no reason to believe that states of personal consciousness cannot produce SEs independent of physical energies. There is no physical law that says you can't create the patterns of meaning and relationship around you using your own brain and focus of attention. Trying to find reasons you can't do this is like looking for your keys where the light is.

THE UNTHINKABLE IS THINKABLE

Jung believed our thought processes are bound by the laws of time and space. We cannot even think about the possible causes of synchronicity. In Jung's words, such causes are "unthinkable." This contradicts Jung's own model of the archetypes. If the causes of these events were unthinkable, then we would be incapable of perceiving the events and thinking about their meaning. It is possible to think about SEs and their causes, but not within the confines of the Jungian model. The denial of personal influence on SE is more problematic than the concerns about the synchronicity-as-mirror solution. In Jung's model, the internal processes of the person are moved about by the clustering effect of the archetypes, until they parallel external events also being influenced by the archetype. The result is the experience of SE. The individual has no choice in the matter. They are swept along without will or choice over the SE they experience. This is inconsistent with the operation of the *I Ching* Jung got the concept from. The individual chooses when and where to consult the oracle. The inquirer also chooses the context of the response by requesting information about specific issues. The frame of reference for the events and their contextual meaning is determined by the operator. The reading centers on personal problems, not archetypal patterns. This shifts the probable causes of synchronicity from the unknowable, to the personal.

Your attention affects the frequency of your encounters with SE. Focusing attention on the possibility of experiencing SE with an attitude of expectancy (expecting them to occur), greatly increases the number of events you experience.

Jung struggled with this contradiction to his theory of archetypal influence for many years. He eventually proposed there may be an archetype of "hopeful expectancy" or "occult influence." When the psyche of an individual comes into contact with an archetype, possibly by personal choice, it caused SE to respond as the person willed or expected. This was as close to personal causation as he was willing to come. This position puts the archetype and its unthinkable power at the command of the individual, which violates what Jung considered an archetype to be.

The concept of archetype is the primary flaw in the model. There is no unthinkable power because there is no archetype. If you look for archetypes in your mirror, you will undoubtedly find them. You see reflections of what you are thinking about.

Don't believe everything you think.

Three

Full
Spectrum
Reflection

SE AND PERSONAL PROCESSES

During therapy, emotion and introspection occurs with depth and intensity. This situation often produces SE. Some therapists have reported mental and emotional synchronicities with their clients so intense, that the possibility of subconscious telepathy was considered. Others noted that some sometimes clients displaced emotions into the production of SEs. These SEs reflected the content of the emotions and experiences back to them. The original traumatic events were converted into SEs, manifested around the client. Others found that SEs often followed states of emotional change that involved fear or apprehension. More growth-oriented emotional states have also been connected with the manifestation of SEs. Some observed that sudden growth experiences are often accompanied by external SEs. Experiences of transcendence are also associated with the occurrence of SEs. It's a full spectrum reflection.

You see reflections of what is happening in your unconscious as well as your conscious thoughts. You will see your own internal processes, your hopes, your dreams, your issues, and your spiritual life.

If there is an energy that drives SE into action, it is the energy of our emotions. Here we walk on the edge of magic once again. I try to be a practical observer. Before I design an experiment, I find out what others have already learned.

SE IN THE LABORATORY

Jung tried to gain acceptance of SEs by associating them with then current PSI (psychic) research. Jung was concerned about criticism for just saying SE exists. He tried to gain credibility by comparing them to PSI experiments being conducted in the laboratory. He chose the work of Dr. R.B. Rhine to associate with synchronicity. Rhine was a psychologist at Duke University. His approach was different from Jung's. Rhine started with a question, not a model. He wanted to know if it was possible for people to influence events by non-physical means. His focus was not on how events happen, it was on if they were real. Jung assumed the truth of his ideas, and then went looking for proof. That's a bad idea with SEs. You find the proof you're looking for, true or not, because SEs mirror your assumptions back to you. They seem to provide proof of your beliefs. Jung declared that Rhine's experiments were a demonstration of SE under laboratory conditions. SE was therefore an empirically real phenomenon. Jung could not accept the outcome of those experiments; people can influence events by an act of attention.

Rhine was a psychologist and researcher. Back in the 1930s a man came to his office with a strange claim. He said he was a gambler. He said he could control dice rolls with his mind. Not all the time, but enough so that it was a noticeable effect that turned the odds in his favor. Rather than dismiss this claim, Rhine did what a good scientist does. He said "show me." They took six pairs of dice; the gambler's task was to have more dice come up with the number six than could be expected by chance. They tossed the dice. Again, and again, and again. It works. The amount of change over random hovered at about 3 percent above chance. The effect was real. Rhine spent 30 years doing rigorous experiments on the ability of subjects to change random events. He was having people produce SE on demand. The research, reproduced and confirmed by peers, states the odds are millions to one in favor of us being the cause of this effect.

He concluded events could be changed in the direction of the subject's desire and attention. These random events included series of coin tosses, die throws, the position objects landed in when dropped in a random manner, the values of randomly generated electrical currents, and the rate of particle release from a radioactive source, among others. In each instance, he found that the probability of these physical events was changed by the psychological expectation and attention of the observers, even though no physical force was detected.

Jung accepted that these were measurements of SE, but not that people have the ability to personally produce SE. He preferred an explanation keeping with his archetypal model. He proposed that there must be some archetypal influence controlling both the experiment and subject, producing the illusion of personal influence. Jung suggested the subjects must have had some psychic way of predicting the outcome of the experiments, then using this knowledge unconsciously to give false outcomes. Given the controls of the experiments, this is not likely. Jung was not able to give an explanation of how his counter theories might operate. They seem to be more pure objection than reason.

Rhine's work went beyond proof of personal causation. He found emotional states, such as interest or boredom affected the subjects' ability to influence SE. (Forwald, 1954) Boredom and anxiety decreased the ability to change the randomness of events in their desired direction. Focused attention and positive expectation increased the occurrence of the targeted events. He found alcohol (Averic, Rhine, 1945) or caffeine (Rhine, 1945) lowered or raised scores respectively. Emotions and personal physiological states can facilitate or inhibit SE.

Several other researchers have suggested that PSI and synchronicity are related phenomena. Some suggest that synchronicity is responsible for all PSI phenomena. A more moderate position is synchronicity may be responsible for only specific ranges of PSI phenomena, such as telepathy (Schwarz, 1969) or clairvoyance. Others suggested SE may be just one class of phenomena of PSI in general. Like many such abilities, it is primarily unconscious. Others (Tart, 1981) speculated that synchronicity needs to be separated from PSI phenomena. He pointed out that because there is no model for the operation of SE, testing hypotheses is difficult. This book will hopefully solve that problem. You are going to test it for yourself.

SE AS PSYCHOLOGICAL FEEDBACK

Rhine's work opened a Pandora's box of possibilities. We now have a direction to look for the causes of SE—us. SEs follow the patterns of the emotions and beliefs of those who observe them. The experiments Rhine did are based on the scientific model. Part of this model attempts to eliminate as many variables as possible. This keeps outside effects on the results to a minimum. The feedback the subjects got from the events they were trying to influence was also reduced to a minimum. There isn't much to relate to about a coin or dice toss. The real world is beautifully complex and rich in events that allow us to experience a wide range of emotional and intellectual meaning. Just as Rhine's subjects influenced events in the laboratory, you have similar effects on events in the world around you. This influence follows the patterns of your thoughts and attention. We all exist in a world of SE, which reflect back to us our conscious, subconscious, and transpersonal processes. You don't have do anything, it's as automatic as your breathing.

We usually don't notice the hundreds of minor SEs occurring around us every day. This feedback system remains unused because we have learned not to pay attention to SEs. Because they don't understand SE is a mirror, most people have no frame of reference for them. They can't see the pattern, so they stop looking. There is no difference between the synchronicity of the house moving, and the way a die falls in a lab experiment. Western culture is based on quantitative reasoning. Thinking this way, an event involving a house should require more energy than one involving a die. Westernized thought is reliable, but limited. It tries to achieve objectivity at the expense of more holistic and associative thought. SE has a logic of its own; association and relationship from which meaning is derived. These are dependent upon the individual's thoughts and experiences of the environment in which they formed. Many religious systems talk about an extra-physical reality with which a person forms an intimate relationship. In the west many have turned to Taoism, Tantra, and aboriginal spirituality in search of this connection to the universe. Western culture has relegated this kind of unified consciousness primarily to mystics and heretics. Instead of being unusual, SE should be seen as a state when the true connection that should exist between the inner and outer worlds is functioning normally. SEs are not the results of a state of psychic imbalance, as Jung claimed. Claiming your own abilities, with a reasoned understanding of how they actually work, is healthy.

Seeing what you believe

The causes of synchronistic phenomena have remained a mystery because they reflect the belief of the observer back to them. They seem to confirm any assumption you care to make. Synchronicity is a mirror of the content of your psyche, made manifest as meaningful events. This is why there has never been a consensus on its causes. Different beliefs cause corresponding patterns of SE. The belief system of a culture or individual is often used to provide an explanation for SE, which take on the pattern of the belief, seeming to provide confirmation. The following example is taken respectfully from Parmahansa Yogananda's *Autobiography of a Yogi*:

Synchronistic Event

Our family moved to Lahore in the Punjab. There I acquired a picture of the Divine Mother in the form of the Goddess Kali. It sanctified a small informal shrine on the balcony of our home. An unequivocal conviction came over me that fulfillment would crown any of my prayers uttered in that sacred spot. Standing there with Uma one day, I watched two boys flying kites over the roofs of two buildings that were separated from our house by an extremely narrow lane.

"Why are you so quiet?" Uma pushed me playfully.

"I am just thinking how wonderful it is that Divine Mother gives me whatever I ask."

"I suppose she would give you those two kites!" My sister laughed derisively.

"Why not?" I began silent prayers for their possession.

Matches are played in India with kites whose strings are covered with glue and ground glass. Each player attempts to sever the string held by his opponent. A freed kite sails over the roofs; there is great fun in catching it. As Uma and I were on a roofed, recessed balcony, it seemed impossible that a loose kite could come into our hands; its string would naturally dangle over the roof.

The players across the lane began their match. One string was cut; immediately the kite floated in my direction. Owing to a sudden abatement of the breeze the kite remained stationary for a moment, during which its string became firmly entangled with a cactus plant on top of the opposite house. A long, perfect loop was formed for my seizure. I handed the prize to Uma.

"It was just an extraordinary accident, and not an answer to your prayer. If the other kite comes to you, then I shall believe."

Sister's dark eyes conveyed more amazement than her words. I continued my prayers with intensity. A forcible tug by the other player resulted in the abrupt loss of his kite. It headed toward me, dancing in the wind. My helpful assistant, the cactus plant, again secured the kite string in the necessary loop by which I could grasp it. I presented my second trophy to Uma.

I don't know Yogananda's relationship with his deity. I believe the events were a reflection of the relationship that existed in his consciousness, and it was his own content that was responsible for the SE. This perspective shifts the cause of the events to the person who experiences them. I don't know that Yogananda's deity exists. I have no proof. I know Yogananda existed. I suppose I'm looking where the light is. In his story the content projected into SE was emotionally complex. It represented both a complete belief system and emotional components of his relationship with his deity. The pattern of the SE started in Yogananda's conscious awareness. He wanted specific events to happen. He produced the emotion, attention, and expectation. The SE followed his pattern. I'm not a Yogananda follower. My mythologies are more personalized. His story does demonstrate the most powerful form of "magic" possible with SE. It is stunningly simple; be grateful. If you look in the mirror of SE and say "thank you," SEs seem to become more generous.

Seeing your reflection in the SE of a series of coin tosses or dice thrown in a laboratory is hard because of the simplicity of the experiment. Only the real world offers the depth and variation of events needed for true work with SE. The meaning of these events is particular to the observer. SE can be very seductive. They can tell you exactly what you most want to hear. That is where your thoughts and emotions tend to be, focused on what you want. You are a modern hunter looking for patterns. Here is an example of an SE that happened while I was writing this chapter:

Synchronistic Event

I was going to a writing workshop in two days. I was more than a little self-conscious about the project I was to present, a book called *The Way Synchronicity Works.* I was concerned about claiming that I had an inside knowledge of the mechanics of meaningful coincidence. The book said that SEs were reflections of people's thoughts manifesting in the events around them, and I had pieced together a model that explained how this worked. I had my license as a psychologist to consider—if I was going to say it, it had better be true.

I was brooding over this as I walked through the parking lot toward my car after work. The sky was dark and overcast; it had been raining much of the day. The flat blacktop was covered with a thin reflective layer of water. I had to watch my feet as I walked to avoid stepping into deeper water. I was considering if I could honestly represent SEs as personal reflections in the environment. Something golden beneath the water under my feet caught my attention. I looked down into the reflection of my own face, and saw beneath it, in the water, what looked like a gold credit card. I reached through the reflection of my face in the water and picked up the plastic card. I brushed water and bits of grime from the surface and read from the bold stylized letters printed across the top of the card "Kirby, Kirby and Kirby."

At first I thought I must have misread the card, it couldn't actually be saying my name three times.

I read again. I had indeed picked up a card with my
name printed on it, plucked from my own reflection in
the water. Under the heading it read:

"Motorcycle lawyers; Licensed in California, we
wrench, ride and litigate."

It reminded me that this was indeed the way synchronicity works. The events mirror our thoughts and concerns, giving the reflections added depth. SEs are like dreams that reveal bits of ourselves and leave us curious. The seductive part is the way we interpret such coincidences. I was looking for validation. I wanted to be told I had the right to say I knew how synchronicity works. I wanted proof that these events are reflections of ourselves. As much as I might like this event to be such proof, it isn't. It may have been a reflection of my thoughts and feelings, but there is no cause and effect proof that make it worth betting the farm on. It doesn't prove my perspective on synchronicity either. I have treated a number of clients with frequent and equally compelling SEs around them. Several have been told by SEs they were Jesus, or God, or victims of cosmic conspiracies. The mirror shows you what you look for. Once you understand this, you can look for, and create, almost any pattern you like.

SE reflect the psychological states of the observer.

Yogananda's experience may have reflected his developmental relationship with his actual mother, which came to be projected in the symbols of his belief system. This does not lessen the reality of his experience. His early positive maternal relationship may be exactly what made it possible to form an intimate relationship with his idea of Divine Mother. The emotional content projected and the pattern of relationship would be the same. I have seen many variations on beliefs about what causes SE. SEs almost always reflect the beliefs and desires of the observer. I have heard people claim SEs were caused by Christ, Buddha, Allah, ancestral spirits, Devas and other complex animistic and hierarchical sources. I know people who swear by their magical rituals and practices. I have also seen exotic explanations such as extraterrestrials, secret organizations, government psychics, spirit guides, and of course, God. Intents range from the benevolent to the malevolent. Many beliefs are contradictory, some so blatantly bizarre that they don't even require serious consideration. In each case, the story SEs seem to confirm is a metaphor for the internal life of the individual. Yogananda held an internal representation of goddess; that is what SE showed him. Jung held one of the archetypes without the possibility of personal influences on events; that is what SE reflected back to him. If a person does not believe in SE, the events reflect this and remain out of conscious awareness. If looked for, they will be found. As the skill of perceiving SE develops, they become progressively more subtle, frequent, and intense, always reflecting some aspect of yourself.

MOVING BETWEEN CAUSAL AND ACAUSAL THINKING

Frame shifting occurs in individuals who have more than one cultural frame of reference. These cultural frames are ways of processing and drawing conclusions from sensory information. Bilingual people often frame shift by using one language for some concepts, and their second language for others. These frames are exclusive. The person can use one or the other at a time, but not both. The brain can't think in two languages at the same time. Frame shifting occurs when the person brings one frame to the fore to process information in a given situation, but when primed by cues from the environment, switches to the other frame. The second frame may lead them to draw different conclusions than the first. It may even change the way they experience reality.

The *New Look* thesis states your experience of reality is changed by your expectations, values, emotions, needs, and culture. Cognitive studies suggest different cultures foster different modes of processing experience. Frame shifting happens when the person shifts his or her pattern-matching style from one cultural frame to another. The brain uses a different set of instructions for each frame. This changes the reality it creates for you. If your most used frame does not process sensory information in a way that looks for pattern matches between internal processes and external SEs, your frame filters them out and the SEs go unnoticed. This isn't a problem if the people around you also have frames that filter out SE. You are all filtering reality in the same way. Everyone appears "normal." Use a different frame, one that allows for SEs, and you literally experience a different kind of reality. Seeing things the people around you don't see is often seen as a mental illness.

Synchronistic Event

Some clients diagnosed as having thoughts of reference, are really experiencing SEs that are projections of their thoughts and emotions. I had a client who suffered from paranoid delusions. He was sure he was being followed by undercover government agents all the time. He said he saw them watching him everywhere. He had no idea why they were so interested in him, but he was sure he was being watched. In a session one afternoon, he was telling me all about it. I tried to convince him nobody was watching him, that there was nothing to be afraid of. I asked him to come to the office window overlooking the street. I challenged him to point out the people who were watching him. At that moment a car drove by with two men in it. Both stared directly at the window we were looking out of as the car slowly passed.

"You see!" my client exclaimed. "There they are, right there!"

I have no idea what those men were actually doing. Maybe they were looking for an address. Maybe they were interested in the building itself. They weren't spies. My client had a diagnosis of paranoid schizophrenia. He had been ill for many years. He had a paranoid delusion of being followed, but the SEs that flowed from it were real. He was looking into the reflection caused by his own illness. I was not able to help him. He did not have the ability to step outside his belief in the truth of his own thoughts. I didn't know how to give it to him. There are moments when I think I see SEs generated by the people I'm with. Sometimes they see the same SE if their frame is not filtering them out. I find it a little unnerving to experience SEs that seem to be made by people unaware of them. I can't tell if the SEs are generated by the other person, or my assumptions about the other person's internal processes. I like simple answers.

The universe is not simple. Being open to SEs in a healthy way means never being fully sure of their meanings.

When I think I fully understand something, I know I'm missing something.

SES ARE NOT FOR EVERYONE

Sometimes when clients can be taught how SEs work, they can put their delusions in perspective. They can stop taking their thoughts so seriously. They can function comfortably in the world of people who do not experience SEs. I have known many wonderful, high-functioning people who understand SEs are a mirror. They play with their world like a child plays with a toy. These people understand it is their world they are helping create themselves. They know they are not creating the world the people around them experience. It is a magical way of thinking, a different frame. I had a friend come to me once complaining that Muggles were driving her crazy. Muggle is a word from the Harry Potter movies. It means a person with no magical ability, a person who doesn't live in the magical world. She was complaining about people who have no SE in their frame of reference. She was lamenting about people around her who seemed to be living in a world of their own fears and insecurities. There were people she loved that kept themselves captive to their own reflections. They didn't know they create the meaning of the world around them. When she tried to explain it to them, they just thought she was a little crazy. She is one of the most grounded psychologists I know. She was not feeling superior; she just wanted to see people free of their self-imposed limitations. She wanted people to come out and play. Expecting people to have an SE frame of reference is like expecting people speak your language. Some people can, some people don't want to.

SE as a rational basis for irrational beliefs

I don't believe in magic. I have seen many things I don't have an explanation for, and many things that are too complex for me to fully understand, but I believe in natural laws. Magic is a very seductive concept. It allows you to stop trying to understand why things happen the way they do. It is a way of saying there are events that operate outside all laws and understanding. To our hunting ancestor, the sun crossing the sky was a magical event. He had no way to learn what the sun actually was, no physics and laws of gravitation. He made up stories to fit his experience. The danger in this is the stories get passed on and accepted as truths. Superstitions can ease anxiety about not understanding the nature of the events around us. The idea of "magic" can be a comforting one. I believe SEs are the foundation of all belief in magic. Although SEs seem magical, they do have some overall patterns and follow some general laws. After I wrote the words you just read, I then left to go on vacation with my family. I was wondering how I was going to explain the difference between magic and SE in a way that was grounded in the SE-as-mirror model. SE itself provided the example I needed.

Synchronistic Event

We were in the town of Seaside, Oregon. It's a tourist town that marks the spot where Lewis and Clark finished their journey at the Pacific Ocean. I was walking on the beach with my daughter, enjoying the natural beauty. As we walked, we were talking about her art. She is an illustrator who often does fantasy work. We were talking about the magical symbols artists create in some fantasy artwork. Whole languages have been created for works such as *Lord of the Rings*, *Star Trek*, and various video games. We were talking about where some of the artists came up with the inspirations for the symbols they created. I told her that most of the symbols in magical artwork I had seen seemed to be based on *The Key of Solomon*, a magical work attributed to King Solomon. It is a magical grimoire probably created in the 15th century, which inspired many other magical works involving circles and mystical symbols. I told her I had a copy published in 1903, supposedly translated from one of the original medieval copies. My father had left it to me. She asked what it was about. I told her that whoever created the original work believed that there were letter and geometrical correspondences for the names of angels and demons, and that there were connections between hours of the day, days of the week, planets, metals, and letters of the alphabet. They made up complex magical symbols to try to tie all this together. I explained that there were talismans and seals for each of the planets. I told her that the one for Mercury was supposed to enhance mental faculties and communication. It was used to summon spirits, and had to be made of a particular metal, at a particular time. That was pretty much all I could remember about the book. I hadn't looked at it for decades. I did explain that I had read that *The Key of Solomon* was a poor attempt to create one-to-one correspondences between languages such as Latin and Hebrew. I told her I don't believe in magic, but that if people of the time did, they probably saw SEs that made them think it worked.

We arrived back at the hotel later that night and were having dinner with my wife, who had been shopping. She handed me a small plastic bag and explained that she had found a store that sold Celtic jewelry. She had bought me a present. In the bag was a small pewter pendant. The pendent had a complex and lovely Celtic talisman inscribed on it. The card with the pendant said it was a magical design for writers and poets. Its magical function was to make thoughts flow into the written word effortlessly. It was made to manifest the content of the writer's mind and intent. I thanked her, and put the gift in my pocket making a mental note that this was a mild SE. I had been talking with my daughter about talismans earlier, and I was having trouble writing my thoughts on SEs and magic before we had left. When we got back to our room I took out the pendant to look at it in better light. I looked at the interlaced geometric design and symbols. I was hoping to find something that looked similar to the pentagrams in *The Key of Solomon.* That would at least give me a reason to write the events down as an SE. There was nothing familiar on the face of the pendant, as lovely as it was. I turned it over. There was a second design on the back. It was the seal of the planet Mercury from *The Key of Solomon.*

This SE gave me exactly what I was looking for, a way to untangle SE and the concept of magic. This SE clearly reflects patterns of thought I had been having. I was thinking about classical ideas of magic, and had mentioned *The Key of Solomon* and the talisman of Mercury an hour earlier. I had been looking for a way to get my thoughts on magic and SE expressed clearly, and I had been given a magical talisman made to enhance writing ability. The pendant was the SE needed to make the ideas clear. The SE was a mirror of my thoughts. The symbols on the pendant were of no significance at all.

I could have been thinking about Mickey Mouse and the meaning of old Disney films and SEs with those themes would have appeared. *The Key of Solomon* is not magical; it's just a book somebody made up a long time ago. They were trying to gain a synchronistic edge. They did not understand they were looking in a mirror. There are no magical correspondences, the scratches we make on metal or paper do not summon unseen spirits to our assistance. Magical ritual and art does focus our attention on our thoughts and intents. Wearing a talisman, a cross, a symbol, reminds us by its presence of the thoughts we have attached to it. Bringing those thoughts to our attention produces the SEs around us that reflect those thoughts.

Maybe our superstitious ancestors belief in magic wasn't all that misguided. I found my inherited copy of *The Key of Solomon*. Doing magic according to the book is a complicated and time-consuming affair. All the ritual objects have to be hand made. In the days before Wal-Mart and the local hardware store it probably took years to accumulate the materials. There were purification rituals, preparations for the location; everything had to be done during specific days, at specific hours. To actually follow the instructions you would have to be obsessively preoccupied with the preparations for a very long time. It was also dangerous. Get caught by the church doing magic in medieval Europe and you were literally toast. It all had to be done in secret. Magic had all the conditions for producing SEs. The preparations kept the magician focused on particular thought patterns for long periods of time. There was emotional intensity to the work, and they were looking for results in the events around them. They probably saw SE based on their thoughts, intensified by their prolonged practice. I do not believe they were summoning spirits or changing lead into gold, at least not literally.

Perhaps there are wise uses for magic. I know people who wear religious talismans: crosses, stars, symbols, and stones thought to have the ability to influence their lives. Some wear their magical items to remind them to be loving and kind to themselves and others. I know many people who participate in religious rituals, which I consider a form of magic. For a time, each of them is reminded of their better natures, that they don't have all the answers. Practicing such magic leaves their thoughts open to the possibility that they are more than they appear to be. When treating a client, one of the primary goals is to restore choice. Most people come to therapy because they want to change. The work is about having a choice about how you think and how you affect the way you live in the world.

Four

The
Diagnostic
Dilemma

SE VS. DELUSIONS

Psychologists and psychiatrists often misdiagnose SEs as a symptom of psychosis. The mainstream mental health community believes SEs are evidence of a thought disorder. If a client attributes a cause or meaning to SE, she may be diagnosed as delusional. If a client reports her thoughts cause synchronistic events, she may sound as as though she has delusions of grandeur. Consider how you might react if a client came to you for mental health treatment and claimed she had supernatural powers. I have seen many clients who have reported SEs and been recommended medication or hospitalization. The mentally ill often do experience synchronistic events more often than healthier populations. Their frame of reference sometimes has no problem accepting things the rest of us filter out. People are often confused about the causes of SEs. This confusion can be mistaken for delusion.

Context is everything. Context determines what additions and subtractions our brains make to our reality. Context determines how we are seen by others. If you claim a flying spaghetti monster created the universe, it is a delusion. If a hundred thousand people believe it, it's a religion. The Mayans and Aztecs believed that they had to cut the hearts out of human sacrifices so that the sun would rise and the crops would grow. Now we know this was delusional, but then it was religion. Many people who have experienced synchronistic events are confused by the lack of context available to fit SE into. There is often fear that experiencing synchronistic events is an indication of some mental illness. People who experience SEs can feel isolated and misunderstood. Some people know the messages SEs appear to be sending them are not true. Delusional people rarely question their beliefs. One client I treated was deeply distressed because his synchronistic events told him he had a central role to play in a worldwide drama. The SEs would direct him to do various foolish things with his money and time that never produced the outcomes promised. He knew the SEs were giving him poor advice. He asked "Why is the universe screwing with me like this? Am I just crazy?" He was not mentally ill, he just didn't understand how SEs work.

I had asked myself the same question years before as I watched a bulldozer load the rubble of a demolished cottage into dump trucks. The question of if experiencing SEs is a symptom of mental illness is no small matter to those who see them. The question of personal sanity can, well, drive people crazy. One definition of a psychosis is a disorder that causes a gross impairment in reality testing or loss of ego boundaries. This impairment interferes with the ability to meet the demands of everyday life. We are going to look at these three requirements and see where SE falls in this diagnostic dilemma.

Reality testing

Let's tackle the question of whether experiencing SE represents impairment in reality testing first. In reality testing we ask, is the mind coming to reasonable best-guess conclusions about how the world works, or are those guesses so off the mark that they may cause the person negative consequences? Let's jump back to our ancestor on the edge of the savanna looking for patterns. Our hunter is wondering what causes the motion of the sun. All life depends on the motions of this bright thing in the sky. Our hunter hopes if he can figure it out why the sun moves as it does, it may provide some useful information. A logical conclusion might be because the sun moves and is warm, it must be alive. Because all life seems to depend on the sun in some form, it must be a god of some kind. The majority of our ancestors believed the sun was a living god. They worshipped it accordingly. It was an obvious fact; all evidence supported this conclusion. The wise and powerful declared any belief to the contrary was a dangerous heresy worthy of punishment. Yesterday's truth is today's delusion. It depends on who is making the judgment and how much latitude they are wiling to give to religious beliefs. The Greeks had their own version of what made the sun cross the sky. The sun was not a god, but they had a sun god, Apollo. He was responsible for driving the chariot that contained the sun across the sky each day. Why would they believe this? Well, somebody had to do it. It had to be someone with god-like powers, and they needed a chariot to carry the thing, didn't they? Couldn't expect a god to carry the sun around by hand now could you? These were obvious logical answers to observed external events. One certainly can't argue with this kind of logic. Someone experiencing SEs must be mentally ill, right? By this logic, all our ancestors were delusional.

Think of the dilemma Galileo found himself in. The church declared that the earth was the center of the universe, and the sun and planets moved around it. Their reasoning was not just that was what visually appears to happen. By that reasoning, the declaration might make sense, except for little problems such as the retrograde motion of some of the planets. No, the church's main argument was that Jesus was born on earth; therefore, the earth had to be the center of the universe. More importantly, God had left the church in charge and it couldn't be wrong. *If* the church was wrong about something as basic as the motion of the sun, it might be wrong about other things. God may not have ordered everyone to kickback 10 percent of their income to the church. The church might not have the right to tell monarchs what to do. If the pope was fallible, people would see the world in a different frame of reference.

Galileo created a simple telescope. He turned it on the heavens and started recording what he saw. He saw directly, not by logical or philosophical inference. He saw that the sun, not the earth, was the center of the solar system. Faced with physical proof, the church declared Galileo a madman and a heretic. It ordered him not to turn his telescope on the heavens again on pain of torture and death. The church was trying to preserve their power and authority. Their belief that they were right was more powerful than objective evidence. No proof, no matter how compelling, would have been sufficient to change their minds. What proof do you have to believe the things you do? Are your beliefs what others have told you to believe? Is there any proof? Do you believe what you think just because you think it?

Galileo found himself in the same position as some people who experience SEs. SE contradicts the accepted notion of how reality is supposed to work. People who report SEs may be labeled as having a problem. Delusions are different from mistaken beliefs. True delusions are very difficult to treat. The therapist must convince a client to trust them to such a degree, that the client is willing to take the therapist's evaluation of what is real over what their own minds are reporting to them. Delusional clients often feel threatened when their beliefs are challenged. The inquisition showed Galileo the implements of torture. Galileo recanted his delusions. It was a very practical decision. If you are going to learn to create and interpret SEs, you will be confronted with delusions every day. This mirroring effect surrounds everyone. People believe what they think. You will begin to see the delusions of others, and your own. How do you tell what is real? My answer has been to understand that my beliefs can be wrong. I am open to reason and proof. I am not open to arguments of faith, not with SEs. I have some trust in the scientific method. Real research results do not state what is ultimately true. Science tells us how likely something is to be true. Science states what the margins of error are. Most importantly, science is repeatable. Any good experiment can be duplicated and the results verified by others. Faith has no margin of error or degrees of certainty. Your task, as the executive ego, is to decide what degree of certainty works for you.

SE and the experience of meaning

The experience of meaning is central to SE. Belief in seemingly psychotic explanations by people experiencing SE might be reasonable based on their experience. SE often muddies the waters of reality testing more than they clarify them. They give meanings independent of how cause and effect reality works, and they can be self-reinforcing. Consider the following experience:

Synchronistic Event

Part of my clinical duties includes doing psycho-educational groups with psychotic clients. During one group, there was a discussion about how to tell if something is real or not. It was not a particularly "on" day for me. I had made the mistake of trying to reason a paranoid client out of his delusion. The client believed he was the subject of persecution by the government. He had "secret" information about the CIA and the space program. I was trying to have him verify facts and think about how probable something was likely to be true. He was a fragile person that needed his delusion of being important. Being kind is often more therapeutic than being therapeutic. But no, I was going to try to reason him out of his long-held delusion. I explained to the group delusions were resistant to change, even from contradicting evidence. That's how to spot your own delusions. Am I accepting my own thoughts as proof? To make my point, I said there were some people who believed they have chips implanted in their heads. The chips monitor their thoughts. Even after repeated medical examinations that show no implants, they hold firm to their beliefs. This was my example of an obvious delusion.

Four of 15 clients raised their hands as declared they knew what I meant. They too had had the chips in their heads, and knew the government was monitoring their thoughts. Three said their thoughts were being monitored from space. One thought the receivers were cast into the concrete walls of the hospital. Four of 15 clients with the same delusion, in the same room, by chance. The odds against such a thing happening randomly are astronomical. I began wondering why the universe was screwing with me, even though I know better. I decided to go with the SEs. I asked if the group minded pursuing the question of chip implants. They consented. I proceeded to try to convince them that the government was not monitoring people's thoughts by putting chips in their heads. I avoided the question of why their thoughts would be so remarkable that the government would spend resources to monitor them. I did not want to wound anyone further. I tried to explain how no such technology exists, not even in wildest theory, and the reasons it was technically impossible. No chip could monitor hundreds of billions of neural connections. Obviously, no one was convinced.

The next night I was watching *60 Minutes*. The lead story was about using technology to read thoughts. Researchers had found that a Functional Magnetic Resonance scanner (fMRI) could perform a kind of electronic mind reading. The fMRI produces real-time three-dimensional images of brain activity. It can record the areas of the brain that are active during various tasks. Researchers had taken a sample of people, put them in the scanner, and asked them to think about specific objects or experiences, such as "screwdriver." The computer stored a map of their brain activity. The fMRI's computer then averaged together all the brain activity maps. This produced an image of what the average brain activity for the thought of "screwdriver" looks like. The researchers created a list of target objects and experiences. The computer then had a list of brain states to compare with new subjects. During the show, one of the *60 Minutes* producers was placed in the fMRI and asked to think of "screwdriver." The computer then correctly identified that brain pattern and printed "screwdriver" on a screen. Of 10 target thoughts tried for the demonstration, the computer correctly identified all 10. The researchers speculated that within five years, this technology will be done remotely with infrared beaming. The target person would not even be aware of the scan. New security scanners would scan the brain activity of people in passing crowds. The computer would look for patterns of emotional distress that might identify terrorists and wanted persons. Big Brother indeed. The technology can't really read individual thoughts, but it can tell what general areas of the brain are active.

As luck would have it, three of the four clients in my group that believed the government was reading their thoughts saw the show. All four took this as absolute proof that their minds are being read through implants. Several of the remaining clients now believed the implants were real, no matter what I had to say.

The delusions of the four clients may have been reasonable based on what they knew of the world. Each of these clients assumed the TV show proved their belief that there were chips in their heads. My position was that the SE was interesting, but the technologies were unrelated possibilities. I have had the privilege and the luxury of an education in these fields. I have been taught how to think systematically about the relationships involved. What if I lived in the client's worlds? Each had come for treatment because their ability to test reality was impaired. They had little education due to their illnesses and lifestyles. They generally had very poor models of how the world actually works. The possibility of an fMRI, or a microchip, reading thoughts doesn't seem that unreasonable without any technical background. The brain fills in the gaps with the closest approximation it has available. The problem is what it fills the gaps with. Making an error based on incomplete information is part of the human condition. Our thinking often has to be fast and sloppy or the game escapes us. Problems arise when we can't reevaluate our situation based on new information. Think about our hunter ancestor stalking a brown pattern in the grass. He has decided it's a deer. He creeps closer. His senses give him more information. It's not a deer, it's a lion. Ever know someone who just can't admit they were wrong? Our hunter can either back away slowly, or poke the lion with his sharp stick and insist it's a deer. We hold onto delusions because of pride, we fear the loss of social status that guessing wrong might bring. We carry delusions because of fear; thinking we are right is more comforting than admitting we don't know. Impaired reality testing happens when you can't let go of believing what you think.

The case of B

Psychologists call SEs ideas of reference, or referential ideas, when seen as a symptom of mental illness. SEs are often mixed with delusions when mental illness is present. The delusions, not the SEs, are the real symptom. How do you tell the difference between a person who experiences SEs as part of a mental illness and a person who is merely aware of them and confused? It is the resistance to change. Consider the following case:

B is a 46-year-old male. B was hospitalized with a provisional diagnosis of Psychosis NOS. NOS stands for "not otherwise specified." It's a way of saying he's psychotic, but it doesn't match the usual kinds of psychosis we diagnose. B reports he has a microchip implanted in his head that, you guessed it, reads his thoughts and transmits them to a secret government agency. He reports getting messages from that agency from TV and radio shows. He believed the actors and on-screen personalities were talking directly to him. He said people on the TV respond to what he is thinking in the present moment. He also reported that the clients in the exercise yard below his window were having his thoughts inserted into their minds. They were talking about what he is thinking without knowing it. He was very concerned that the power of his mind is damaging those around him.

The most common treatment for B would be medication, which he may well need, and a course of therapy that confronts his delusions. But what if B is not delusional? What if he is accurately reporting his experiences? What if his delusions are based on misunderstanding SEs? Let's look at how B came to his beliefs. My experience of B was that he was a highly intelligent, loving person, capable of great insight. He had a psychotic break in his early 20s that lasted for six months. His records indicated he had fully recovered. He may have had pre-dispositions for schizophrenia. After his recovery he had educated himself, built a career, and had a social life. He had a very active spiritual practice. He had studied many schools of mysticism, and was practicing several forms of meditation at once without monitoring or instruction. He also began experimenting with hallucinogens mixed with these meditative practices to get more "bang for the buck." His goal was to become what the Buddhists call a bodhisattva, a divine teacher of compassion. He was trying to dissolve the boundaries of the ego, on the theory that the ego is what separates us from awareness of the divine. This would dissolve the ability to discriminate between the outer world and the inner world.

EGO BOUNDARIES AND REALITY TESTING

This brings us to the next criterion for a diagnosis of a psychotic disorder: loss of ego boundaries or a gross impairment in reality testing. B may have already had a predisposition for ego boundary distortions. He had a previous psychotic episode. Hallucinogens disrupt the brain activity that tells us what experiences are internal or external; they can disrupt ego boundaries. He had a stated goal of dissolving his ego boundaries. He was using every means available to do so. He believed that sacred intent would protect him from poor choices. This was a set up for a perfect storm. Ask and you shall receive. B reported his problems started simply enough. He had been meditating to music on the radio. He noticed if you strung together the themes of the songs, they seemed to follow what he was thinking. After observing these SEs for a while, he decided they were not just his imagination. He began to wonder what was behind these SEs. He strained to fit together what the underling pattern might be. He wondered how it was possible for such a thing to be happening, and why to him. Someone or something must be reading his thoughts and changing the radio broadcast content in an attempt to communicate with him. It was this thought that sent him down the rabbit hole.

Soon, he had the revelation that he was in conscious communication with something that was talking back. The SEs began to assume paranoid and grandiose tones. A personal mythology around government conspiracies and secret technologies developed, along with delusions of why he was chosen. The SEs expanded from radios to TVs, to other people. SEs eventually included anything he paid attention to. Stories of messages from gods and demons came and went. His work and friendships drifted away as he chased more cosmic promises. He was eventually hospitalized.

B suffered a breach in ego boundaries and a failure of reality testing. He intentionally assaulted his ego boundaries with time-tested methods of breaching them, and succeeded. He did not transcend his ego boundaries. Transcendence implies moving past them while leaving them functional. He tore a hole in them. B disrupted the neural programming that allows us to distinguish internal from external. What was internal and what was external had become blurred. The result was an explosion of real, objective, SEs that bore the pattern of his confused thoughts. I know his experiences were real, not just part of a psychotic process. I spent time with him, watching them happen around him. It's an interesting experience, watching someone bend their reality around their thoughts. When in session, an SE would happen that patterned on what he had been saying. He would immediately say it was proof of one of his beliefs. I would respond that it was a reflection of his thoughts, not a proof of his thoughts' reality. It was like watching someone have an argument with themselves in a mirror. Think about B's story from a slightly different perspective, one that allows for the projection of internal meanings into external SEs.

B was meditating and doing drugs. He had disrupted the neurological process that maintained his sense of the internal and external. Because of this, his mind was projecting its content onto external thoughts of reference—SE. How this crossover from internal states into actual events occurs will be explained in later chapters. B had disrupted his normal frame of reference. His mind was no longer filtering out normal SEs. B recognized some of his thoughts and feelings reflected in the music on the radio. He started to wonder how this was possible. His mind was trying to pattern-match an explanation and predict what will happen next. Many meanings then appeared in the stream of the SEs as possible explanations for what is happening. He was seeing his thought processes manifested in SE. One set of SEs might reflect the thought that maybe he was talking to god, another SE that these were technologically advanced beings, another that he was communicating with spirits. Eventually he settled on the explanation he thought made the most sense. The SEs told him he had a chip implanted in his head and there was a government conspiracy behind it. This seemed the most plausible explanation to him. It became the dominant pattern. The SE then seemed to confirm this new reality. B was looking in the mirror and seeing his reflection in the whole world.

At this point, B's reality testing had failed. The story he has created would fail any attempt to confirm it, but he still believed it. The SE themselves were being mistaken as proof of the delusion they merely reflect. Treatment for B did include bringing a psychiatrist into the treatment team and putting a floor under his feet with medication. Imagine the state of anxiety he must have been experiencing and the neurological damage such prolonged stress levels can cause. Sometimes you need to bring people down for a landing. The next step was to challenge the delusions compassionately, seeing if he had enough ego strength to re-assess his beliefs. Challenging a delusional belief system that has been re-enforced by SEs is often a daunting task.

With SE, what seems reasonable is often irrational.

SE feedback from the environment helped shape Bs delusions. He was operating from reasonable assumptions based on his experience. He had just been confusing causal reality with acausal events. In his case, the treatment was fairly straightforward. I proposed to him the reflective nature of the SEs. I asked him to consciously focus on a pattern of his choice, and then look for its reflection in the SEs around him. He chose the metaphor of a chess game, and was soon reporting SEs involving bishops, kings, and chess symbols. B was able to accept his thoughts could cause specific patterns in the world around him. In a few months, B was able to let go of all explanations for what was behind the SEs. He was able to learn that the stories the SEs told him were metaphors for his own subconscious processes. He still experienced SEs, but could now discriminate between personal and objective meanings. When I last saw him, his reality testing had been restored. He was functioning well in the world once again with his new understanding. I wonder if his ego boundaries will ever be quite the same. His frame of reference has been permanently altered. SEs are now normal for him.

SE OPERATE INDEPENDENTLY OF A PERSON'S STATE OF MENTAL HEALTH

The mainstream psychiatric explanation of B's story is that he was genetically predisposed to schizophrenia. He had a psychotic break. Medication and therapy had restored him to functionality, but that he was still experiencing thoughts of reference as a residual symptom.

Sometimes when I present the story of B, I am asked why use an example of someone who had a history of mental illness. If I'm trying to present examples of people experiencing SE, why not just pick a high-functioning person as a clear and simple example? Neither people nor SEs are simple. People rarely have a single motive or objective for their actions. We are not consciously aware of most of our thought processes. We don't fully understand ourselves because our complexity would be overwhelming. Tracking every computation in your personal computer would leave you too overwhelmed to make decisions. The meanings we derive from SEs are similarly complex. We never see all there is to be seen, or know all there is to know. We do what we do best; look at complex and incomplete patterns. We take our best guess about what they mean. Then we act on that assessment as if it were reality.

Synchronicity is messy. It is a mirror into the unconscious.

There are reasons why we are shielded from the unconscious. We have defenses to keep us from being overwhelmed. Grandiosity is often a defense against the anxiety of helplessness and inferiority. If someone such as B shapes himself into a grandiose delusion by following SE, it is because he is already using that defense unconsciously. The SEs have performed one of the functions of psychotherapy. They have made the unconscious conscious. They reveal the defense, and the material underneath.

Being aware of SE is not an indication of mental illness. It is not an advanced set of perceptual skills. It is not an indication of spiritual achievement. It is a particular way the mind matches patterns and derives meanings between the internal and external worlds. Our senses give us information that is both incomplete, and in amounts that are overwhelming. Our decisions are always best guesses based on a reality that has had much deleted, edited for context, and added to by the brain. It is a messy process because to be precise and accurate takes too much time. For our ancestors, he who hesitated became dinner, or missed the chance to catch dinner. Being wrong was not that important. Being able to make a decision and act quickly was. If our ancestors ran from a movement in the grass they thought was a lion, they increased their chances of survival. Messy pattern misinterpretation worked in their favor. If they set traps for small animals only where they were sure the animals would be, there would be only a few chances to catch a meal. If they guessed, put many traps down, even in places they were less sure about, the chances of a catch got better. Guessing is messy, but it increases our chances of a positive outcome. When people are suffering from delusions, they are often trying to get away from the uncomfortable uncertainty of some part of their experience. They can't tolerate not knowing for sure, so they foreclose on the situation by picking one explanation and sticking to it. It solves the problem of things feeling messy and out of control. But it also can prevent adapting to new information and experiences.

SE AND CULTURAL PROGRAMMING

Modern western societies ignore SE. We don't teach our children about the connection between their inner and outer worlds. If they are very young, we allow "magical thinking" and tell them stories about how wishing sometimes makes things come true. We leave out that the world mirrors their drives, emotions, and thoughts. As adults, we have enough problems dealing with our own. We expect older children to give up the belief that their internal world affects the external reality. We call this an act of maturity. It is really an act of cognitive castration. If children learn to suppress awareness of SEs, they have trained their brain to filter out SEs from conscious awareness. The resulting adults operate in a linear world that is much less messy, much more predictable, but ultimately less rich and full of opportunities. This more limited way of experiencing the inner and outer worlds offers the illusion of certainty usually reserved for the delusional. It makes for a less adaptive ego structure with ridged but more fragile boundaries. B was a person who could have functioned well if it were not for some poor methods of self-exploration. Once he had fractured his ego boundary, he found himself with no way to orient himself between the internal and external worlds. It is difficult enough for any person to cope with a psychological crisis that seems purely internal. B had to cope with both internal and external worlds becoming confusing and disorienting at the same time.

What if B had not been trained as a child to form such ridged separations between his inner and outer experiences? What if he were used to SEs happening as part of his normal reality? What if he knew about SEs from childhood, was taught SEs by his parents, by his schools? Would he have become delusional? Certainly, the emotional charge would have been less when the world began to respond to his thoughts. He might have seen an increase in the frequency of SEs. He might even have taken the opportunity to analyze what internal content was coming up and gained some personal insight. He might not have gotten himself tied up in a psychological knot chasing his own mental tail.

Synchronistic Event

A few years ago, I was driving through the San Francisco area with my daughter. She was home for college vacation, and we were enjoying catching up with each other. During the ride, we encountered a string of SEs that reflected back to us pieces of the conversation we were having. Each time I pointed out the connection of the event to what we were saying, she would make some small acknowledging comment and continue with the conversation. Eventually, I pointed out an SE and she just looked at me with a sweet, yet patronizing look. I asked what she was thinking. She said, "Look dad, you have been telling me about synchronicity all my life. It's just not that interesting. I understand how it works, my friends and I play with it sometimes, but its kind of your thing. I don't really have the time to bother with it."

I was a little stunned, and more than a little impressed. SE was just part of her ongoing perception of the world. She was raised with it; she had it completely in perspective. She was politely acting as if I were trying to explain what a metaphor was to an English major.

MAKING THE UNCONSCIOUS CONSCIOUS

Sometimes we make things messier than they need to be. Many SEs are simple, direct reflections of emotions and thoughts, and are not easily subject to deeper interpretations. There are many shallow and un-important SEs around us all the time. There are many shallow and un-important thoughts as well. Sometimes the bird in the mirror is just a bird in the mirror. Like dreams, the more one pays attention to SE, the more frequent and more meaningful they become. Like the unconscious, the more intently we peer, the greater depth and complexity that rises to meet us. Therapies such as Freud's psychoanalysis and Jung's analytical analysis have a primary goal of making the unconscious conscious. This is no small undertaking, as the majority of our processes remain un-conscious no matter how much time we devote to trying to understand them. When doing therapy, part of my task is to keep in mind what the client's goals are. Therapy should not become a free form and unending wandering about. People's internal wonderland is vast. Exploring it can consume as much time and resources as a person is willing to commit. SE reflects the content of the personal unconscious and the collective as well. SE can easily become a distraction. Like the magic mirror in Harry Potter, one can become lost staring at reflections of one's deepest desires or fears. The observing ego's job is to sit on the fence of the internal and external worlds, to balance both, and to meet the demands and needs of each of them. Synchronicity can be thought of as a sort of "cheat" that allows the observing ego to view aspects of the internal and external world at the same time. It can become a formidable distraction. You can become so fixated with the image in the mirror that you forget your "real" life. B became trapped staring into the mirror.

My approach is to provide the reader with different depths to the explanatory fiction I have created. It is up to you to decide what your goals are, and how deep down the rabbit hole you want to go.

Exploring SE is exploring yourself.

You are vast, complex, and beautiful. In the following chapters, we will be descending gradually deeper down the rabbit hole. Any journey that tries to describe where the inner and outer worlds meet tends to become more metaphorical and mythological the deeper it gets. SEs often give the feeling that we are almost there, only to find the next unexpected turn opens to more than we had anticipated.

Five

Synchronicity and Enlightenment

"A human being is part of the whole...the universe. He experiences himself, his thoughts and feelings, as something separated from the rest—a kind of optical delusion of his consciousness. This delusion is a kind of prison for us, restricting us to our personal desires and to affection for a few persons nearest us. Our task must be to free ourselves from this prison by widening our circle of compassion to embrace all living creatures and the whole of nature in its beauty." —Albert Einstein

RECOGNIZING YOURSELF IN THE MIRROR

When I first started to write this chapter, I thought I had a few simple and clear ideas to convey. I was going to tell you in simple terms how you are connected to the wider reality you think is outside yourself. Enlightenment is an understanding that separateness is an illusion. It can be an actual experience we have, sometimes called satori, divine unity, being one with god, or ascension. These experiences last for moments, and they alter lives forever. Nobody lives in these states of unity. Even Zen masters consider themselves fortunate to reach satori a few times in a lifetime. I was going to begin this chapter on SE and enlightenment by telling you that SEs are partial experiences of satori. SEs are a small-scale satori, tiny hints that you are not a separate being, that you are, in your deepest identity, god. Friends have told me it would be a great selling point for the book, that there is a huge market for books on spirituality. The original idea for this chapter was to sell you the idea there is only one being: you. I'm going to describe a set of ideas that our ancestors evolved and passed on to us, ideas about how we are connected to the universe. If ideas such as enlightenment and opinions of what spirituality means don't appeal to you, feel free to skip this chapter. You don't have to understand your universal connectedness to use SE as a mirror. You will need to understand SEs are a mirror to avoid coming to believe what you think. Things are not true just because you believe them. Likewise, SEs are not to be believed or followed blindly.

I want to empower you, give you an understanding of your connection and abilities in a balanced and grounded frame of reference. SEs provided me with a perspective changing experience. SEs are harmless. Ignorance isn't.

The case of J, a cautionary tale

A client came to me for an assessment. J looks 10 years older than his actual 60 years. He has three serious illnesses that he knows will be fatal within the next 10 years. J has had a difficult life. As the end of his life approaches, he is grieving over all the things he never had. He is alone, owns nothing, sees no hope in his future. My task was to assess his current mental status and recommend which services might help him. In my second interview with J, we were talking about his personal history. He was clearly depressed about his situation. He gradually opened up to me as he realized I actually cared about people and was trying to help.

His health records indicated several serious symptoms of mental illness, including delusions. These assessments did not match the person I was sitting with. He was depressed, but his thoughts were clear, his concerns well reasoned, his emotions appropriate for his situation. Toward the middle of the session, J said, "I know I'm not going to get any better. I can deal with my situation. Its all the other stuff that bothers me."

I asked him what "other stuff" he was talking about. He told me it didn't matter because I wouldn't believe him, nobody ever believed him. I spent some time making sure he knew I was not going to judge him and although I might not believe what he wanted to tell me, I would really listen to his story. When he believed there was enough of a connection between us, he shared his burden. He told me that he was one of god's chosen people. Usually when a patient informs me they are god, god's representative, or some variation on the delusions of grandeur theme, there are familiar patterns. Sometimes the patient is manic; their brains are racing so fast the state of elation causes them to believe they are god. They may be high on their own brain chemistry. This costs them dearly. The racing brain activity literally burns out their neurons if it goes on too long. J was depressed. If anything, his brain activity was lower than it should have been. Most delusions have a reason. They protect the person from something, some pain they can't function with. Clients who believe they are god, or chosen by god, are usually scared and hurt. The defense against vulnerability is sometimes delusions of divinity. J felt his own pain and powerlessness. My gut told me something else was up. I was having a good day. I managed to do the most therapeutic thing; I listened.

J told me he had no idea what god had chosen him to do, or why. According to J, there were lots of chosen people like him. There was no ego about the way he explained it. He didn't feel blessed. It had ruined his life, driven away everyone he had ever been close to. J said God tormented him, for some unknown reason, by changing events and people around him, causing meaningful coincidences. He believed God talked to him through the context of events. TV programs were speaking to him in real time; what was said by the actors was always a commentary on what he was thinking. He couldn't bear to be around people because they always spoke his thoughts as he had them. God made them do this without them even knowing. He said it was like the whole world continually revolved around what he thought and felt. He believed God must have chosen him for some special purpose. It must be true, why else would God expend such cosmic power just to make the world dance in the pattern of J's thoughts? There was no other possibility. J had never been taught to think in any other pattern. He had spent the last four decades trying to cope with being made the center of the universe, trying to figure out what God wanted from him. He had been surrounded by intense SE for all those years, seeking an answer, looking into the SE mirror, lost. He looked for God, and never recognized himself.

I was not able to help J. I arranged supportive services and completed the assessment, which should have, but did not contain a recommendation he attend an SE education class. No such classes exist, yet. In what little was left of our session time, I tried to explain the concept of SE, and that he was looking at a reflection of his thoughts. It was a futile gesture; you can't change someone's frame of reference that drastically in an hour. He probably thought I was crazy. There was no way to give J the reasoning and background he needed to recognize not God, but himself, as the source of the SE. Explanations matter; they give you ways to think about causes and effects. Explanations allow you to match patterns, to predict. Explanations can free you or enslave you. J, if you're out there, here's what I wanted to tell you:

You have an amazing ability. You effortlessly create SEs all around you. You are not alone; everyone creates SEs. You do this with such ease that even your most fleeting thoughts create SE reflections. Your dreams and fantasies, the simulations your mind creates to process experience, all appear in those SEs. These are all forms of thought. You decide which thoughts are objectively real. Your job is to not believe everything you think. SEs reflect the full range of your mental activity, even activity you usually filter out of conscious awareness. They are a window into the unconscious and the transpersonal. SE is a full spectrum reflection of your inner life. Being aware of how SE works presents you with the dilemma of living in a world of people who, for the most part, do not share this frame of reference.

SE AND THE EVOLUTION OF RELIGION

When I finally bumped my head against SE enough to understand I was walking into a mirror, many things I had read about spirituality suddenly made sense. Have you heard the joke about the Dali Lama? He walked up to a hot dog stand and asked them to make him one with everything. One with everything. There are religious doctrines created to keep people under control and to maintain civil order. You can spot them pretty easily; they consist mainly of behavioral instructions and commands. Jared Diamond describes in *Guns, Germs, and Steel: The Fates of Human Societies* the evolution of the concept of a single, all-powerful God. When we lived in tribal groups without fixed laws, we generally had social communities of about 60 people. This is the kind of society our ancestral hunter lived in. One of the reasons we developed these marvelously fast and complex brains was to be able to keep track of the other people around us. We survive because we cooperate with each other. Cooperation means being able to keep track of what the people around us need and want. It takes a biological supercomputer to run internal simulations of all the relationships involved, and figure out who is being fair and who is cheating. With groups larger than about 60 people, the internal social tensions become overwhelming. People begin to have conflicts, factions develop, and parts of the group split off and leave to live and hunt somewhere else. We can't keep track of everyone in larger groups. This makes it impossible to make good pattern matches about everyone, so we break up into smaller groups. We answered this problem by creating a social technology that allowed many more people to live together. We created law. Tribal groups came under the law of a single king. The king had the power to negotiate and coerce tribes into cooperation. Kings needed to justify their authority over clans and tribes. Tribal cultures believe in spirits. Each person and clan usually allied with a spirit they hoped would help tip the SE scales their way. Bears are tough and versatile survivors. There were bear clans wherever there were bears; in ancient Europe, Asia, and in both North and South America. There were wolf clans, lion clans, horse clans. Some tribes allied themselves with their dead ancestors. After all, not having the limitations of the living, the dead might be in a good position to lend a hand. When tribes went to war, a common event, the spirits fought and the strongest spirit gave victory to its people. There was much "Our spirit animal can kick your spirit animal's ass" mentality.

How was a king supposed to maintain authority over such a spiritual zoo? No matter what spirit a king claimed to derive his authority from, there was always someone claiming he had a more powerful spirit animal. This undercut the king's authority. What made kings possible was the first great religious con. The kings declared that there was a king of the spirits. This new head God had power over all the tribal spirit animals, and this king God ordered obedience to the human king. There were, of course, a few details to fill in to make this all work. The king had to be the head priest so that nobody else could claim they knew the God's will better than the king. Disbelief had to be declared heresy, couldn't have folks asking for proof of the unprovable. Heresy usually meant torture and a death sentence. This cut down on disbelief quite a bit. Later, when societies became larger and more impersonal, kings declared themselves Gods and demanded direct worship. This usually entailed demanding people give them goods and services. The king became the law. The law became the religion. These doctrines are all about controlling behavior and keeping order. If you can substitute "The king orders you to" for "God wants you to," and the command still makes sense, you are looking at a man-made frame of reference. Placement in heaven or hell, or more favorable incarnations, has replaced open death threats, at least in some of the world. These doctrines still focus on manipulating behavior. SEs can mirror these beliefs because we carry our beliefs as thoughts.

RELIGIOUS BELIEF VS. STATES OF CONSCIOUSNESS

Some spiritual doctrines don't focus on behavior; they focus on achieving states of consciousness. They change the frame of reference to create experiences. Christian Gnosticism, Islamic Sufism, Zen Buddhism, and the shamanism of our ancestors often focused on creating states of ecstatic union. In these states of consciousness, the practitioner experiences existence without boundaries. The subject/object relationship we experience as separateness ceases to exist. You become one with everything. This connection is not something you earn; it is what you already are. SEs are not something you learn to create, you learn to recognize you are already creating them. I have heard people ask if someone was "enlightened," as if it were a possession that enhanced their value. Enlightenment is the recognition of your essential unity and connection with existence. You don't have to earn it, you are it.

Spirituality is not based on a merit system. Grace is the nature of existence.

Bodhidharma was a monk said to have brought Buddhism and the doctrine of enlightenment to China in the 6th century.

Hearing of Bodhidharma's reputation as a monk, Emperor Wu of the Liang dynasty summoned him to court. The emperor asked Bodhidharma:

"Since becoming emperor I have had many temples built, had many sutras (sermons) copied, and many monks ordained. How much merit have I gained by these actions?"

"No merit at all," answered Bodhidharma.

"Why no merit at all?" Asked Wu.

The monk replied, "All these are but impure motives done for merit; they mature the paltry fruits of rebirth as a human or a god. They are like shadows that follow the form, having no reality of their own.

The emperor then asked, "Then of what kind is true merit?"

He answered, "It is pure knowing, wonderful and perfect. Its essence is emptiness. One cannot gain such merit by worldly means."

"What is this sacred truth's first principal?" asked Wu.

"Vast emptiness, nothing sacred," replied the master.

The emperor then asked, "Who is this that stands before me?"

"I don't know," replied Bodhidharma.

Displeased with his responses, the emperor had him banished from court.

The emperor thought spirituality was a behavior. Earning it meant spending money and performing good works. Bodhidharma teaches enlightenment is the experience of your real nature, not something you accumulate. In Bodhidharma's philosophy, our mental conceptions of what is spiritual can only limit our experience of what the spiritual is. We can become like the emperor Wu, who thought that the manipulation of objects and behaviors lead to spiritual merit. You can't buy enlightenment, but there sure seems to be a lot of people willing to try to sell it to you. Enlightenment is your understanding of the scope of your connection to everything. Enlightenment is rational, demonstrable connectedness within your own consciousness. It is the thought that you are an isolated being, unconnected with the events around you, that doesn't make sense. Changing to this frame of reference can happen after spectacular experiences of unity, such as the experience of satori. More often one learns enlightenment in stages as a person's frame of reference gradually becomes more inclusive. The emperor asks Bodhidharma, "Who is this that stands before me?"

When the sage answers, "I don't know," Wu takes him for a fool and throws him out of court.

It's the question that doesn't make sense, not the answer. Bodhidharma answers from the enlightened frame of reference. He lives in a frame of reference where there is only one being, one existence, one consciousness. Believing each person is somehow separated from the existence around them, made no sense to him. The question seemed irrational. Emperors often like to think they know more than everyone else. It helps with the nagging feeling they have on the inside that they are really regular people. Bodhidharma has a wider frame of reference. He experiences a universe that is one continuous living energy. He is a set of temporary waves on the surface of this infinite sea. Wu's "Who are you?" question supposes the universe is divided into separate beings. Bodhidharma has no way of answering the question because separation is an illusion for him. He might have said something such as, "I'm you, dummy, the chair you're sitting on, the room you see, the servant serving you wine, everybody and everything you have ever experienced." Probably safer to tell the emperor he didn't know and walk away.

I love that story, long commentaries have been written in Buddhist literature about all the meanings it can convey. I don't believe for a moment that the encounter between Wu and Bodhidharma actually happened. People tell stories to pass on ideas, enshrine what seems important in religion to give it credibility, attribute things to gods so that authority will outweigh the demand for proof. An encounter between a legendary enlightened master and a materialistic God-king becomes a legend, passed down in scripture and sermon for a thousand years.

SE as a demonstration of connectedness

SE can teach you your seamless connection to the rest of the universe, that you are one. It can demonstrate the separated, individuated, isolated existence frame of reference is the illusion. Instead of asking how our connection to SE is possible, why not ask for an explanation of how it could possibly be any other way? I want you to stop thinking of SEs as unusual events. We match patterns. Our brains don't like patterns that we can't recognize. We are hard-wired to react to the unknown with a danger signal. The unusual attracts our attention, becomes important. We also learn from the successes and failures of others. Emperors and enlightened sages all have an association of having "succeeded" in some great endeavor. We associate their success with having done something that assures their survival. Wu is the alpha male leader of the pack, there is no doubt his genetic pattern will be passed on and his needs will be provided for. The ideal king is the protector and provider of order that serves his people's survival needs. Stay close to the big dog, he can help you stay alive, watch what he does, learn from his successes. Belief in the power of gods to assist us is a logical extension of this way of thinking. The concept of enlightenment takes a radically different direction. There is no road to follow, no ticket to buy from someone else, no way to lose it. Your innermost identity is not just connected to everything, it *is* everything. That includes all the sort of death and taxes conditions of life we would rather didn't exist. SE can show you your connection, by showing you yourself, but it won't allow you to delete parts of your experiences from existence. There is an old Zen saying: "Before enlightenment you chop wood and carry water. After enlightenment you…chop wood and carry water." This literally meant before the satori experience people have to carry out the mundane activities of everyday life that support their physical existence. Ahh, but after enlightenment everything changes; except that you still have to carry out the mundane activities of everyday life that support your physical existence. I was disappointed to learn this. Like the emperor, my ego hoped it was like a finish line I could cross and all the problems of living would be resolved. Life is not about completion; it's about living.

SEs are not about making problems go away, they are about experiencing more fully the life you already have.

The Buddha never described his experience, saying only it was beyond thought and had to be sought by the individual. He never gave any detailed instructions, and told his followers to stop reading books on spirituality and to ignore the priests. He said not to worry about what happens when we die, that it takes care of itself. He said to take care of each other, to be kind and compassionate to other people. Doctrine doesn't matter, beliefs don't matter, love matters. Why would he say such an illogical thing? Because it is logical, it's the most rational statement I have ever heard a teacher make. From an enlightened, unified, frame of reference, those people around you *are* you.

The world you live in IS you. Be nice to yourself.

When my dog Sol was a puppy, he chased his own tail. He thought it was something following him around, didn't know he was connected to it. One day he caught his tail and bit down hard. It was an enlightening experience for him.

The evolution of the concept of enlightenment

How do you actually have "the experience" of enlightenment? What is in your way? In Bodhidharma's day, the thought was thinking was in your way. It's a catch 22. If you think you need to become enlightened, you are thinking that you are not already, so your experience follows your thought. Your thoughts are in your way. SE behaves this way, reflects what you believe. The Zen answer at the time was to tell the students aspiring to enlightenment they had to stop their thoughts. Good luck with that. I think of Bodhidharma as a kind of Buddhist Paul Bunyan: a larger-than-life figure in larger-than-life stories. Ideas about how to become enlightened evolved into teaching stories. For example; Here's another tall Bhodidharma tale:

> Bodhidharma sat in zazen (meditation) facing the wall. His student (Hui-k'o), who had been standing in the snow, approached Bhodidharma and cut off his own arm as a gesture of the intensity of his desire for enlightenment, and said, "Your disciple's mind is not yet at peace. I beg you, my teacher, please give it peace." Bodhidharma said, "Bring the mind to me, and I shall set it at rest."

> The student declared, "I have searched for the mind and it is finally unattainable (He can't find it.)"

> Bodhidharma responds, "I have thoroughly set it at rest for you."

The student is lost in thinking like emperor Wu. He has been trying to do something to get something. Bodhidharma is telling him to stop chasing his tail. Stop thinking there is a lack of connection, and there won't be one. You already have the Buddha nature, stop screwing it up by looking for it.

Nike Zen; Just be it

Dogen Kigen (1200–1253) was one of the first Japanese masters to make the journey back to the root of Zen in China, then return to Japan to revitalize the practice. In his masterwork the *Shobogenzo*, Dogen makes one of his most insightful statements during a translation from the Chinese of the Nirvana sutra. The original text reads:

"All sentient beings without exception have the Buddha nature."

Dogen renders it this way: "All sentient beings *are* the Buddha nature."

Dogen reinterprets the term "sentient" to mean the Buddha nature itself, extending the Buddha nature to the universal. He makes all of existence part of the Buddha mind. The Buddha mind is sentient, all things are of the Buddha mind, therefore all things partake in that sentience:

> Hence, all mind is sentient being: Sentient beings are all Buddha nature. Grass and trees, states and lands, are mind. Because they are mind, they are sentient beings. Because they are sentient beings, they are Buddha nature. Heavenly bodies are mind. Because they are mind, they are sentient beings. Because they are sentient beings, they are being Buddha nature.

Dogen is saying there is only one vast, living being. No separation was ever possible to begin with. Even our personal thoughts and illusions of separation are part of the whole. Imagine a sheet of plain white paper in front of you. Pretend this piece of paper is the universe, all of time, all of space, every possible thought. Draw a small circle in the center with a pencil. In the circle, write, "This is me." Did this separate the paper in the circle from the rest of the paper? No. You created the idea of separation between areas of the paper. The actual paper has not changed. You can draw any idea you like on the paper, its still the same paper. Make as many different circles as you like; its still one piece of paper. SE is a way you draw on the paper. You draw what you choose to think about. When I draw on the SE paper, I use a pencil. I don't believe in permanent unalterable thoughts. Delusional people tend to draw on the SE paper with ink, hard to erase, and easy to draw yourself into a corner with. Enlightenment tends to erase permanent lines from the paper. It erases lines in your mind, in your heart, and between the self you think you are, and the only self there really is.

PRACTICAL ENLIGHTENMENT

I'd like to finish this chapter on a practical note. While I was writing the first drafts of this book readers and editors repeatedly asked a question that astonished and perplexed me. They wanted to know what practical use synchronicity was to readers, why they should be interested. Synchronicity is a tool of self-knowledge and a new awareness just wasn't, well, enticing enough. So, I spent some time thinking about how to make synchronicity seem interesting. It felt a bit comical, like trying to figure out how to make water interesting to fish; they already swim in it but probably don't actually think about it that much. Here's what I came up with to get you interested:

Most of my life, I have been a spiritual tourist. Like many curious people with the privilege of access to information, I have wandered, however shallowly, down the spiritual paths left behind by other people and cultures. I have been a consumer of many spiritual goods, follower of many wonderful and silly fads in consciousness, been taken by, and taken in by, both the traditional and new. I'm pretty lazy and impatient when it comes to the claims of spiritual achievement and promises of becoming a master of consciousness. I don't want to practice something for years before seeing results. I don't have the faith to wait lifetimes for liberation while practicing devotions, or the purity to wait for my rewards in heaven. I never achieved enough trust to place my life and belief unquestioningly in the hand of a spiritual master, no matter how well endorsed and commercialized the workshops and retreats. Yup, I'm a westernized consumer. I want it now, I want it cheap, and I want it easy. As a psychologist, I'm dogmatically research-oriented. If you think something is an effective therapy, show me the research. If someone tells me something works, even if they don't know why, demonstrate it. Sooner would be better than later; I grew up watching TV and get bored with things longer than a commercial break that don't seem to be going anywhere. Sad but true.

Enter synchronicity. Synchronicity works. If you realize it exists, and look for it, you find it. There's no complex philosophy needed, it's as simple as a mirror. It works now, just start looking. If you haven't already experienced SE in your life before, or started experiencing it since you started reading this book, I'd be very surprised. There is no esoteric discipline required, no teacher to sit at the feet of, and, horror of horrors, no money to spend.

Synchronicity offers a window of self-discovery that works best in the context of the life you already live.

Before SE, you chop wood and carry water. After SE, you chop wood and carry water. SE demonstrates your connectedness; they are a mini-satori. SE reminds you of your essential connection to the whole. If you choose to use SE to walk a spiritual path toward being one with the universe, take care. SE will reflect any spiritual fantasy you choose to entertain. You can create moments when every event in the universe seems to align with your thoughts and emotions. All lines and boundaries seem to have been erased; these moments seem perfect, infinite, and eternal. In the next moment, you realize you have to use the bathroom, the shopping has to be done, and you forgot to call the phone company to check on that problem with the monthly bill. SE, like enlightenment, includes the details of everyday life.

Six

Satori in a Can

SE AS COMMUNICATION WITH YOURSELF

You have many choices about how to experience SE. In the previous chapter, I talked about synchronicity as a minor manifestation of enlightenment. SE can act as a kind of mini-satori, indicating your conscious connection to more unified aspects of yourself. SE show connections between aspects of yourself that are not immediately apparent. We think in relationships. Often when an SE happens, I wonder at the meaning, often wasting my time, trying to understand what use any particular SE can be. This misses the more important use of SE, as a way of communicating with yourself. It is easy to become caught in utilitarian logic, looking for the profit, the survival benefit to us as individuals. We sometimes miss deeper connections that do not seem particularly concerned with our survival as individuals. We can forget that we are collective beings. It is the relationship between us, between each other, and the objects we mis-perceive as separate from us, that SEs often reconcile. You are already more than the tiny area of brain activity that forms personal consciousness. You already have a relationship with the wider whole of your being that is the totality of all possible experiences and relationships. That relationship is what you expect it to be. Like the friends we make, it can be close and generous, or at times, difficult and challenging. As a psychotherapist, it strikes me how responsive we are to each other in our relationships. Parents, children, couples, and friends seem to react to each other in the ways we expect. We take on complex roles for each other with remarkable ease. In family and couples' counseling, I often see very enmeshed relationships. The individuals have unconsciously taken on roles for each other that blur their psychological boundaries. This is not an inherently good or bad thing. People in love often finish each other's sentences, and seem to know each other's moods and needs almost telepathically. This a beautiful thing to experience. On the other hand, co-dependent relationships that support each other's weaknesses out of insecurity cause much personal suffering. Sometimes people forget they have choices in the way they form relationships. Your relationship with SEs will depend largely on how you feel about being part of a unified collective consciousness. Is your relationship fearful or friendly? Do you expect SEs to merely reflect your conscious desires and thoughts? Do you expect more than just being able to direct aspects of SEs for your amusement and benefit? What kind of relationship with SEs do you actually want?

GETTING WHAT YOU WANT FROM SE

Let's dissolve some barriers. The moment I am writing this sentence, and the moment you are reading it, is actually the same moment. Time is not a separated thing, moving from disconnected moment to moment. It is also part of a greater collective, an all-inclusive whole. This allows SEs to happen in real time between when I am writing this, and when you are reading it. So, if you choose to, you can read this, or anything else, as if it were created for you in your present moment. As I have been writing this chapter, I have been having some difficulty collecting my thoughts. I need an example of SE that reflects a relationship to the whole that is personal. I also wanted to make a case for SE being able to provide actual opportunities and answers when you need them. I'm trying to make a case for the whole, experienced in satori, as being capable of being an actual relationship that is responsive to your needs, not just an impersonal reflection. There are a number of books on the market that claim SE as a manifestation of "cosmic" consciousness. Some of them claim you should always trust SEs to come up with directions and answers to life's problems. I would like to believe this is true, but my personal and professional experience has shown me that personal delusions run rampant in SE for many folks. At the moment, I need a clear example of an SE that shows they have a personal relationship and can provide the opportunity to have needs met. So, I'm at a stuck place in the writing, until:

Synchronistic Event

The phone here at the house just rang. The call is from a close friend. Kieth has called to tell me about an interesting SE he has just experienced that he thought I might want to write about in this book. Now, I'm tired, and a little frustrated at the moment with my inability to remember a specific SE to demonstrate how SEs can unexpectedly provide something you need. My life is filled with daily SE, but I haven't been writing them down lately, so I don't have one that directly reflects the thought pattern I need. When I'm tired I can be, well, a bit slow. So, I reluctantly ask him to tell me about his SE. At this point, I have completely missed the synchronicity of needing an SE that demonstrates a relationship, and having my best friend call me to tell me about an SE. One of Kieth's many hobbies includes running a Karaoke business. He said he went to a local record store looking for a newly released CD to include in the show. When he arrived, the record store was closed, and he was unfamiliar with the city. He decided to ask the first teenager he met on the sidewalk if he knew where the record store had relocated. The person he asked not only knew the new location, but worked there. He was walking there at that very moment, and offered to walk Kieth over. The store not only had the music he was looking for, but he was given a large discount because he now knew a store employee! He said that he knew this was an SE and that he was supposed to tell me about it. He walked outside to smoke a cigarette, and found he had none. A person who had been in the store approached him and said "Hey, I know you. I was at one of your shows. They then handed Kieth some smokes without being asked. SE was handing him everything he needed.

I listened to his story. When he was done he asked if I could use it in the book. I said I didn't know, but that I'd write it down and see if it fit in anywhere. I thanked him and we set a time to talk in a few days when I wasn't so preoccupied. I was actually a little annoyed at the interruption. I came back to my keyboard, here now, in this moment with you. I started to read what I had just written, and was wondering how I was going to find an SE that characterized the spontaneous fulfillment of a need in a way that seemed to be based on a personal relationship. I drank the 5-hour energy drink I had been using for motivation, and when the caffeine raised my IQ a few points, I realized what had just happened. SE had literally called me on the phone to provide exactly what I needed at the exact moment I needed it. As I was trying to speak with you in your present moment, SE reached out to demonstrate you can get some semblance of what you need from SE.

Context is everything with SE.

By context, you can infer relationship. When I teach SE, I always try to set a context for the listener. This sets the tone for the relationship. I speak from the perspective of a storyteller. This frees you from the need to determine if the story is, in the strictest sense, true. The idea is for you to make this story about SE true for you. The actual events of an SE are usually straightforward. The meanings you take away from them are as vast, complex, and full of relationship as the time you spend thinking about them.

Your sense of time and the ability to recognize patterns is created by the way your brain processes information. As we shall see in later chapters, we have more than one mind, more than one computer in our heads. You are constantly engaged in creating new realities, running scenarios, matching patterns, and considering alternative possibilities. SE reflects all of this vast processing activity simultaneously. You get to choose which of the vast possibilities you want to validate and manifest as SEs. Sometimes SEs show you your own uncertainty. SEs are story-tellers. The best storytellers incorporate enough of the listeners' known experience to make the story plausibly true.

As I'm writing this I'm trying to set a direction and tone for your relationship with SE. The SE of this afternoon doesn't seem to be co-operating with the direction I was originally heading in this chapter. De-pak Chopra, in his book *The Spontaneous Fufillment of Desire: Harnessing the Infinite Power of Coincidence*, makes a wonderful case for SEs being available for the fulfillment of your personal needs. I didn't want to give you that impression. I see SE more as a reflection of the totality of your thoughts, even your unconscious and transpersonal processes. Yogananda's perspective on SEs also runs more in the "SE is your friend and can provide what you need" camp. His perspective is the positive SEs he experienced were the result of his relationship with the divine. I'm still not a big believer in outside intelligences that direct SEs. In fact, I'm deeply suspicious of anyone who claims SEs result from personal relationships with unseen supernatural forces. Yet here I sit, trying to convince you that you are a unified being, SEs are a reflection, your energy creates them, and not to believe things just because you think them. All the while, the SE flowing around me contradicts the story I'm trying to tell you. SEs have been illustrating my material as I write, but today seem to be pulling for a mythology I don't completely believe. One of the most powerful of all human motivations seems to be the search for spiritual connection. For most religions this manifests as a need to feel close to a personalized parent-god figure.

Synchronistic Event

In my time, I have been trying to make a case for you being god yourself, at least one connected aspect of it. As I'm beginning to type a long-winded explanation of this, SE pops up again on the internet radio station playing in the background. The song "What if God Was One of Us" by Joan Osborne is playing.

"What if God was one of us?

Just a slob like one of us?

Just a stranger on the bus

Trying to make his way home."

SE can be quite playful. Allan Combs in *Synchronicity: Through the Eyes of Science, Myth and the Trickster* points out that many cultures see SEs as mischievous. At the moment, SEs seem to be pointing out that you are the one who will write your own story, and poking some fun at me for making assumptions on how you should tell your own tale. You will have your own relationship with SEs. Personally, I find dealing with tricksters more fun than forming relationships with divinities. Divinities seem to format SEs with less of a sense of humor. People can get touchy about anything that criticizes what they see as their spiritual path. As previously described, religions, the inherent vehicles of our created divinities, really have little to do with spirituality. Neither do schools of meditation, philosophy, gurus, or anything else that takes your attention out of the present moment of your experience. Spirituality is an experience of connection. It is the degree to which you experience your wholeness. SEs are one manifestation of that connection. We shape that connection by limiting it to our own thoughts and assumptions. We tend to think there is a spiritual path, a goal, some state of consciousness we have to achieve. No wonder the tricksters of the universe play with us and try to teach us a sense of humor. It's really quite funny, being an aspect of the one being, and thinking there is anywhere to go, or something to do, to make us more of what we have always been. There will always be people who will try to skillfully insert themselves into this silly misperception. They provide further distractions and instructions on how to get where you always have been. Entertainers usually get paid for their services, or for their books.

HAVING A RELATIONSHIP WITH YOUR WIDER SELF

So, here we are. You can play with SEs, create your own, or use them to explore your innate connection with the one being you already are. As long as you don't take yourself too seriously, SEs won't either. SEs behave much like a good friend that way. SEs can tell you a lot about yourself you don't necessarily see on your own. Some of us are content with an amusing taste of unified consciousness. You may read this book out of curiosity, see a few SEs over the next weeks because you are paying attention, then lose interest, and the SEs will fade away. You may become interested in the possible use of SEs to provide you with things you desire. Or, like some of us, you might want to know just how deep this rabbit hole goes. Unitive consciousness exists on a spectrum. At the shallow end of this pool is existence that knows nothing of interconnectedness. People can function quite well and fulfill their biological and genetic mandates without ever experiencing a real connection to their universe. You can worship the god of your choice, or cultural default, without ever realizing you are the object of your devotion. In slightly deeper waters, you can live in a universe in which your thoughts are reflected back to you in SE. This doesn't mean you have the personal moment-to-moment experience of being a unified being. That experience, satori, is at the deep end of the pool. That experience requires a relationship which dissolves personal ego boundaries. It's a very personal, intimate, and powerful ecstatic experience. Satori is also well within your normal range of experience. Now, I understand that the theme of this book has been telling you wonderful things about yourself and your abilities. Much of this story is a little hard to believe, but it's a true story nonetheless. How much of this story is true is left up to you to verify by making your own SEs. Remarkably, if you can experience SE, satori is also within your range of consciousness.

Satori is a full-scale SE experience. In the usual run-of-the-mill SE, you experience a partial synchronization between your thoughts and the world around you. If you analyze the structure of the SE, you find deeper layers of your own thoughts brought to consciousness by the SE. There are always echoes of deeper processes, and no SE can reflect the totality of your internal states. Not until you realize it is possible. Consider this: what would happen if you could push the intensity and frequency of SEs to the most extreme imaginable limits? Imagine; every event and object in the universe falls into a perfectly synchronized SEs around you. More than that, every thought that fabulous supercomputer in your head produces, suddenly synchronizes as well. The distinction between inner and outer worlds disappears as the pattern of each perfectly reflects the other. Satori. Hopefully, you won't be driving when this happens.

THE NEUROLOGICAL BASIS OF SATORI

Each culture has different words for this experience of collective, unified awareness. Each term has different flavors and connotations, and there are many disciplines that lead to this end. Usually, satori requires decades of guided, slow progress, under the instruction of a meditation master....

Synchronistic Event

Oh, damn! SE just won't leave me alone to pontificate in peace this afternoon. This is what I get for writing with the radio on. I was about to go on about how you can achieve satori with a few weeks of meditation if you understand what you're trying to do neurologically. I was going to say we are in a consumer-oriented, fast information society, and these states of consciousness can actually be treated like a video game you're playing on your own bio-computer. SE on the radio beat me to it. An ad for Joysticq.com just played. It's an online service "For those ready to commit to the total Zen of the video game experience." I was a little apprehensive about presenting instructions for shaping the brain into producing a satori experience as if it were a game. But, that's what I'm about to tell you. What did that last SE really mean? Probably that I've had too much caffeine. Rhine was right. Stimulants seem to increase the SE effect.

Later in this book, I'll describe how to fine-tune your production of SEs. You will learn to make SEs appear more frequently, or less, depending on your mood and attention. For now, I'm going to turn down the radio on my end and tell you how to produce a satori experience. Many works on meditation caution students that such exercises should be done under the instruction of a trained master. Even so, some never achieve this experience after decades of practice. I think you should be able to learn to turn this state on within about six weeks of conscientious effort. If not, you need a different instructor.

You are the area of the brain just behind the forehead. The prefrontal cortex is the part of your biocomputer that is the conscious executive function. The rest of the brain, as cosmically complex as it is, is mostly automated processes that send information to you. Your personal awareness evolved with the express purpose of being able to oversee the general processes of the rest of the brain. You make decisions on how the automated processes should proceed with their work. You decide what patterns are being scanned for in the grass. You command the movement routines and motor areas that make your body run toward or away from what you decide is out there. You have more control over what your brain does than you think you do. When you visualize what you want, you cause the occipital lobe to do complex computational miracles. Your brain constructs models of the objects you want to manipulate in your mind. When you talk to yourself, you command the temporal lobes to create verbal dialogues you then evaluate for accuracy. You have networks of mirror neurons that allow you to accurately recreate models of other people and their perspectives in your memory. These emotional computations enable you to feel what they feel. The limbic system that produces your emotions reacts to the inner verbal messages that you, in the prefrontal cortex, give it. When you have an emotional reaction, your job is to feel it, then choose if it fits your understanding of your situation. Your brain follows your lead. You have a substantial degree of influence on the states of consciousness the brain delivers to you. You are the driver, you get to steer this vehicle.

In the previous chapter, I proposed that you are already an enlightened unitary being. The illusion of separateness is the result of the way the brain processes information. To survive and pass on your genetic code, your body needs to out-think situations it encounters. Your job is to steer the thought processes. This includes those computational processes that regulate the artificial experience of being a separate being. Your body evolved to do things such as chase an antelope across planes of high grass, moving with speed over a variable terrain, in changing weather conditions, looking to match changing patterns all around you. The amount of calculation needed to do this "primitive" function is staggering. There really isn't much hope of creating computers with that much power in our lifetimes. But *you* do it automatically. You create the environment you are sitting in right now. You create the meaning of the words you are reading. You pattern match the lines and curves of individual letters into complex thoughts. Your brain creates reality. You have bil-lions of sensory nerves pointed out into the environment. Each one is a digital sensor. Each nerve sends rapid and varying pulses of on and off signals, electrical signals, to the sensory processing areas of your brain. That miraculous supercomputer is receiving trillions of bits of digital in-formation each second. The automated areas take as many as 30 or more kinds of sensory streams, and weaves them together into a virtual picture of the universe that eventually is sent forward on massive data transmit-ting bundles of nerve fibers, to you. Your brain creates your reality.

As mentioned previously, your brain does a lot of deleting of infor-mation along the way, and adds information it thinks you might find more relevant. The brain becomes like a good internet search engine. It tracks all your previous searches and tries to give you only results that are relevant to things you have previously searched for. For you, this means the reality you are experiencing has been engineered to fit the specifications of what you choose to think about. We only see a mas-sively simplified "comic book" version of reality. We experience reality as a performance on a constructed stage in our theater of consciousness. The Buddha reportedly said the universe is made of thought. He was right. Before any understanding of the computational model of the brain, be-fore computers, before modern neuroscience, he was right. The reality you are experiencing at this moment is a data signal of thoughts. And you, dear reader, have a significant amount of control over that thought process.

The universe you are experiencing right now is a construct built in your brain's memory.

There is a stage, a theater, in memory, on which that amazing brain of yours builds reality. You too are part of that production. To chase your antelope, significant other, or spiritual path, you need an idea of who you are. You are on stage at this very moment. What you believe is a separate self, is a computational model of yourself placed on the stage with the rest of the reality constructed around you. Remarkably, you have the ability to modify not only the reality that is on the stage, but you can change the representation of yourself, and your relationship to the reality you are constructing. You can choose to temporarily alter the construct so that you deactivate the parts of the programming that cause a sense of separation from the rest of the universe. Satori is stopping the computational processes that place the illusion of a separate self on the stage.

Synchronistic Event

Ok, SE got me again as I'm writing this. I have been listening to music from the internet over my iPod as I write. As I wrote the bit about shutting down the part of the computer responsible for the illusion of a separate self, the music stopped. The little computer in its cradle is now showing a blank screen with a tiny apple logo in the center. The little computer just partially shut down. Wait a moment...there, its back on. Satori is pretty much the same; partial shutdown and then restart.

To accomplish this, you use your attention to create a condition in which you temporarily shut down your conscious thought processes. In your mind, you have constructed a model of the world, and in that model is a model of yourself. You move the models around to be able to think about both navigating in the outside world, and to think about your relationships. You use these models, in the same way a child uses a dollhouse to rehearse family roles through play. The child's play of today becomes the adult life enacted in the future. But who is observing your play? If you are on your stage, who is it that understands this and watches that actor from the audience? Metacognition is the ability to think about thought. This ability enables you to think about your thought processes. This too seems to be an executive pre-frontal lobe function. So, if you turn all this off, where are you? Everywhere. Your awareness becomes based in the automated processes of the unconscious, without a sense of personal existence. What you experience is existence without the decisions and judgments of the executive function. This entails more than just shutting the executive functioning down. We turn the frontal lobes pretty much off and run on automatic pilot much of our lives. When you do very routine tasks, your executive functioning is often not being used. We don't really remember most of our lives. We store fragments that have been highlighted by emotional valence. We remember when we have to make decisions. We tend not to have a tape recording of our entire waking life. You have automated most of the responses you have to routine daily situations. I have known psychiatrists who were very competent, and were practicing mostly from memory, using very little conscious thought or executive function. They had learned their professions well during decades of practice. So well, the complex decisions they made required no conscious thought. We exist in our memories, literally. The stage you have created, where you stand in the midst of the world, is constructed in areas of your brain's memory. Your thoughts and experiences seem to be happening in the present moment, but they are not. There is a delay between when things happen, your brain deconstructing them, deleting and adding data, and the reconstruction of reality on the stage of your consciousness. Researchers can now use fMRI scanners to watch the brain doing this in real time. Displayed as three-dimensional computer images, your thoughts look like lightning storms passing through areas of the brain, trillions of bits of data being processed in waves.

Much of this process of constructing your reality is based on the pattern matches you have been making throughout your life. Your brain is amazingly responsive to the instructions you have been giving it. What do you suppose would happen if suddenly you stopped filtering data from the senses? What if what was constructed on your stage was not subject to the deletions and additions the mind makes to the sensory data it is receiving? You would experience the universe as it is really presented to you by your senses. This is satori. No executive function is instructing the supercomputer to filter out some patterns and add to others. Reality as it is. No automated pattern matches doing you a "favor" by constructing your reality according to what you expect to find, or desire to locate. Satori means being fully and directly in the present moment of your experience. My stage has modified some of the programming that my self-object is constructed from. Compared to some, my self-object allows for being part of the stage itself and the objects on it. The set of processing instructions that say the inner world of thoughts is separate from the outer world of events, has been re-written. My programming now allows more diffuse experiences, such as SE. The universe is thought. Duality is not a natural condition; it is a set of programming instructions used to interpret experience.

Don't believe what you think, choose what you think.

INDUCING SATORI

There are three approaches to getting the mind to be fully in the present moment, inducing a satori experience. The first path is mostly passive. The person just allows thoughts to surface into awareness without direction or intent. The second path aggressively directs thought to a chosen pattern and holds it there. The middle path guides thought and attention in a general direction, but also gives the mind a wide berth to wander. It is a middle path because it moves between the extremes of complete passivity, and over-control. All operate to clear unwanted processing instructions from memory.

The first approach is to gradually de-program automated processes by allowing the brain to catch up on its back-log of processing. Long-term memories take years to fully consolidate. The brain stores experiences in an area called the hippocampus. This area is connected by huge data tracts to the neurons in the cortex where long-term memory is stored. Breaking down an experience into sensory data bits and associating it to other matrixes in memory for long-term stable storage can take years. Your brain is constantly working on the consolidation of experiences. These computational processes take internal resources, just as running any computer program requires processor time. Much of the way we act toward the world is based on trying to process previous experiences into some usable pattern in memory. This is why some people tend to repeat the same patterns in their lives and relationships.

The mind has not yet processed previous experiences and is trying to replicate experiences in the world to work through consolidation processing still going on.

This first approach takes the longest. The strategy is to use the executive functioning as an auxiliary processor to help clear the back-log of memory consolidation tasks. You put the computer at the front of your brain at the disposal of the automated processes in the back of your brain. This is the simplest and probably the oldest form of meditation. You sit in a quiet place where you will be undisturbed. The space has to be without distractions. You are trying to lighten your processing load, not create more by attending to demands from the environment. The position you meditate in is not terribly important. You need to be comfortable so that you won't be distracted by messages from the body. Lying down only works well if you can prevent yourself from falling asleep. Most manuals on meditation recommend a sitting position of some kind. Some suggest using a pillow to raise your butt up a little to take the strain off your legs and back. Whatever works for you. You just close your eyes and pay attention to whatever thoughts and feelings come up. You have a stream of consciousness that is always flowing. You have internal dialogues with yourself, images, stories you tell yourself. What you are experiencing is a stream of data about what tasks your brain is processing. We think in pieces of our sensory information. This data stream responds to your attention. You could even use it as a place to look for SEs if you like.

SE happens in your thoughts as well as in your environment.

Your task as the executive here is to be presented with information, and then to decide how important it is. You give the instructions about how important a thought is. You tell the rest of the computer if it needs to continue processing those thoughts as a high priority. In this meditation, your decision process remains passive. Whatever comes up for you in the meditation, you observe and assign no importance to it. Whatever your meditation presents to you, you let it pass by. Its all just data. This does two things. First, you are assigning a low emotional valence to the thoughts. This lowers the priority it gets for consolidation. That lightens your processing demands. Secondly, your undivided attention is actually applying additional processing power to the thoughts. Once you become aware of them, it takes less time to put them into long-term storage. Most of what we think is fairly repetitive. Processing through them with meditation frees up your computer to do other things.

Eventually, the brain gradually clears your stage of the various props and objects that have been taking up your attention. Your theatre becomes empty of the ghosts of previous productions. You find a moment to be between productions in memory to experience a stage empty of thoughts. Gradually, this meditation clears thoughts that obsess on the role of your self object as well. The long-term rules you use for pattern matches become, for a few moments, suspended.

There is a moment in which you will experience nothing. Not the room you are in, not a sense of yourself, not even the conception that there is someone experiencing a concept of nothing. There is a quiet moment in the void. Then the data stream from your senses rushes back on stage. This time, without the filtering and pattern-matching programming running. This time, without the programming that defines you as a separate being, without separations in time and space. Everything synchronizes in a moment because you are not in your own way. Descriptions are fairly useless at this point. Bliss, cosmic consciousness, satori. Any description of the experience tries to define it, to match it to a known pattern. The experience itself tends to be short. The automated responses of the brain are already busily rebooting the rest of your programming at this point. The body is designed to operate in a world that needs representations of who you are on your stage of consciousness.

The experience of being a separate person usually seems to return first. This is closely followed by a return to linear time and space. With that, thought and pattern-matching return. There is a kind of emotional and sensory hangover that lasts for a few hours or days. The world seems brighter and clearer, as if the sensory channels have been somehow purged. There is a feeling of being cleansed in a bright world that has never known anything but a state of grace. And there is an experience of indescribable gratitude. All this fades over time. The experience stays in memory, but life and the experience of the world soon move our processes back to something close to our old patterns. Old neuro pathways reassert themselves, but you are left with knowing you are not necessarily the limited set of processes your brain describes for you.

Cooperating with yourself

Current research on the effects of meditation on mental health indicate positive effects on stress management and overall functioning. Meditation, and lowering the processing demands we place on ourselves, may be one of the best prescriptions psychology has to offer. Unfortunately, even something as benign as meditation can be abused. There are shorter and more aggressive paths to clearing one's inner stage and quieting the mind. One of these is to sit in meditation and assign the mind an impossible task, then keep demanding it accomplish it. As the executive function, you can command the mind to solve problems you have chosen to focus on. Your attention to the problem you assign sets the priority it receives from your computational resources. The more you choose to obsess over a problem, the more data processing resources are assigned to it. Normally this is a good thing. If we fall in love with someone, we may obsess over how to win their love in return. If you set a goal in your life and are driven to achieve it, your odds of success get better. But, what if you knowingly assign the mind an impossible task?

One of the tools of Zen meditation is the assignment of a Koan as the object of contemplation. A Koan is a verbal puzzle that has no fixed solution. A master might instruct a student to answer the question "What is the sound of one hand clapping?" The student then drives themselves to extremes in meditation trying to answer an unanswerable question. Neurologically, the technique makes perfect sense. Instead of gently assisting the mind to clear up current data processing demands, clearing the stage of memory gradually, the student overworks the mind until it collapses. Neurons use a lot of resources. They run on blood sugar and oxygen, as your muscles do. You can jog every day, and your legs get stronger. Most people don't run until they completely exhaust their body and they collapse. Stories about people who have reached satori through Koans usually include how over-the-top obsessed they were with solving the riddle. They become so obsessed that they turn all of the mind's resources toward solving the unsolvable. Neurons get tired, too. The experience of meaningfulness deepens as more neurons wire and fire together to work on the problem. The developing network takes over large areas of the brain's processing. The student continues to push for an answer until everything on their inner stage is involved is solving the Koan. Eventually, all their pattern-matching programming is devoted to this single problem. Even their self-object becomes determined by if they will be able to resolve the pattern.

There is no resolution. There was never intended to be one. It's a trick. The strategy is to make the brain associate so much of its internal processing to this one problem, that it will collapse when the neurons becomes exhausted enough. The stage is cleared because the mind doesn't have the neurological resources to keep it running. Typically, Zen stories of satori have the explosive experience triggered by some mundane sensory input from the environment. It could be the sound of a bell calling the monks to meditation, the sound of a stone swept by a broom striking a piece of wood, or the sensation of the master smacking the student across the face with a sandal. The "trigger" is not the cause. The student's mind has collapsed, he has become the void and dissolved his individual programming already. The "trigger" is merely the first sensory input entering the stage completely unfiltered and unchanged. It is the first direct sensory experience unfiltered by other computational processes.

I'm not a Roshi. I'm sure a real Zen teacher would have a lot to say about the need for a teacher. A real Roshi would also point out the dangers an unsupervised student faces when trying to achieve satori. I heard a story of one Roshi in Japan who decided to update to more modern Koans. He assigned one student "How do you stop the Bullet Train by doing nothing." Poor guy became so obsessed with solving it, he tried to stop the train by sitting on the tracks. Did not turn out well. A real Roshi might say this is an example of why sticking to the traditional instructions in a supervised setting is best. My advice is don't do anything extreme to begin with. Sitting on the train tracks, poor decision. Crashing your neural network to catch a cosmic buzz, poor decision.

Be nice to your brain. Work with it, not against it.

THE MIDDLE PATH TO SATORI

The last method for inducing satori is a hodge-podge of several techniques I have cobbled together based on my understanding of how your brain functions. I'm going to give you just enough of the procedure and rational for you to tailor it to your own needs. Choose a comfortable sitting position. Staying upright helps keep you awake. Choose a regular spot to meditate where you will not be disturbed. You are trying to cut down on unexpected demands for attention from the environment. A familiar location will mean you will soon not have to think about where you are. If you know there will be no lions jumping out of the grass at you, you soon forget to be interested in your surroundings. I meditate in front of a blank white wall, eyes open. Zen meditation spaces are sparsely furnished so that there are no visual distractions. Keep your eyes open so that your attention is in the world. You are trying to produce a synchronization of the inner and outer experiences. Closing your eyes also makes it too easy to fall asleep. Choose a sitting position that is comfortable, which you can sustain for an hour if needed. If you have a comfortable sitting position and choose not to move, not even scratch your nose, sensations from your body will cease to be a distraction in a half hour or so. The brain has this wonderful mechanism that diminishes repetitive signals you do not act on. If you hold still, send the same sensory signals from the body to the brain long enough, the brain starts to ignore the signals from the body. Getting comfortable seems more important than forcing the body into submission. Work with yourself. Synchronizing means not treating things as though they are outside objects that need to be bent to your will.

When you feel steady in your seated position, you will have a mildly floaty sensation. That's your brain starting to follow your lead and ignoring some of the body's repetitive sensory messages. Pranayama are breathing exercises said to direct energy during meditation. They provide a practical way to regulate brain activity. Because neurons use as much as twice as much oxygen as other cells, their activity can be regulated by regulating your breathing. Now, there are always people who take things to extremes. If you tell them to gently slow their breath to lower their brain activity, they hold their breath until they turn blue. The idea here is to stay in a relaxed, pleasant comfort zone. Slowing your breath and breathing from low in the abdomen will naturally slow your heart rate. As your body slows and relaxes, the jumpy, insistent quality of your stream of thoughts slows and evens out. Your brain evolved to make intelligent choices about resource management. Given the choice between non-critical data processing and physiological needs of oxygen, it keeps your body functions intact. The brain puts off unnecessary neural activity for another time. Knowing how to regulate your breath provides some immediate conscious control over your brain activity. Reducing brain activity helps clear the clutter from your stage. Doing it gently and without discomfort keeps you from creating more activity to deal with the discomfort.

Stopping all thought is impossible. Zen meditation literature claims that a master can stop thinking by following the breath for 10 seconds. About that time people tend to congratulate themselves on not thinking...ooops! There you go thinking again! Setting yourself impossible tasks creates more problems than it solves. You never have full conscious control of your thought processes. The brain is always active. Work with your brain and physiology with the tools your body provides. Use the brain's tendency to ignore repetitive signals to remove most of the sensations of being in a body. Use your control over the breath to signal the brain to slow unnecessary thought. When you have been able to achieve a relatively calm and comfortable state for a few sessions, your brain will have learned how to go back there automatically when you meditate. You won't have to concentrate to stay there.

The last part of the meditation is to gently direct your thoughts to... nothing. This part isn't so easy. Nothing is an idea. Real nothing can't be thought about. When you think about nothing, you are thinking about a thought you have constructed and labeled nothing. You are trying to construct a true blank spot on your internal stage. As in passive meditation, all kinds of thoughts and ideas will rise and ask for your attention. Your task is to direct your attention back to nothing. At first, you will bounce from a normally cluttered stream of consciousness, to thinking about nothing, and back. With some practice, you will be able to gradually pass over the other thoughts and internal objects on your stage in favor of thinking about nothing. This is similar to the way Koans work, but much gentler. There is no obsessive quality, no mental force. It is just an amusing game you play with yourself. You are not trying to force the mind into a desperate struggle to find a solution. You are slowly clearing the clutter from your stage, turning down the lights, relaxing in the safe and quiet theater of your mind. When you find you are thinking about something, you just return to thinking about nothing. Eventually, the data stream subsides and you spend time moving between thinking of nothing, and realizing the thought of nothing is in itself something, and trying to leave that behind. I used to think about deep interstellar space, delete the stars in my mind, think about the void itself. Then, later, delete even the dimensions of space itself. Doing this for long enough empties the stage as effectively as turning the mind off by creating an internal collapse. It is more of a slow dance than mental combat. It usually works within about six weeks. My re-entry experience had a simple sensory trigger. Silly, really. My thumb twitched, and the universe was reborn whole.

Seven

The Big Picture

"Time is the moving image of eternity." —Plato

UNDERSTANDING THE POSSIBILITIES

Even if our ancestral hunter on the savanna knew he was one with the world, the lion out there somewhere in the grass would just as soon eat an enlightened person as any other. We are still individual people trying to survive. How you describe SE to yourself gives you an advantage or disadvantage. The lions in the grass are part of the same unity that you are, and from their perspective, they are the center of the universe. Lions, and the other people around you, are looking into the same SE mirror you are. The cats are having their thoughts reflected back to them as SEs, just as you are. Your advantage comes in understanding the nature of what is happening. The lion produces SEs, but is unaware of them. Its brain can't process the level of complexity and pattern-matching yours can. The lion, and most people around you, don't understand how SEs work. People can be educated, lions generally not. This chapter is going to present you with a science-based model of the universe that will be the basis for understanding SE as a technology. If you are satisfied with knowing SE is a mirror, skip this chapter. If you want to know exactly how SEs are possible in the real world, read carefully. Here is where the ride starts to get wild.

Knowledge matters. Knowledge, correctly applied, is power. Your grassland ancestor is out of breath. He's scared and is shaking so badly he can barely stand. He has been running for his life. A pattern he thought was an antelope in the tall grass wasn't. He had the decision, committed to the attack on the usual partial information his senses provided. He ran forward with his sharp stick, poked into the grass with all his strength, and hit the lion in the side of the head. The hunting charms around his neck didn't protect him. The ancestral spirits didn't warn him. The tribal shaman's rituals didn't put the game where he needed it to be. Our ancestor ran until he vomited. The lion didn't chase him; not enough meat to bother with today. Our ancestor is seriously considering kicking the shaman's ass when he gets back to the village. This particular ancestor of yours was the first scientist. He decided to stop taking the word of others for how the world actually worked, and demanded proof. Your ancestor went back to the village, kicked out the shaman and the king, and began experimenting to find out how the world works.

Your scientist ancestor had his people dig holes throughout the tribe's territory, and had piles of the stones they found brought to him for examination. When he was done, he had a pile of stones. He had no idea what to do with them, and soon the shaman and king were back in business. Knowing SEs are a mirror is like making a pile of stones; ok, I got 'em, now what do I do with them? Add some knowledge. Your tribe, your modern day tribe, humanity, has done something amazing. They dug some holes in the ground, re-arranged the rocks they found, and used the materials to create spacecraft that flew to the moon, and safely returned their pilots to the earth.

Synchronistic Event

As I wrote the last sentence, a commercial for live 365, the internet radio station in the background began. Its first lines; "Huston, its one small step for man, one giant leap for mankind." The famous first words spoken on the lunar surface.

Have you ever wondered what the universe actually looks like? The entire universe, all at once, all hundred billion galaxies? You are an inseparable part of this great unity, albeit a tiny part of the whole. So what do you look like from the largest possible vantage point? Google image search "large scale structure of the universe." There it is, in all its cosmic glory, the actual structure of the universe. You can even see time-lapse animations of its development in the past 13.7 billion years. This wide view took computers to create. Astronomers plotted the distances and positions of all the objects in the sky, and fed the information into a computer. The computer created a three-dimensional map to show us what we really look like. The images are stunningly beautiful. Billions of galaxies form vast strands in space, creating structures resembling the neuron networks in your brain. It has an organic, almost living order and complexity. I would rather make speculations based on science than religion. Real knowledge is repeatable and verifiable. It is also in a statistical sense, likely to be true. SEs will reflect the religious myths you have been taught, or chosen to believe. My profession fosters restoring client's personal choice, not on dissuading them from their beliefs. My bias lies with empirical science, and where that ends, I have my own beliefs that are as delusional as anybody else's. Science has always been at war with faith in one form or another. We are going to go on a short tour of the universe as science currently sees it. After that, we step off the verifiable trail into likely explanations of SE that follow from what we now believe to be true. I have no faith. It would keep me from understanding the truth of how little I actually know. If you have ever wondered if science or religion has the more likely truth, consider this: every religion from the beginning of time has claimed to be the divinely inspired and complete truth. All have claimed their model of the universe came directly from God. Every description they have given us of the actual universe has been wrong. In the hundreds of thousands of pictures and descriptions, they have left behind, in the words of proclaimed prophets, saviors, teachers, and self-appointed divine representatives, not one has left a simple picture of the universe we live in. Science has done that.

TIME IS A VARIABLE

Truth does not change over time, but our depth of understanding does. Dogen declared the unity of all things as Buddha nature. Einstein was one of the first to emerge into scientific adulthood with the same truth. He declared matter and energy are the same stuff, light is a constant, but time is a variable, and pointed to a unity almost mystical in nature.

"Since the general theory of relativity implies the manifestation of physical reality as a continuous field, the concept of a discontinuous particle cannot play a fundamental part, the particle can only appear as a limited region of space in which the field strength and/or density of energy is particularly high."—Albert Einstein

Einstein: the name conjures images of genius and complexity, but the basic concepts he gave us came from a beautiful, almost child-like wonder and imagination. Dogen told us all things were the Buddha mind, and that mind was an inseparable unity. Einstein declared the same basic truth. There is no such thing as separate objects. Space is a field of energy, like a vast fabric. Particles of matter are just areas where the fabric is in motion, or bunched together. Nothing separates objects; they are all one. There is no empty space; separation is an illusion. Einstein's next revelation to the world was that because there was no separation between the energy field that is space and the matter it is made of, matter and energy are the same thing. Unity rears its head again. You, the book you are reading, the light and heat in the room at this very moment, all the same energy, all part of the same field.

We are localizations of the universal energy field.

The reason the environment provides me with SEs that reflect and illustrate material I write about in real time has nothing to do with any special ability or spiritual status. I have learned, in my better moments, not to think of myself as separate from my environment. The result is, on occasion, I'm aware I'm not. SEs are the reminder.

EXPLANATORY FICTION

We are about to descend into the rabbit hole. If you poke around the internet, you will find blogs talking about people's various theories about how SEs work. Most of it is just silly. Most try to explain SEs using ancient spiritual mythologies, or speculate on influences and energies that have less than empirical data to support them. Most models of SEs fail because they are operating either from a religious mythology, or from obsolete science.

Most models of SE are reflections of how the person thinks it should work.

SE usually accommodates people by reflecting the fantasy back to them, right or wrong. Good experimental science usually does not start with answers. It starts with questions such as, How does SE work? It then takes what is known, clearly distinguishes it from what is not known, and makes up a good story about what might be happening. That story is an explanatory fiction. It accounts for all the information, then makes a good guess. That story is then tested with experiments to try to find out what is real. Real is important because it allows us to make predictions about how reality actually works. The frog in this custard is explanatory fictions, like religions, don't have to be true to be useful. I believe most religions are complete fantasy, and, most religions are inherently beneficial and useful. Even if factually incorrect, they give a social pattern and personal direction that has allowed civilization to exist. The explanatory fiction about SE I am about to present has no more validity than any of the other explanatory fictions about SE, with one important difference. You can personally test it by using it to create your own SE. This does not prove the explanation is correct, just useful. From this point forward I will be telling you a good story, not a factual explanation. I hope you find this story both entertaining and useful.

THE EVOLUTION OF TIME AND SPACE

Isaac Newton gave us the first truly scientific model of the universe. All bodies move according to laws of motion and gravitation he defined mathematically, giving a model with predictive value. His model believed in objects being separate from each other, in "empty" space, with gravity being a mysterious force acting at a distance between them. Newton's 17th-century model described a universe that acted like a vast clockwork mechanism. Exactly what gravity was evaded him, but he described its effects. There was no need for a creator of spiritual forces to run the universe; it was a machine with knowable laws. This is still the way the majority of people view the universe. This mechanistic view fails with SE because it leaves you looking for the "force," the gravitational "energy" linking you with the SE around you. Time to advance to the 20th century.

Einstein solved the gravity problem. There is no gravitational force. Not in the sense of a separate energy acting between objects. Imagine a trampoline. It's made of a piece of strong fabric stretched flat by springs attached around the edges. Imagine that the fabric is the fabric of space itself. This is the same space that all matter is made of, the "whole cloth" of the universe. Place a heavy bowling ball in the center of the trampoline. The weight of the ball creates a depression in the center. The curve in the fabric is steepest near the ball, and becomes nearly flat again at the edges. Congratulations, you now understand how gravity works. Gravity is not a force acting across space, it *is* space. The mass of any object, say, a planet, curves the surrounding fabric of space. It's almost as if to create the matter of the planet, you had to pull space into a knot. The knot pulls the surrounding fabric out of shape, makes a depression that objects close by can fall into. SE does not result from a force radiating from you. The energy of your presence is producing curvatures in the structure of time. I sincerely hope the idea that you are powerful enough to bend time sounds strange and outrageous. Without understanding how this is possible, it should. Back at the campfire on the savanna, our ancestral hunter is listening to visions of the re-instated tribal shaman. The shaman says people are capable of re-arranging those piles of rocks into rockets that will fly people to the moon. Clearly the shaman is nuts.

So, turns out all that mystical clap-trap from our ignorant ancestors about unity and one being was correct after all. Empty space is not empty, and can even be bent. The next step down the rabbit hole is letting go of how you think time works. For Newton, time was a constant; it progressed the same everywhere in the universe. That time must be a universal constant was as obvious in the 17th century as the earth being flat was in 3000 BC. Both were wrong. Time is a variable, and its rate changes. SEs are all about the way time moves and changes the relationships between events. If you are stuck believing time is only the clock-on-the-wall, one moment at a time, steady, linear, boring, non-varying, Newtonian clockwork kind of time, you're playing with the same old pile of rocks your ancestors were stuck with.

People have generally heard things get weird when you get close to the speed of light. When you travel at high speeds, time slows down. For example: A middle-aged man decides to leave the earth to travel in space. His trip will take 60 earth years to complete, and he leaves behind a young son. The traveler makes his round trip close to the speed of light. Time passes much slower for the traveler, so while for him only a few months have passed, 60 years have passed on earth. He returns to find that his son is now older than he is. The rate time passed for the father was different from the rate of time passing for his son. Did you know you couldn't fall into a black hole? As you get very close, time begins to slow down. As an object gets very close it virtually stops in time, moving so slowly an eternity must pass before it reaches the theoretical singularity at the center. Time moves at a different rate at your head than at your feet. It's all relative. Relative to the amount of energy you have. Time is passing by you, literally. Time moves at 186,000 miles a second; that's the speed of light. Space is expanding through a dimension we call time. Time is an actual dimension. We think of space as having three dimensions, and time is the fourth. Time slows down when you get close to the speed of light because you are catching up to the rate time passes. You are approaching the rate at which the physical universe expands through time. Motion changes the rate you pass in time.

It takes a lot of energy to approach the speed of light. The faster you go, the heavier you get; the energy it took to speed you up becomes part of your mass. This is why being hit with a bullet does more damage than dropping your house key on your foot. The bullet weighs more when it's moving. You might say, "That's ridiculous. That would mean if I weighed more it would be the same as moving really fast. By that reasoning I could slow down in time by just being heavier." Congratulations, again. You now understand Einstein's general theory of relativity. When you bend space, you bend time as well. Time and space are one. On a heavier planet than ours, the mass of your body would be greater. This increase in relative mass because of proximity actually changes your rate of passage in time. The more powerful the field, the slower the relative time rate. This holds true for the earth as well. Two extremely accurate atomic clocks have been synchronized with each other, and then one flown around in an aircraft at a few thousand feet for a few hours. When brought together, they showed different times. The differences were infinitesimal, but enough to demonstrate the principle. Theoretically, because of the difference in position in the gravitational field of the earth, time moves at a slightly different rate at your head than at your feet. The difference is small, but it demonstrates that time is a variable, not as constant as we usually think it is.

SPACE, TIME, AND SE

Let's break out that piece of paper that represents the entire universe again. Pretend you have a piece of plain white paper in front of you. You are enjoying your god-like view of the universe in your hands. You now know the sheet of paper is not just space, but time as well. Space and time are a unity. You now hold all of space, and all of the past, present and future, in your hands. This thin sheet, this fabric membrane, is where we tiny mortals live. Pretend for a moment the sheet is truly flat, has only two dimensions of space. Up and down on this flat universe don't exist. The people who live on this flat universe have no concept that it is possible to go over or under anything—that is unthinkable. Flatlanders have to go around each other. Science describes objects in terms of an event; various energies come together for a moment to give the appearance of something behaving in some way. In our flat universe, events are objects. The Flatlanders see the events around them as objects on the page moving in time. For them, cause and effect is seeing where the objects came from, and that motion carries them forward. Space and time are one. From your god-like perspective, imagine placing a pencil point on the paper. This causes quite a stir for the Flatlanders living on the membrane. Having no concept of there being three dimensions, it seems to them like an object, an event, just appeared out of nowhere. SE feels that way to us. The event appears in our universe, with no traceable cause and effect. The SE is an event, it has meaning, we notice it, but how did it get here? Lift the pencil point. The object/event on the membrane disappears for the Flatlanders. The best and the brightest of the Flatlanders then engage in speculation about what just happened. The Flatland scientists speculate about how much energy it must have taken to alter all of Flatland time and space to create the event. Such reality-bending power and intelligence baffle the Flatlanders. Under their two-dimensional physics, to accomplish such a feat requires truly cosmic amounts of energy. One Flatland psychologist suggests their minds are not capable of understanding such events. He does correctly guess the causes of this Flatland SE come from outside Flatland time and space.

Now we are really going to confuse the Flatlanders. Put down your pencil-of-the-gods. Imagine instead that you are holding a cone. Touch the tip of the cone onto the paper again. Like before, an event seems to appear out of nowhere for our Flatlanders. Start slowly lowering the cone through the paper. The extra dimension allows it to pass through the paper without disturbing it—wouldn't want to be tearing holes in time and space now, would we? To the Flatlanders the area on the paper where the SE event appears widens to become a circle of events. As the cone descends, the circle of events becomes more inclusive. The shape of the cone is becoming the pattern of SE events on the paper. The Flatlanders can only see in two dimensions. They may see the pattern of the circle in events, but have no concept of the overall shape of the object causing the changes. They see the events, but can't see the object that causes them. When the cone has passed all the way through our paper version of time and space, the SE suddenly stops. The Flatlanders have no cause to trace, no trail left on the paper. This is about the time they start talking about gods and spirits.

ARCHETYPES AND THOUGHTFORMS

We are going to talk about Jung again for a moment. Archetypes. Your cone-of-the-gods caused events to cluster around the shape it outlined as it passed through the paper. Jung got it half-right. He thought of archetypes as object-like "somethings" that cause SE to cluster around them in patterns of meaning. He saw them as things that underlied the creation, and made universal patterns. Let's scale that idea down just a bit and give them a new name.

These objects, the cone you were just playing with, are thoughts. Mystics call them thoughtforms. Take a thought, and think of it as an object with its own mass and energy. A thought with a form, a form of thought, take your pick. Enlightenment says its all thought in the universal mind. Thoughtforms are localized, not universal. You make them with your mental activity. They have more dimensions than physical objects, and they cause SE effects around you. Yes, this implies that you exist in dimensions outside of the physical universe. You are much more than you can sense.

Some part of you is already operating outside the limits of time and space.

But, sadly, this does not prove we are universal creatures. We have very real limits. The energy in your physical body does make its own gravitational field. You are bending space-time just by existing. Theoretically, this tiny curve in space affects the motion of objects across the universe. You could even calculate out how much force your body exerts on the moon, the sun, or a distant galaxy. But, realistically, the effect is so small you would have to use math tricks such as scientific notation to fit the number on a piece of paper. Jung's idea of archetypes was universal. The idea of extra-dimensional objects making SEs makes it seem as if such objects would have to be universal. They would have to be universal thoughts, universal thoughtforms, archetypal thoughtforms. That makes them universally big and powerful, right? Not even close.

Remember the cone you were just playing with? Lets pretend the sheet of universal paper in front of you is huge, the size of a football field. The cone fits in the palm of your hand. Pass the cone through the paper again. Only the tiny area the cone touched formed SE events for the Flatlanders. The rest of the football-field-sized paper universe was unaffected. SEs are generated locally. Your thoughtforms, centered around you, cause the effect. The cone has more dimensions than the two-dimensional paper. Your thoughts have more dimensions than the four-dimensional physical universe you sense. You don't have to move the pattern of the entire universe to create SE. You only need to affect the tiny area of the paper you are standing in. Jung was wrong.

Archetypes are not universal. You make them. They are localized, temporary, thoughtforms.

Silly String Theory

"Ok," you might say; "Why isn't science telling us about all these extra dimensions?" Science has been shouting about extra dimensions for a while. String Theory is one of the latest contenders for the possible "universal theory of everything." The name String Theory comes from the model's attempt to describe sub-atomic particles as loops of energy. Like the strings on a musical instrument. These loops vibrate at various frequencies. The way they vibrate determines what kind of particle they appear to be. One String Theory idea states these loops are sewn through three-dimensional time and space much the same way threads are sewn through fabric. To do this, the strings have to exist in more dimensions than the physical plane. Remember Flatland. The only way to sew a loop through that plane would be for the loop to exist in three dimensions. There would have to be an "up and down" for the loop to be able to pass through the two-dimensional plane. Mathematical models can describe objects and events that occur in more than four dimensions.

String Theory declares the universe has 11 dimensions. Things get even stranger; some of those dimensions are as small as the strings themselves. The particles in the atoms you are looking at are made of tiny universes, like our Flatland paper, crumbled into tiny sub-atomic wads. Extra dimensions do not have to be universe-sized, cosmic things. They are localized, like us. Tiny, like us. Inseparably connected to all dimensions, like us. Your thoughtforms do not have to be universal to have the extra dimensions needed to create SE.

You are more than one universe. Assume your god-like view of the paper universe again for a moment. The sheet in front of you has only two dimensions, no thickness. Call it a membrane. Imagine the paper is elastic, stretchy. Using your god-like powers, you can bend the membrane, make curves in it, and fold it. Pretend you have bent the membrane so that all the outside edges touch; you have transformed it into a sphere. The Flatlanders have no idea their two-dimensional universe is now shaped like a soap bubble; a thin membrane of curved time and space. String Theory tells us our universe is a bubble blown from the big bang; a bubble 13.7 billion light years across, expanding at the speed of light. We live on a membrane expanding through time at the speed of light. When I was a child in Sunday School, we would ask annoying questions, such as, "If God is all-powerful, can God make a rock so big that he himself can't lift it?" Scientists are asking similar questions, such as, "If all the energy in the universe were at a single point before the big bang, time would have been stopped due to the requirements of special and general relativity. So what came before the big bang? If there was no time and no space, what was before that? If space and time, all 11 dimensions of it, were created as the big bang expanded, what was it expanding into?"

M- AND N-SPACE

M-Theory is an aspect of String Theory that tries to explain what happened before the big bang. It proposes our universe is an expanding bubble floating in "M-Space," which has more dimensions than the physical universe. Picture a soap bubble floating in a room. We are the bubble, the room is M-Space. At least we are not being ferried across the room in a chariot at this point. So, how did our bubble get there? M-Space may be literally eternal, no beginning, and no end. It would have more dimensions of time and space than we can envision. We will leave the origins of M-Space alone, lest we start an endless round of what dimensional chicken or egg came first. According to the M-Space model, we are not the only brane floating around. There, energy branes can collide at single points. This causes cosmic releases of energy that result in "big bangs." These collisions blow bubble branes like the one we live in. Our universal bubble probably isn't the only bubble floating around in M-Space. There may be many universes just like ours floating beyond the 13.7 billion light year edge of our bubble, and we may even be subject to our bubble someday bumping up against or merging with another.

Explanatory fictions are wonderful starting points for the imagination. Once one realizes we are playing fast and loose with partial patterns and unverified information, we can create our own worlds of possibility. Some of the M-Theory models speculate M-Space may have so many brane universes in it, M-Space may be more like foam than an empty space with the occasional bubble. Yet, if a schizophrenic client believes the universe is a bubble in god's bubble bath, we take it as a psychotic symptom. The client doesn't have the advantage of being able to express his ideas in mathematics. Good scientists think a lot about where science and philosophy meet and inform each other.

Seemingly not to be outdone, M-Theory is now being one-upped by yet another extra-dimensional model. In N-Space, an infinite amount of alternate probable universes exist. Just when I thought science could not possibly get any stranger, humanity's best physicists are telling us there are parallel universes where Elvis is literally still giving concerts. N-Space solves the problem of how progression of events through time is possible at all. N-Space attempts to explain how existence navigates through probable events by stating there are an infinite number of membranes, all of them parallel universes. Each parallel membrane is a possible instant in time. How far away is the parallel brane where Elvis still sings? Close, very close. All parallel branes co-exist with each other in the same relative space. Two objects existing on different planes can exist in the same space at the same time, without interference with each other, because they are composed of the localized densities of different fields of energy. String Theory uses this assumption to speculate that there may be an infinite number of physical universes, all on different branes, existing in the same space, but only minimally interacting with each other. The distance in physical terms is about equivalent to the diameter of the smallest possible quantum of matter.

In the physical universe, gravity happens when the mass of an object curves space. If there is an object in M-Space, it curves time itself. The cone-of-the-gods you were playing with was an M-Space object. Past and future events cluster around the M-Space object. These are not universal alterations in reality. They are not as Jung might have suggested, archetypal, just extra-dimensional. They are local. They are your thoughtforms. Your thoughts, centered in areas of time, in locations in physical space. The events that cluster around these M-Space objects are SE.

You're doing it right now.

Your thoughts bend, ever so slightly, the M-Space that supports all of physical time and space. Least this sound too implausible even for this philosophical model; String Theory currently states that much of the mass of the universe is tied up in "dark matter." Dark matter is, well, dark; we can't measure it directly. It can only be detected because its gravity affects visible matter around it. Most of the mass of the universe is dark matter. Gravity from dark matter formed galaxies from nebula of dust and gas. Stranger yet, String theory believes that gravity may not be confined to our dimensional brane. Gravity is the weakest of the forces, so weak in fact, that it is 1×10 to the 39th power weaker than magnetism. One explanation for that incredible weakness is that the particle responsible for gravity, the graviton (which no one has ever seen or figured a way to prove or disprove) is not "sewn" onto our physical plane the way other particles are. It may be that the graviton is not so much weaker, it just travels through many branes as well as ours, and has much of its energy distributed amongst many parallel universes at once. One of the hopes for CERN, the 10 billion dollar high-energy particle accelerator, is to create gravitons with so much collision energy, that we will see them leave our universe. Science is speculating about gravity-based telephones to communicate with parallel probabilities. Anybody on your side got tickets to the Elvis concert?

YOU EXIST IN MORE THAN ONE PROBABLE UNIVERSE AT A TIME

Here is where our model train of SE departs the station of probably true physics and the fun really starts. You exist in more than one probability at the same time. Physics and science fiction speculate about parallel probable universes in which some other copy of us exists. Whenever a Sci-Fi TV series runs out of plot, they jump the characters into some parallel universe to confront evil-twin versions of themselves, or an alternative parallel future that has to be changed. You are doing this every moment of your life. Nature is always more elegant and efficient than human imagination. We imagine that these parallel branes are separate. We would have to somehow jump across the distance between them. It's much easier than that. You, not copies or variations, exist on an infinite number of probabilities at once. SE happens when you navigate through these probabilities. You have a natural on-board computer that has evolved to match patterns. It is also navigating through dimensions of probability. Make me one with everything, and all the possible probable variations of everything.

In N-Space, probability becomes a dimension of space and time. You already move through N-Space because you exist as a unity with all dimensions of the universe. In N-Space the distance between one probable universe and the next is literally a measure of distance. SEs happen because you have traveled to a spot in N-Space where that combination of unlikely events is happening. You have traveled in probability. How's that for a demi-godlike power! Wow, how far and fast can we travel in parallel probability? Not all that far, unfortunately. We don't produce much gravitation, and we don't move very fast. We also don't travel far in probability. I may finish this chapter in the next few hours, or go out for a walk. The distance to either probability from where I sit at my computer right now is very short. Either event is close in probability, a short distance in N-Space. When I am 80 years old, I may receive a Nobel prize, or a Hugo award for the writing I am doing at this moment. Now, that's a far-fetched idea! Literally, the distance in probability to reach either of those events is vast.

We are much like planets moving through space. Our tiny mass curves space-time around us, just a bit. That curve in M-Space causes events to cluster around us, just a bit. We also move through space as planets in an orbit do. We move through the probabilities of N-Space. Planets spin and wobble, changing their direction in orbit, just a bit. We change our focus of attention, changing our path through probability, just a bit. Knowing how to create that "just a bit" can give you a profound advantage in your travels through life. All this extraterrestrial Physics 101 has a purpose. It gives you a way to think about what is happening around you. It gives you a working explanatory fiction; SE is a mirror. "Ok, it's me." You might say, "Now what?" Now you learn to manipulate the actual SEs. Gravity: "What SEs are my thoughts and emotions attracting?" Movement in probability: "What direction am I moving through SE events based on the direction of my thoughts?" How do I create more effective thoughtforms? Change SE in the directions I choose?" In the next chapter, we begin taking the pile of rocks we have been digging out of psychology and science, and making you your spacecraft.

Eight

More to You Than Meets the Eye

"The earliest evidence of anything like mythological thinking is associated with graves.... Burials always invoked the idea of the continued life beyond the visible one, of a dimension of being that is behind the visible dimension.... I would say that is the basic theme of all mythology—that there is an invisible dimension supporting the visible one." —Joseph Campbell

THE BRAIN AS A COMPUTER

This chapter is going to describe exactly how you manage to create thoughtforms that carry your thoughts and emotions into the world as SE. Rearranging that pile of conceptual rocks into a spaceship capable of altering reality sounds like a lot of work. Relax, its already done. Nature was making biological computers long before humans appeared on the evolutionary scene.

Lucky you, nature already gave you a built-in, starship-grade set of multi-dimensional forms. During an educational group, a client asked, "Is it true we only use 10 percent of our brains?" This question is a leftover from bygone days when we didn't understand much of what the brain does. We use it all, nature never maintains what the organism doesn't use. You use all of your brain, but you are not consciously aware of what most of it is doing for you. We are like Flatlanders who only see narrow dimensions of a multidimensional universe. In this case, the universe is us. I love learning about the brain. Your brain's complexity and brilliant functional design is awe-inspiring. And, we are not consciously aware of a millionth of what it is doing for us every moment. It functions for us automatically. It does what all good advanced technology does: carries out its functions, freeing you to pay attention to more important things. The multidimensional aspects of you work the same way. They are not normally conscious. They can be made conscious if you focus on them. But, generally, they perform their miracles for you without you having to do anything at all. Good technology.

Making things that are unconscious, conscious is one of the goals of psychotherapy. The view of why to do this has changed. In the perhaps not-so-good days of Freudian therapy, clients were supposed to bring up their emotions freely. Many therapists still believe in "venting" emotional energy. It's as if your brain was a battery needing discharge. Modern brain function mapping tells a different story. The brain is a computer. By consciously paying attention to your thoughts and feelings, you lend the extra processing power of the frontal lobe to the task. You can augment your unconscious powers by putting your attention into the process. This chapter is going to give you ways to think about those extra-dimensional parts of yourself that create SEs. You will then have a way of consciously focusing attention on them. We are going to build you a model of your SE starship in your mind. That model will be the control panel you use to create your own patterns of SE. We are all Flatlanders. We don't see these multidimensional spaces directly. Please don't mistake the thoughts I am going to give you for the actual reality. The actual reality is far more amazing than the explanatory fiction that will allow you to consciously create SEs.

SE is an "ask and ye shall receive" kind of phenomena. You don't control the minutia of each event, anymore than you control the firing on an individual neuron. Ahh, but the effect of having a couple of billion of them firing together when you ask—spectacular. That kind of mass action *is* under your control.

Synchronistic Event

I spent Sunday morning working on parts of this chapter. My focus was consciously "How do I make the writing come alive?" There was going to be a party for Linda, my writing coach, that evening. My wife, also a writer, and I would be joining a group of Linda's grateful students to celebrate her new novel *Dead Love*. At the time, my wife was working on the plot for a novel. The plotline has a heroine who inherits a strip club and has to solve a murder mystery. We spent some time that afternoon talking about how that might work in real life. Before we left for the evening, we sat together in front of the TV watching an episode of *Supernatural*. The story was about two brothers who suddenly discover their lives published in intimate detail as they lived them, as a series of books. They look up the author, who is shocked to learn the characters he has been writing about are real. He has been working on the next book in the series. In that one, the brothers look him up and confront him. He was sitting at the computer writing that the brothers were at his front door, when he got up to answer the front door, and found himself confronted by the brothers. Writing comes alive.

It gets stranger still. At the party, Linda read a passage from her book about one of her characters. She describes him in detail, his body, his face. The

fictional character lives in Amsterdam, in a house-
boat, on a city canal. He is a photographer who specializes in publishing pictures of tattoo art. After
the reading, she announced since reading the draft
of the book in your hands, she has experienced an
explosion of synchronistic events that mirror her
thoughts. Including recently meeting the character
just described at a literary conference where they
were both faculty. She said it was as if her writing had come alive and he had just walked off the
pages. Physically, the real person was exactly as
she described him in the already-published book—same
face, same body. The actual person is a well-known
photographer; like the character, he is known for
his photographs of tattoo art. His close friend and
associate is the man whose work inspired the novel.
She had never met this photographer or seen his work
before. She kindly endorsed the model of SE-as-mirror
to the group. Seemingly, just to top off the "writing comes to life" theme, in case there was any doubt
left, my wife reported an interesting conversation
as well. She was talking to another writer about the
plot she was working on, the heroine inheriting the
strip club, needing to know financial details of such
an inheritance. The other partygoer declared, "Oh, I
can help you with that; I unexpectedly inherited two
strip clubs!" Writing come to life indeed.

Creating SE is as seamless and automatic as those miraculous functions your super-computing brain does for you automatically at every
moment.

Creating SE is so automatic you can't turn it off, ever.

I get funny looks from some people when I tell these stories. What can you say to such events? They are unbelievable, until you know how to create them. When I get one of those incredulous looks, I tell them what I'm telling you now. Soon, they are seeing them too. Some people even take the shaky first steps out of the fear of their own connection and power into creating SEs by conscious choice. Some people come out and play in the joy and wonder of the amazing power and beauty of what nature has already given them. Here's how your automated SE starship works.

YOUR OTHER FORMS

Imagine taking out your universal piece of paper again. The entire physical universe is a sheet of paper, a two-dimensional plane in front of you. Now take out that cone-of-the-gods you were baffling the Flatlanders with. Pass it through the plane, and you get areas of SE. Doing this in your imagination seems somewhat academic. What's your connection? That multidimensional cone isn't imaginary. The cone is you. You have, for lack of a better term, a "body," in M-Space. This other form is composed of the folded and compressed dimensional energy of M-Space, just as the matter of your physical body is condensed dimensional space in the physical universe. Your M-Space body has miraculous complexity and functionality, just as your physical body does. It also has the advantage of existing in dimensions that are the foundations of physical time and space. It is responsible for curving the event structures in time that create SEs. Your M-Space body is a living thoughtform. The energy of that dimension is…emotion. You have an emotional energy body that curves SE the way matter on the physical plane caused gravitation by curving space-time. Your emotions create SEs. So, why hasn't anyone been telling people this? Our old friends the mystics, shamans, and magicians have been talking about this body, the astral body, for thousands of years.

So I'm supposed to be a scientist basing the model I'm teaching you on evidence. Now I'm suggesting emotion is an actual dimension underling your physical reality. When I say this the bells on my brain's built-in BS detector start going bing, bing, bing, bing. Neuroscience has proven beyond any reasonable doubt that our emotions are the result of mid-brain, limbic system, computational processes in the brain. There are four basic human emotions: love, anger, fear, and disgust. We know what areas of the brain generate them, and which neurotransmitters they depend on. With all science currently knows about the brain, nobody has any idea why you are conscious. I don't have a good answer for how it is possible massively complex computations in that beautiful brain of yours become emotions. There just isn't a good testable explanation for how your physical emotions are connected to the energies of your M-Space astral body. Mystics and clairvoyants tell us there are receiving centers in the body called chakras that pass energy between the physical and emotional bodies, making them act together. Look them up on the internet. There are many drawings. I don't believe it. The scientist part of me says "We have scanners that can watch the protons in your brain wiggle, see the almost unimaginably faint magnetic fields your neurons make when they fire. We can measure your degree of emotional response by the changes in your skin conductivity. We don't see any trans-dimensional energy." We know your amazing "matrix" computer of a brain produces your conscious experience. There is no way to measure anything in M-Space. If it exists, it might be made of chicken soup for all we know. Or, it could even be made of emotional energy.

THE BRAIN AND EMOTIONAL ENERGY

Your brain has evolved in stages. These stages determined the structure of your on-board supercomputer. The oldest part of your brain is at the brain's core. In it are sensory switching stations and computational centers that run your basic body functions. It doesn't think much, and is mostly automatic. This area is often called the reptilian brain. This area of your brain responds to physical stimuli and biological needs in the immediate present moment. It has no notion of the passage of time. This area's consciousness is like being aware of just physical space-time. It has no thoughts about what might be, no planning, it is stuck in the present moment. Your mid-brain generates your emotions in the limbic system. This evolved later to process experiences from the present moment into longer-term patterns. Emotions are thoughts about patterns in time, and the likely results of those patterns. Emotions are a way of thinking outside the present moment of time and space. Emotions drive our actions, interpret our experiences, and link our past, present, and futures. Emotion operates outside the limits of space-time. The limbic system takes the needs of the more primitive, simpler, brain beneath it, and manifests them as emotions. In M-Space, your emotions become thoughtforms, literally embodied emotional energy. Your M-Space astral body manifests the emotions generated by the physical you. Physical thoughts become M-Space thoughtforms. These create SEs based on your emotions.

I have a passion for understanding what is real, and for what works. Science tells us what is probably true, based on experience. When a better explanation comes along, we use it. Thinking about creating SE in terms of your emotional body works. It looks to me as though the shamans and mystics were almost right. The mystical traditions view the astral in terms of spiritual development. Higher emotions such as love and devotion contain more consciousness and energy. These bend event space and cause longer range and more spectacular SEs. Magicians understand emotion as energy, not in moral terms. We are all magicians, like it or not. It's automatic. Let anger and fear run your life, your energy produces SEs that reflect those emotions back to you. Focus as much as is practically possible on love…well, you get the idea. I have treated patients who are unabashed criminals. Some even brag about being evil and drawing power from hatred. I'd like to blame *Star Wars* for this dark-side-of-the-force attitude. Truth is, we all have the same four core emotions. Love, anger, fear, and revulsion. They are generated by specific areas in the limbic system. Neurons that fire together, wire together. Emotions are motivating; they drive our actions through time. If someone decides to get themselves motivated by calling up anger and fear, it works quite well. Emotion can focus attention; it calls for a response, an action, an event, an SE. Which SEs do you want to be most prominent around you? The clients I have treated who keep their anger and fear on cause their limbic systems to wire for those emotions. They get better at being fearful and angry. It becomes a habit. Your starship tries to remember your chosen instructions, which way you have chosen to travel, and how you want to respond to the patterns around you. Your M-Space body makes SEs based on your brain's emotional responses, which are partially a matter of choice. Most of the "darkside" clients I have treated have been in prisons. Most were proud of the strength their anger and fear gave them. Their incarcerated worlds exactly mirrored the emotions they had chosen in the SE of their lives. I have also treated people who, having practiced creating the emotion of love, were just as dysfunctional. Love has the advantage of creating very positive-feeling chemical states in the brain. It also can make one blind to warning signs in relationships, and in the world. We are complex critters. We have all our emotions because nature, in its unimaginable intelligence, found what works best, a responsive balance. Our basic four emotions can be recombined in a dazzling number of combinations and intensities. All colors can be made from combinations of red, yellow, blue, and contrast.

SE ARE DRIVEN BY EMOTIONAL CONTEXTS

SE tend to come in emotional colors. Before you drive yourself batty trying to figure out what each detail of an SE means, start with the emotion it created in you when it happened. You're seeing the effect of a thoughtform created in your emotional, M-space, body. Your emotions are being directly translated into SEs. To create SEs with an emotional theme, focus on the emotion you want to manifest. Conscious attention from the frontal cortex cues the mid-brain limbic system to create that emotion. It also instructs areas in memory that process incoming sensory data to pattern match for that emotion. Somehow, this entire pattern becomes replicated in the astral body that then creates the curves in space-event-time that become the actual SEs. Your brain is pre-set to see the pattern, sees the SEs, which calls your attention to the SEs. Attention causes the cycle to start over again. Before you know it, usually literally before you know it, you are creating a series of SEs around a chosen emotional theme.

Now you know where the control panel is. Let's look at some of the knobs and dials for a while. If you Google image search "human aura," you will get images of people with egg-shaped clouds of transparent colors around them. Some are drawings, modern or ancient. Others look like actual photographs of the human aura. If you read the literature about the aura, it will tell you these colors are actual emotional astral energy. This is the aura claimed to be seen by some clairvoyants, and which many religions depict as a light surrounding their favorite divine beings. These are depictions of emotional M-space energy that change with your emotional state. How is it possible to photograph extra-dimensional energy? Its not. The pictures are fakes. The expensive aura-displaying equipment for sale on these sites are just digital cameras with a computer program that draws on the pictures. Nice fantasy, but no, none of the pictures are real. The pictures themselves are useful, though. They give you a model to use to understand how you create SEs. The aura is emotional energy that surrounds your emotional body. Think of it as the electrical field that surrounds your physical body. The aura is an egg-shaped field filled with masses of color. These colors are the emotions you are experiencing at that moment. As the moment-to-moment emotional process goes on, these colors change to match changes in emotion. A sympathetic emotion might fill your aura with bright blues and greens. If you become angry or hurt, the aura may change to reds and browns. The aura correspond to minor changes in mood that are transient. They are largely a reaction to short term environmental effects and their immediate processing. Your emotional body, being much denser, does not change as rapidly. It represents the major psychological patterns and complexes of the personality. These are the long-term developmental consequences of your experience and choices. Changes in the aura are easy to make; it reacts emotionally from moment to moment. These changes create small, short-term SE reflections. The mass in the emotional body itself is much more powerful. Its effects are long-term SE patterns. It creates entire emotional mythologies, complex SEs that persist and repeat. These are the emotional processing patterns of the limbic system areas of your personality. These are core drive states. Learn to choose your emotional states without being driven by them, and you have partial mastery over creating SEs.

Auras and hallucinations

I used to see auras. Well, for about a month anyway. I had fantasized about seeing auras for decades. I first became enamored with the mystical literature about them when I was a pre-teen. I read the theories, looked at the pictures, practiced the meditations, tried everything, saw nothing. I grew up and became a psychologist. I learned that seeing colors around people was probably a neurological cross-wiring in which data from another area of the brain was incorrectly sent to the visual cortex. Then I met someone who taught me how. It took about an hour to learn. The guy taught me to look for the faint outline of the energy shell around the body, not to look at the body itself. Hold the image in your mind of where the aura should be, then look for the outer edges. Marvelous! I was soon seeing faint traces of the aura and its colors whenever I concentrated enough. I could see them around anyone, anytime. Faint traces that I had been assured would develop with practice into full-blown Technicolor visions. You would think that I would know better than to fall for this, but I did. One afternoon, about a month later, I was sitting in a large meeting. It was one of those deadly boring mandatory staff meetings where nothing new is said and no issues are resolved, other than set times for other meetings that will be just as time-consuming. I started to pass the time by looking at the auras of the people at the meeting.

I was asking myself how it was possible for my brain to notice a non-physical energy. More importantly, why wasn't I getting any better at it? The traces were still as faint now as they had been a month ago. Then I remembered a piece of research I read as a teenager. Psychics who said they could read auras tried to read the aura of a person behind a partition. They were to read the space above the person they couldn't see directly. Problem was, the subjects had been snuck out of the room by the researchers, so there was nobody in the room to read. The psychics reported auras for the people they didn't know had already left the room. I started to get that "Could you really have been this stupid?" feeling. I looked across the room at a blank wall. I imagined a person standing there. I looked for an aura around the imaginary person. Yup, there it was. I was seeing something that wasn't there. Try it sometime, you'll see it, too. Here's how it works. When you imagine something, your brain uses the same areas to create the imaginary image as it would in creating a real image from your sensory data. Brain scanners show that the same areas of the visual cortex become active when you imagine a screwdriver, as when you look at an actual picture of one. The only difference is the strength of the activity in the cortex is less, and the image is fainter. When I looked for an aura expecting to see one, I was holding an image in the visual cortex. I saw the faint traces of the pattern I was looking for. More disturbing, I didn't question what I was experiencing, even though my training should have told me what was happening. I wanted to believe in what I saw, I made the mistake of believing what I was thinking. Never look without question on any of the thoughts you choose, especially when creating SEs. We tend to believe our favorite stories.

YOUR MENTAL BODY

You have yet another, more powerful, extra-dimensional body. I mentioned N-space, a set of dimensions where all possible probabilities in time curve back on themselves into a single moment. In this dimension, you don't just curve events around you, you travel in alternate probabilities. In mystical traditions, your N-space form is called the "mental" body. It gives the form to your emotional energy. It makes the form in thoughtforms. And, true to pattern, its abilities match structures in your brain. Your cortex, that massive grey area of neurons on the outermost part of your brain, is where your heavy-duty processing gets done. The frontal cortex is the conscious part of you that makes decisions. The cortex receives data signals from the emotional limbic system, then processes them into meaning. The cortex is the place where you think about what patterns probably mean, and what effect your actions will probably cause. You use your mental body to direct and interpret energy from your emotional body into action in the world. You use it to move through probability. You can literally think SE into existence by choosing the direction you allow your thoughts to move in. Focus on a picture you like. Look at the elements in the picture. This creates thoughtforms in your aura. Focus long enough, and the process continues even after you turn your attention elsewhere. These more persistent thoughtforms change your direction in probability. Soon, the elements of the picture start showing up as SEs, even after you have stopped consciously looking for them.

The primitive lizard brain in the center controls basic impulses such as the sex drive, and pleasure-seeking. It drives the emotions into action, such as looking for love. They in turn enlist the cortex into figuring out the complex social and physical actions needed to find a partner. The entire system has information flowing both ways. Physical to astral to mental, and mental to astral to physical. What we want affects how we feel, which affects how we think. How we think affects how we feel, which affects what we want. All of it gets reflected in SEs. Your part is consciously choosing which parts of it to boost with your attention. There is a strong professional movement in psychology right now for empirically based treatment. Instead of just applying the methods you know and understand treatments must be for specific problems and backed-up by research that proves they are effective. When I was studying for the licensing exam there was an actual instruction that said if the test asked what the specific treatment for a disorder is, and you don't know, say CBT. It was most likely to be the answer. CBT stands for Cognitive Based Therapy. Short version: you can control what you feel and how you react by consciously and deliberately choosing what you think. That's how you create SEs. Thinking about emotional expression and regulation in terms of a possible emotional body and aura works in the same pattern as CBT. Psychics say people who experience a lot of anger have dark auras. A psychologist would say that anger is actually a prevalence to use neuron-pathways devoted to that emotion. A good therapy for anger would include changing the way the person thinks in order to change their emotions, to change their cognition. This would have the brain use the pathways for the unwanted emotion less often. Over time, those unused pathways are trimmed away, a process called neurological pruning. Or, you could claim more positive emotional energy is being built into the aura and emotional body, replacing the negative. Mythology is other people's psychology. Both science and mythology express observed patterns, but in different languages. Good science tends to describe patterns in exact detail, and refrain from describing what it cannot test or observe. Myth and mysticism enjoy a greater freedom. They are free to describe patterns and experiences that can't be tested. Alchemy developed into modern chemistry. Astrology became the mother of astronomy. Each told stories to explain events. These stories turned out not to be accurate, but parts of them were true. Both had an essential belief: our emotions and thoughts are connected to the events of the physical world. Astrologers still say our moods and thoughts follow the influences of planetary motions. In a sense, they believe in a gravitational influence, a kind of mental and emotional gravitation, affecting people and events. Only the really, really, naive alchemists tried to turn lead into gold. Real alchemists were trying to use the symbols of elements to manipulate their own emotional and mental states. Gold was a metaphor for enlightenment. The elements the alchemist manipulated were their own emotional and mental bodies. Our medieval ancestors were using M- and N-Space long before the physics of the late 20th century proposed String Theory. Their language, like the language I'm using now, was only as accurate as their best educated guess.

EXPANDING PERSPECTIVES

One of my favorite mind games changes my frame of reference. It takes me out of accepting the perspective I usually use. I call it "tour guide." I pretend I am showing someone from another time, or from another cultural perspective, the world around me. Imagine showing Julius Caesar around your town. Dress him up in street clothes and give him a tour of your life. Explain the world to a 9th-century European peasant, or to our ancestral hunter. Pretend to see through someone else's eyes. Make that brain of yours use its mirror neurons to create a new personality. Be someone who doesn't have the same limitations and set of pattern matching instructions you do. The world starts to look really new and interesting. You could even pretend to be someone who produces SE and sees the world from a unified perspective. Here's a perspective-changing SE that happened to me a few months ago:

Synchronistic Event

I was pretending I was a tour guide to an enlightened being. Not just any old enlightened being;
this was an alien who had never had any concept of
not being a unified being. What can I say? I got bored
pretending to talk with historical figures. I had been
trying to explain the behavior of the people around
me to him. He was telling me how the experience of
knowing everything is an extension of the same consciousness. Then I experienced a moment of slippage
between what I was pretending to be, and who I usually am. I sat down and turned on CNN. Larry King
was interviewing a fundamentalist religious leader
who was lobbying for his particular us-against-them
perspective. There this guy was, seated across from
the host, glass of water on the table, talking about
what God wants people to do and be. He was a well-
educated and respected spiritual authority. For an
instant, I saw the situation from the perspective of
the enlightened alien still constructed in my memory,
and burst out laughing. This guy actually thought
he was separate from the people he was advocating
against. He believed he was separate from the glass
of water on the table in front of him. The man had
never experienced anything, in his entire life, anything, that was not the one being. Yet, there he was,
this spiritual authority, with no clue he was talking
about, and to, himself. He was telling everyone his
views on how to follow a spiritual path that never
leads to recognizing yourself. He was telling people
to follow someone else. Someone he just happened to
know more about than other people. It was like watching an old episode of *Monty Python's Flying Circus*.

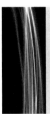

It was the absurdity of the common place exaggerated
to the point of comedy. For a moment, I saw it from
the perspective of the person I was pretending to be.
For a moment, SE followed the pattern of the pretend
person I had created.

*Sometimes the best way to get what you need, is to take from yourself what
you already have.*

COMMUNICATING WITH YOURSELF THROUGH SE

When I was a child, I loved *Star Trek*. One of the nice futuristic touches in the show was the talking ship's computer. You could ask a question into the seemingly empty air, and the starship would tell you the answer. The starship had such massive computing power it could simulate a personality the crew could talk to. The computer controlled the starship. Your brain can do the same thing. Your mind is multi-dimensional. The frontal lobe "you," is only a small part of the total mass of your brain. The rest of it is as alert and present as you are. Your starship talks back, too. It can use SEs as a language. SEs not only reflects your thoughts, they allow you to communicate directly with the unconscious. SEs show you directly what your subconscious thoughts are. Some people communicate with their unconscious by watching their dreams. You have the ability to communicate with your unconscious by creating SEs.

The unconscious can be a cooperative partner of the conscious. Many people have had the experience of not being able to find an answer to some problem or question, to remember some name or word. They forget about the question, then at some later time, the answer just pops into awareness while they are doing something else. The subconscious has been looking for the answer while conscious attention has been turned elsewhere. It then provides the conscious with the information when it has been located. You ask for the information, your computer lets you know when it finds it. We tend to treat the unconscious as though it's a stupid servant. Find this, get me that, a collection of automated systems that sometimes helps, sometimes interferes with our wishes. Freudians said the unconscious was a dumping ground for unacceptable impulses, a psychic trash heap. Way to go guys; treat the universe's most complex and miraculous computational system as a garbage can. The modern computational model of the brain is a clear improvement. It can demonstrate how your starship-quality computer works, in a general sense. Both models miss something essential. It's alive! Seriously. The unconscious is physically larger than the frontal lobes, it has better access to sensory information and memory, it follows many of your instructions, and it is constantly trying to communicate with you and do things for you, including communicating through creating SE.

Synchronistic events pattern off your emotional and mental energy.

These energies do not distinguish between patterns produced in the conscious or unconscious any more than the electricity in your computer cares what part of the mother board its running through. SEs reflect the totality of your mental processes. You can read the unconscious patterns of your mind, or talk to them, through SEs.

We are the path we walk. The dramas of our journey are played out in our emotional and mental lives. Some of these stories are determined by our predetermined genetic and environmental inheritances. Much of the path is a story we are writing ourselves from moment to moment. You can use SEs to make alterations in the path you travel. We have limits. Some distances in probability are too far for us to travel. It is unlikely mankind will ever develop actual starships. The state of theoretical physics at the moment leaves no conceivable way to move a ship faster than the speed of light. It would take 200 times the total energy output of the entire civilization to get even a small ship to the next star system within a human lifetime. Nature has better technology than we do. You're born with it. Your brain is a better computational system than any we can even remotely hope to design. We may have fusion reactors in about 70 years that can convert a few grams of matter into energy, enough to power a city. The sun is a natural fusion reactor. It has been converting 11 million tons of fuel a second into energy for billions of years. You already have a vessel capable of faster than light speeds. Your emotional and mental bodies are made of fields of energy that already exceed the speed of light. The thoughtforms you create with your thoughts, emotions, and attention are already traveling faster than space-time. They encompass it, locally. You are already in your starship. SEs are the on-board computer telling you how the ship is functioning, waiting for your directions. Your spaceship doesn't travel in anything as mundane as mere physical space. Your vessel transverses universes of probability. Forget about that pile of rocks at your feet. You are what you were dreaming of building all along.

Nine

Mystical Mumbo Gumbo

COMMONALITY OF MYSTICISM AND SCIENCE

This chapter is about how you communicate with different parts of yourself. Even if you fully understand that you are a unitary being, you are still only experiencing a tiny fraction of yourself at any given moment. The part of you that experiences reading these lines has its own moment in time and location in space. I have mine as I sit and write them to you. Ultimately, we are part of the same being. But we have separate windows into that unified being from our own physical perspectives.

The energies that make up our forms seem separated by time and space. This is an illusion created by our brain's limited ability to process information. All energies are part of the same underlying dimensional fields. Einstein was one of the world's greatest mystics. He stated a simple truth; all is connected and all is relative. Matter is a form of space. A particle is just a place where the local density of the space is a little higher than the space around it. Look at the clothing you are wearing. Imagine the fabric is space. Pinch a bit of fabric between your fingers and twist it a bit. That's a particle of matter. Think of the fabric as stretching for billions of light years, across all of time and space. Every particle in the universe is a twist in this fabric. It's all the same fabric. Currently physics is debating which particles are more twists in the fabric, which are threads of the fabric, and how those threads are woven together. Seems the fabric of the universe is a blend of many dimensions. Some threads are woven more tightly from some dimensional fibers than others. Time functions in much the same way. Einstein declared that space and time were inseparable parts of the same fabric. The matter in your body is part of the same fabric of space-time as mine. The moment in time you are reading these words is part of a larger blend of dimensional time. I am writing these words on part of the same fabric, in the same universal present moment in time, but on a different area of the fabric.

You are clothed in these fabrics right now. You wear time and space, multiple dimensions the same way you wear clothing. They move with you, bend as your thoughts bend, and change as your thoughts change. Like a comfortable shirt or a well fitting pair of shoes, you forget they are there, moving with you, part of you. We remove these fabrics occasionally, re-cloth ourselves in them, and mistake them for the totality of our being. You can see the effects they have around you as SEs. In some ways, SEs are like wearing a long flowing robe. You move, and the fabric flows in the space around you. If you were half-asleep, you might see the motion and not realize you were moving the cloth. You might think the fabric moved by itself, or was being moved by some mysterious force. Mysticism and science have a common goal. They look at the motions of the fabrics around us, and speculate about what caused the motion. Mysticism, literally the study of the mysterious, found its general answer long ago. In a broad, general sense, we are the fabric, and we are the forces that move them. There is only one being. But, the devil is in the details. It seems that the overall unity has no single individual awareness, no personal consciousness. Individual consciousness requires a focus in selected areas of the fabric. You, the human being reading these words now, and I, the human being writing them in my present moment, experience only our infinitesimally small, individual, parts of the greater fabric.

The universe is always more complex than it appears to us.

We can understand that everything is connected, but we can only be consciously aware of tiny parts of the whole at any given moment. Even in deep satori, you can experience the full connection, but not the details. The universe may open to your senses, but you are still not aware of every particle of dust blowing in the sand storms on Mars. You know you are one being, but you are not tracking every hydrocarbon atom in the methane oceans of Titan. You become aware of your individual SEs, and some of the SEs in the world around you, but never all of them, never the vast SEs of all things. SE remains mysterious because, as individual beings, we were not evolved to process such vast amounts of data. Science realized something mysticism was never able to fully grasp. The best way to understand how the universe works is to be incredibly humble about your own understanding. Philosophy and religion have some common psychological foundations. Yes, there's a personal rant about religions coming again. Please bear with my skeptic's perspective for a few moments. I have a problem with not believing what I think, or what other people think. Good scientists have some of the personality characteristics that make good priests. Characteristics that good priests, philosophers, and mystics often lack.

ADVANTAGES AND DISADVANTAGES OF THE SCIENTIFIC PERSPECTIVE

Let's use that supercomputer in your head for a moment. On your stage of internal memory, that place where you construct reality, imagine a scientist standing on a stage. Make him, or her, somewhat of a comic extreme, a stereotype. Perhaps yours has a lab coat, a pocket full of different colored pens, thick glasses, and an air of personal distraction and disorganization. You're creating this reality, whatever works in your world. Next to him, materialize a priest. Rather than just any priest, we are going to borrow a parody. This priest is a true believer in a ridiculous fundamentalist religion; the fast-growing church of the Flying Spaghetti Monster. I'd love to claim I created this religion, but it was first thought up by Bobby Henderson as a satirical poke at The Kansas Board of Education. Your Pastafarian priest is dressed in the sacred robes of his religion, a pirate costume. Now, in our internal theatre of the improbable, we ask both our newly created thoughtforms, "What causes global warming?" Our scientist fumbles around for a self-conscious moment or two, then begins to write long strings of math on the blackboard that materializes behind him. "Well," he begins, "We performed a meta-analysis of 1,400 different studies on the relationship of reported atmospheric temperature variation, taking into account 35 separate variables that affect energy distribution of air masses under different seasonal condition, and looked at amounts of solar radiation and carbon dioxide production during a 75-year period. Statistical analysis indicates a .P value of .92878 within a 6 percent margin of error on a confidence band of plus or minus 5 percent."

My eyes began to glaze over just writing that. What your little scientist is doing is admitting the limits of his understanding. He is describing, in painstaking detail, the precise limits of what he understands, and how probable it is that his understanding is true. Good scientists are never sure. Good scientists know how likely something is to be true, under very precise and limited conditions. Good scientists give you such exact information, that you could perform the same experiment, in exactly the same way, and get the same results. If you don't get the same results, and you can explain why, in detail, a good scientist changes his mind about what he believed was probably true. Not only does the good scientist change his mind, he is overjoyed at having learned something new, to have helped the process of investigating the mysterious. Science is an inherently humbling profession. Now we ask our Pastafarian priest the global warming question. Here's his response:

"First I'd like to state my humble thanks to our lord, the all mighty creator of the universe, the Flying Spaghetti Monster, or FSM as we affectionately worship him. His power and wisdom are beyond all human understanding. Did I mention I represent him? Global warming is caused by the FSM. He is upset with humanity for its iniquities and immorality. Global warming is the result of not following the word of the FSM. You see it is all very simple. FSM is fond of pirates. If you look at a chart of global warming trends, you can clearly see that over the last century the pirate population is clearly in decline. Fewer pirates, more global warming. The FSM is obviously angry with humanity for its persecution of pirates. That's why we Pastafarians dress as pirates. We are performing a divine service to humanity by increasing the number of pirates and spreading the word of the FSM. We are FSM's chosen people; we need donations to spread the word, hand over yer booty, arrrr."

Pastafarians, of all denominations, have simplistic answers to complex problems. They are usually sure, in an absolute sense, of the answers they provide. They make declarations about the nature of reality that cannot be tested, can't be verified, and they stick by them. Pastafarians often declare their humility and humble service to their FSM, while forcing their way of thought on others. Philosophies and religions have positive aspects to be sure. But, all tend to declare the nature of your reality for you. A handy service if you would rather cruise the infinite universe of creative possibility on someone else's autopilot program. The problem is, unverifiable beliefs limit the way you consider alternate possibilities.

Science has a matching problem. A yin to mysticism's yang. Some followers of the scientific method have made science itself a religion of sorts. They take the easy, self-assured way out. Some devotees of science declare that their way of investigating reality is the only valid means of determining truth. Some priests of physics believe that, until something becomes verified by experimental investigation, it is not true. The problem is, science isn't supposed to work that way. The scientific method is a humble method. It tests one small, very specific set of conditions at a time. Then it asks others to test the same conditions again independently. If results are reliably reproducible, a small bit of probably true information is added to the knowledge base. Scientists tell themselves stories about reality, just as philosophers do. Good scientists know they are telling stories. They are never sure. The way science is supposed to work is to allow for the possibility of anything not specifically ruled out by valid research. Science is supposed to be where dreams, speculations, experiences, and assumptions, are tested with an open mind. The true scientist is open to alternate probabilities, but sides with the preponderance of evidence. Your conscious awareness evolved as an area of computational processing able to deal with uncertainty. You are never fully aware of the whole of your situation. Your senses always provide you with an overwhelming amount of information. There is so much more to you than a mere conscious awareness can hold at any given moment. The brain evolved to keep the body alive, and to pass on its genes to the next generation. The consciousness it evolved to help you limits and processes the information you receive. You exist in a data stream that constantly dances between being fast, and globally oriented, but lacking in detail, and being slower, more accurate, but missing global connections.

This is the true existential dilemma; to tolerate the ambiguous nature of existence, to remain flexible, to keep moving, to never truly be sure, to find wonder and joy in existence.

You are never going to be sure about SE. You are able to create them, but the more detailed your analysis of them, the more complex they will become. Your powers to create your reality are spectacular, but as an individual consciousness, there are local limits to your abilities. I'm going to start to explain some of the more amazing capacities you have, and to put them into a workable perspective. If I did this from the perspective of spiritual and mystical philosophy, it would sound like mumbo jumbo to the scientist on my stage. If I stick to the minutia of verifiable empirical data, the joy of our situation disappears; the awe and wonder are darkened by seeing only what we know is already there. I like Pastafarians. They often have a delicious sense of humor, whether they realize it or not. I would like to offer you something other than science or philosophy. Please allow me to present you with a good meal.

Gumbo is a traditional Cajun dish. It has no definite recipe. Each cook boils the best of his ingredients, shrimp, fish, okra, chopped vegetables, even sausages and shellfish, all in a broth of seasonings that often remain the savory secret of the chef. Gumbo emerged from Louisiana, where a crossing of French, Native American, African, and Caribbean cultures all brought together their own spices and ingredients to the cauldron. There is no scientific formula for gumbo, and no global rules about what it must include. Generally, it is a savory, satisfying celebration of creativity. It tastes good. Rather than being created from a standard recipe, gumbo emerges from the relationship the chef has to his culture and ingredients. To taste a good gumbo is to enter into a relationship with the creator, not to merely consume a product. There are many delightful ways to serve it. Today we are serving SE gumbo. Dip a spoon beneath the broth, and you might find a flavorful chunk of neurophysiology. The next spoonful may have bits of String Theory. The broth may be seasoned with perennial philosophy, personal experience, and the timing of SE that appeared and were added to the stock. Gumbo doesn't require belief.

HOW SE ARE CREATED: A UNION OF SCIENCE AND SPECULATION

In previous chapters, I described your brain as a starship-quality biocomputer. Your experience at this moment is entirely composed of the data processing stream your brain produces. As you read, the universe you are experiencing is actively constructed in the partial lobes, analyzed, altered, given emotional valence by the limbic system, and passed on to you up in the prefrontal cortex. You talk to yourself about what you are experiencing through activity in the temporal lobe, then you alter the data stream to match for different patterns based on what you, up front, tell the rest of the brain about what's important and what's not.

Let's take the starship metaphor a step further. Your ship is composed of your physical body. It is made of the fabric of physical space. Think of your senses as reporting on the movement of the fabric beyond the cluster of fibers you think of as your personal consciousness. Your starship has sensory systems that orient you in time and space.

Your vehicle is much more sophisticated than a mere physical body. It is made of at least two other fabric blends. M- and N-Space have their own fabrics, and you are made of them as well. M- and N-Space have more dimensions than physical reality, and the fibers that make up the matter of these multi-verses have their own type of consciousness. M-Space matter is literally made of dimensions of emotional energy.

SEs happen because your brain's processes create changes in your MN-Space forms. When you change these forms, you change your course through the infinite probable universe membranes you are traveling through. Yes, your starship is already in motion. Currently, String Theory is considering the possibility that some particles, like the graviton, are shared between different physical realities. Excited visionaries are speculating that perhaps we can create "gravity phones" that will allow us to speak to parallel alternate universes. Toys. You are already equipped with something vastly better. You exist in an almost infinite number of alternate universes right now. Your MN-Space bodies exist over areas of time and space. They exist over areas of probable parallel universes as well. You are moving through these probabilities the way you move through physical time and space, effortlessly. When you create a pattern of SE by applying attention, emotion, and thought, you are doing much more than just bending time and space. You are doing more than creating reflections of your thoughts; you are navigating your travel through alternate probabilities. Your thought and emotion creates changes in your MN-Space forms. These changes cause alterations in the directions you travel through the infinite probabilities around you.

You already exist in many parallel universes. You travel through them unceasingly, you always have. A little closer to conventional string theory; our normal movement in time results from quantum movements from one probability to the next. We move so fast through these probabilities, we blur them into the illusion of a continuous timeline. When you arrive, for a moment, in a probability that reflects your MN-body's energy, SEs happen. Your psychological state reflects the probability you have arrived in. It appears that the inner and outer realities parallel each other. You not only already communicate in other realities, you travel there. The MN-bodies reflect all of your unconscious processes. They make no distinction between conscious and automated processes. Because of this, you can track the SEs they create, and use the SEs to communicate with your unconscious processes. Think about that for a moment. You are already powerful enough to use the events of the environment as a way of communicating with deeper levels of yourself.

THE PRACTICAL LIMITATIONS OF SE

As odd as it may seem, with all this range in probability, we have very real and concrete limitations. Some probabilities are just too far away to reach. We live within the limitations of our physical world and circumstances. I work with the mental health needs of prisoners much of the time. It's tempting to dismiss people by saying their circumstances result from the choices they have made. It's not that simple. As a forensic psychologist, I'm interested in the circumstances that have led a client to be incarcerated. Some people literally follow courses in probability that lead to dead ends. The limitations life can place on people are real, and as the Buddha said, suffering is real. After I had struggled working through my masters program, I went to the graduation ceremony. The keynote address was given by the then secretary of education. Part of his speech was about seeing people who had become prisoners of their own lives. He said the reason education was so important was because without it, people become trapped in their own limitations. In society, if you are not born rich, or very lucky, you have to either start a business or learn a skill to survive well. He described, eloquently, the way circumstances people live in often determine their outcomes. Many people become too busy surviving to follow the life paths they would have chosen. Many people never learn they have choices about their direction. Some people never find out they are navigating their own course until they are so far ashore from their desires that return is improbable. I read many correctional file histories to determine who my clients are, and what kind of probabilities they have arrived from. Statistically, it is easy to determine who will probably wind up incarcerated. There are actually formulas to calculate how much free will was probably involved in the commission of a crime. You can factor in poverty, lack of education, environmental exposure to crime and deprivation, parental drug use, learning disability, genetically inherited intelligence, or lack thereof. Overall, you can predict pretty well who is going to end up with their choices severely limited. But, we do have choices. Some of the most remarkable stories of recovery I have witnessed have involved seemingly miraculous SEs that have offered second chances to people looking for them. We are never completely limited by our circumstances. When someone has changed their way of thinking about their circumstances, often their circumstances change in response. It's a reciprocal relationship.

SE exists to give you an advantage over the starkness of mere cause and effect. You are not a ship dead in the water with no wind, drifting on the current of random events. You are navigating by your own attention and choice. Realistically, you can even determine, in a general way, how much of a change of course you are normally capable of. Time to dip the spoon in the gumbo again. My understanding of Rhine's work with producing highly targeted SE is that, under normal circumstances, you are probably altering the actual events around you by 3-5 percent without trying. My experience has been there are spikes in that rate that are much higher. Some of them feel like course corrections of 60-90 percent. These are the rare, attention-getting SEs, not the low-level background SEs.

Synchronistic Event

SE has once more provided an event that illustrates what I was writing. I was trying to think of a good recent example of an SE that demonstrated a spike, and another that represented a more common background SE. I had been writing this chapter for a few hours, and need to stop. My daughter was at work, and asked me to pick her up and give her a ride home. She would be providing babysitting for my son so I could continue writing these lines to you. On the way home, she asked how the writing was going. I told her I was trying to set up telling the reader how to amplify their SEs by displacing their conscious awareness directly onto the astral (MN) dimension. I explained that I wanted to give them a way to make SEs appear so blatantly, it would seem as if they were manifesting their thoughts automatically. She listened, and then said, "Oh, dad, I have something for you." She held up a large zip-lock bag. Allan Combs was absolutely correct when he pointed out that SEs seem to have a sense of humor all their own. When I wrote the section in this chapter that included the Flying Spaghetti Monster, I printed Wikipedia's entry for FSM for reference. It includes the official Pastafarian pictures of the FSM. It depicted FSM as two large meatballs surrounded by a mass of impossibly thick spaghetti tentacles, with a dash of red spaghetti sauce. Vencenza was holding up a plastic bag with the FSM sealed inside. "A woman at work brought too much food for everyone. I thought you might like some," she said. The bag had two large meatballs surrounded by the thickest strands of tentacle-like spaghetti I have ever seen, and a dash of meat sauce. It was not just the food, it was the arrangement. As it sat in the bag, it was arranged exactly as the drawings of the FSM were done. The FSM was literally staring out of the bag at us. "Vin," I said, "that's the Flying Spaghetti Monster." She turned the bag to face her and looked at it. She giggled. "So it is!" I asked her if she had set this whole thing up, and she assured me the SE was completely random. When I arrived back home, I hurriedly dropped the bag on the desk here next to my computer. It landed on the FSM article I printed out. The FSM in the bag is now sitting next to the picture of the FSM, virtually identical. I had been handed my example of a spike SE.

The example of a background SE followed right behind the FSM.

Synchronistic Event

As I sit writing this, an internet radio commercial just came on for a pet supply service called "Paw Nation." At that moment, our Jack Russell Terrier, Sol, came bursting into the room, flinging the door back, my son in close pursuit yelling, "Doggie!" That was the example of a background SE I needed to compare to the spike SE. Trickster indeed.

STEERING SE

Navigating through SE, like steering a ship, has two elements. The first is the direction of the course in probability you take. Your navigation system, like so much of that miraculous brain of yours, is mostly automated. Your emotions and thoughts automatically change the energy of your MN-bodies, which direct your course through the parallel probabilities around you. You automatically steer through probability until events mirror your thoughts. Your relationship to SE is an automated response to your thoughts. Second is the amount of energy you are expending to propel your forms through probability. Ships have mass, even MN-ships. You can't turn a large cargo ship on a dime. Some of us are carrying a lot of emotional cargo. Here in the San Francisco Bay area, we see large ships coming into port every day. Once under the Golden Gate Bridge, they are met by tugboats. These smaller craft, with powerful engines, maneuver the larger vessels once in harbor. Their extra energy provides the ability to make tight course corrections. They place the larger ships into the exact berths the pilots direct them to. Your MN-vessels normally don't need extra help to navigate the wider dimensions of probability. Our pre-human ancestors did not need our extensive prefrontal cortex to survive and pass on their genes to the next

generations. But, being consciously aware, being able to make finer decisions about the patterns around us, gave our ancestors an edge. You, the
consciously self-aware part, are the edge. You are the extra energy. Your
attention is the tugboat that directs the larger part of your being through
the infinite dimensions of probability around you. You decide what you
think, what feelings you validate, what push your automated processes
need to reach the destinations you choose.

You are in an amazing situation at this very moment. You exist in a
neurologically created representation of reality. Even what you think of as
yourself is a complex computational process added to the inner stage of
your consciousness. Are we more than this? You will never be sure. Being
sure forecloses on possibilities, makes your thoughts inflexible. Being sure
lowers brain activity. Unquestioning belief makes you dumber. It lessens
your actual degree of consciousness. Amazingly, that is exactly what many
belief systems demand—unquestioning faith. Dumbing-down people
makes them easier to divert and direct. Without having to declare the
best way to make gumbo, I'm going to give you a recipe for dramatically
increasing the intensity of SEs around you. This is the recipe I used, the
formula that caused the proliferation of SEs in my own life.

No one has a good answer for how your astral and mental forms con-
nect to your physical body. The classical and perennial models have failed
to show any empirical proof of their theories. More modern philosophers have borrowed from theoretical physics. They suggest the physical
is in a state of quantum entanglement with the MN-Dimensions. Many
have proposed that thought and emotions are part of this complex entanglement. Perhaps these entanglements anchor consciousness to brain
processes. Nobody really knows. I'm going to propose an elegant theoretical cheat: you have a soul. Or, more accurately, there is a soul that has
you. It is easy to conceive we are purely physical beings. Experience and
consciousness existing as computational processes on stages of memory
is pretty much the accepted norm in neuroscience. SE tears huge, gaping
holes in this linear time and space model. I'm having a snack right now,
a warm bowl of leftover FSM. Explain that with a brain-based model!
Yet, we are clearly on that neurological stage at this moment.

THE MEANING OF THE DREAM

The soul is the trickster. Its energies are love, wisdom, and intelligence. It is your highest quality. It is playful and joyous. It delights in our attention as we delight in our children. Now look out at the room around you. This stage of reality is maintained by your causal form, as is your placement on that stage. Ultimately, behind the physical, the M- and N-Space bodies, that causal form is you. You are dressed in the fabric of the other dimensions. This mythology not only solves the problem of your experience being brain-based, but SE being a real external phenomena. The soul becomes the real brain, out there in indescribable hyperspace. Everything else is the result of its processes. As I said, an elegant cheat. It just puts off unanswerable questions to a higher level of explanatory fictions. This is the force that plays with you through SEs. It is the part of you on the other side of the illusion. Let's start playing with this trickster.

Your conscious awareness is a deep source of energy. The prefrontal lobe is in effect a booster processor, an extra CPU core the brain uses for particularly difficult problems. When you dream, the brain is engaged in memory consolidation. Your motor systems are put off-line, so you don't walk around the house while you're walking around in your dreams. The meaning of dreams is usually the emotional feeling of the dream. Emotions are clothed in different symbols that become the context and objects of the dream. Experiences become an algebra that represents the brain trying to "solve" and file away for future reference your experiences and reactions. In conventional dreaming, only a portion of you is brought on-line to assist in the processing. Usually you become conscious in the dream, but large parts of your self-awareness are still dormant. Parts of you that know your mother can't turn into a fish, and that would wonder what was happening when reality shifts and changes, remain off-line. The brain creates these realities on the stage of your consciousness, in areas of memory, then puts you on the stage to see how you react, to lend processing power. These stages are, for lack of a better term, quantum-entangled with your MN-bodies. Dreams have a powerful influence on the energy states in the MN-forms.

Freed from the distractions of the physical world, dream states can create pure representations of thoughts and emotions not available in the waking world. How would you experience the joy, or terror, of being able to fly in the real world? How would you replicate the unresolved night terror your two-year-old self felt when it realized it was mortal? The brain can do all of this safely in the metaphor of a dream state.

Because your actual consciousness stems from the causal body, you have the ability to bring your full self-conscious awareness on-line in any combination of your physical or MN-forms. You can bring your full, lucid, self-awareness on stage during dream states. Our ancestors, and some of our contemporaries, believe that the state of fully lucid dreaming is actually leaving the body and traveling in other worlds. Current research on lucid dreaming suggests that you become fully conscious in the dream state when you bring your prefrontal cortex fully on-line during the dreaming. Astral travel or a trainable neurological process? I'm taking another bite of my FSM. Not bad, the meatballs are vegetarian.

Conscious dreaming

In lucid dreaming, you have full conscious awareness at your disposal. You wake up in a clear, real, alternative universe, a parallel probability. You know you are dreaming. Lucid dreams tend to be much more stable than conventional dreams. They act more as physical realities do. Your presence seems to be what makes this so. Your unconscious is not reality-oriented. It changes the data it receives from the senses, adds, subtracts, and alters the neurological information without much regard for actual reality. We live in a representational hallucination. You are the part that is reality and consequence oriented. You are the part that has the responsibility to decide what is real and what is imagination. You make the important decisions. When you enter a dream state fully conscious, you bring a tremendous amount of auxiliary processing power onto the stage. Your presence stabilizes aspects of the dreamscape because you are the reality function. It becomes more concrete, vivid. It becomes more like the reality you are accustomed to functioning in while you are awake. You experience universes that are created from your unconscious processing. You have your full personal resources and memory available to you during these little adventures. You become a conscious co-creator of your universe. This is an incredible opportunity. You can fully experience anything you need or want. With some practice, it becomes possible to enter into conscious cooperation with the unconscious that sets these stages for you. You live adventures in universes created just for you. You have experiences that re-enact the issues and experiences you need to process. You play in created probabilities, and clear the minds back-log of processing. Gradually, these environments become more responsive. As you integrate conscious and unconscious functions, you can take over aspects of the creation of the lucid dreaming universe. Eventually, you stand on the stage of a universe you have created, and which changes to meet your every thought. It becomes possible, for short periods, to be a causal creator of your reality. Perfect SEs.

Time to stir the pot a little. There are traditional schools of meditation and shamanism that teach students to walk between the worlds this way. Some of them even recognize that the distinctions between the personal unconscious and external reality are pretty irrelevant. SE crosses these boundaries constantly. Trying to separate them can make you crazy. But, that is the essence of your task. You decide how to navigate in environments that are a mix of personal reality and objective, a collective existence. Most mystical traditions advise having a guide if you are going to start walking the planes of consciousness regularly. It's sort of the ancient version of having a psychoanalyst if you are going to interpret your dreams. Some of the Tibetan schools have warnings about astral traveling. I think of them as astral travel advisories. The primary cautionary note is that you can get addicted. Let's assume the classical mystical position for a moment. These aren't dreams. You are actually displacing your consciousness fully onto other planes of reality. These universes are natural ecosystems. They have their own inhabitants, civilizations, critters, gods, demons, spirits, and rules. There, you are not subject to the same mundane rules and limitations of physical life. It's exciting, interesting, enticing. You can virtually be a god, don't have to pay taxes, transcend death and pain. There are no rules limiting your behavior, you do whatever you want, be whatever you want. Your astral body can take any shape you like. It is virtually indestructible, needs no food, never gets sick, and never ages. And, if you want to believe such myths, it can be used to ride out the death of the physical. Naïve practitioners can mistake all this for reality, and come to prefer the lucid dream state over waking reality.

A congresswoman and more than a dozen others were shot in May 2011 by a very disturbed young man. From what I understand, it sounded as though he was suffering from paranoid schizophrenia. Clearly, he was psychotic. In his journals, authorities found he had been practicing lucid dreaming. Socially awkward and isolated, he preferred these dream worlds where he could be empowered and unchallenged. He had learned to create universes there, and gradually came to believe that his astral universe was the real world, and that we existed in a dream. I suppose it's easier to shoot 18 people if you believe they are not real. But they were.

My profession is to recognize and diagnose mental illness. I spend much of my day determining the state of reality testing in clients with various psychotic disorders. Meditation and dream work are positive, integrative, and therapeutic. It is the lack of information, the inability to keep an open and reasoned mind, not being grounded in physical life, that leads some people into strange places. Crazy and spiritual are not related. We dream because we are meant to dream. We evolved to be able to dream to assist us in processing the experiences of our lives. If we can walk other planes, design other universes, it is because there are advantages in being able to do so. SE exists to assist you, not to make decisions for you. You determine how to react to your reality. Traditional schools of magic and meditation also recognize that these other worlds underlie the foundations of physical reality. Traditional magic across the world works by having the practitioner journey to the other worlds, gain knowledge, and undergo transformation. Saints and mystics, profits and magicians, change the events of this world by becoming conscious on the next. Placing your awareness directly in the MN-Space bodies increases the energy available to create SE drastically. Your thoughts and emotions become considerably more effective at steering you through the probabilities that create SE.

CHOICE IS A BITCH

Your decisions about what you think and feel are what direct your course through SE, and through life. There is a story by Karen Kwiatkowski posted on the wall of one of the offices where I see clients. In the story, an old Cherokee warrior is telling his grandson about a battle that goes on in each one of us. He tells his grandson that within each of us there are two wolves. One dark, the other light. One is evil, full of anger, rage, jealousy, sorrow, self pity, jealousy, doubt, resentment, lies, inferiority, and selfish ego. The other wolf is filled with love, joy, hope, security, selflessness, peace, hope, humility, kindness, empathy, truth, and compassion. The grandson asks his grandfather, "Which wolf wins?" The wise old man replies, "The one you feed."

When you displace your consciousness directly into one of these MN-environments, you will always be given a choice. You will decide how you react to the circumstances of the universe you find yourself in. Who do you want to be? Choices in these environments have consequences here in the waking world. Even if they are merely dreams, your decisions instruct the automated aspects of the unconscious how you would like to perceive the world. You are programming your mind to react according to your example. There is a karmic logic to it all. Behave in a lucid dream as if you are the center of the universe and no one else matters, and your brain will filter your reality to match that pattern. SE will follow your lead and present you with events that make you feel isolated, misunderstood, disconnected. Behave in astral environments as if they are real, treat all you meet with courtesy, respect, and kindness, no matter what the situation, and SE will show you your connectedness. You will have directed a course based on how you treated those other aspects of yourself.

If you feel you need to know the exact meditations that produce out-of-body experiences and lucid dreaming, search the internet and visit a local metaphysical bookstore. They should be more than sufficient to get you started. Following is an experience I had after a few months of traveling in these dimensions, before I had much of a clue.

I had been re-reading the *Bhagavad Gita* that day. Prince Arjuna returns from exile and finds his kingdom usurped. The story is rich and complex, but the crux of it is Arjuna finds himself about to engage in a great battle against many of his friends and relatives. Two great armies face each other across the battlefield. Arjuna finds himself in a chariot between the armies agonizing about closing a battle in which many of his loved ones will die. He can't reconcile his warrior's duty to secure the kingdom with the suffering his actions will cause. Fortunately for him, his charioteer is his close friend, the god Krishna. Before closing the battle, Krishna instructs him on fate, the duty to uphold righteousness, and the discharge of one's moral duty in the face of personal loss. He talks Arjuna into fighting the good fight. In my copy of the book, there are richly illustrated color plates. They depict two vast armies of warriors, chariots, and horses facing each other. They are clad in armors of shining gold. They are valiant warriors, strong, brave, immaculately groomed, and disciplined. Every shield, each weapon is a masterpiece of engraved metalworking. Every horse and chariot are the perfect example of the craft of war. All is clean, bright, ideal, and holy. A romanticized view of war to say the least.

That night, I woke to a burning sensation on the back of my hand. I opened my eyes to brilliant sunlight, looking down at my hand resting on a railing. My skin was dark and red, the hot sun almost baking my flesh. I knew this was a dream, and took a few moments to marvel at the reality of the sensation. Then I noticed my forearm. It was clad in dirty leather armor. There were tarnished, spiked, bronze plates riveted to the leather at intervals. The plates were well dented and worn, and the leather had been repaired many times. This was not a good portent of things to come. The ground seemed to lurch, and looking up, I found myself in a chariot. Two horses were nervously jostling against the reigns of the charioteer next to me. I had a sinking feeling in my gut as I looked across a wide battlefield at two opposing armies ready to be joined in battle. These were not golden armies of legendary warriors. These men were grubby, wearing mismatched armor, with scarred and dented shields and weapons. Their faces were grim and frightened. And then there was the stench. Sweat, leather, filth, and neglect. My own leather gambeson stunk over unwashed padding and clothing. I could feel my body dripping sweat down my back beneath it.

In racks on the resin-stiffened leather sides of the chariot were my weapons. Bow, arrows, battle-serviced spears, and a set of bronze swords. On a hill behind the opposing forces was the wall of a fortress. I remember thinking the armor and battle standards looked more European than Asian. I was sure I didn't want to experience whatever was coming next. Intending to flee, I turned to step off the chariot, and found my way blocked by the shield-wall of the men behind me. A flag was raised over the fortress, and the two lines of men and chariots began to move forward. I knew what was coming next. As a charioteer, my line would gradually speed up to a gallop. The armored horses would crash into the opposing line at full speed, opening a gap for the foot soldiers to follow. My duty was to drive as deep into the enemy forces as possible, then kill as many as I could. If I was lucky, very lucky, and very savage, I might live long enough for the others to reach my position.

We were already moving and picking up speed. The field was muddy, and full of ruts that bounced the poorly suspended chariot and made standing difficult. The charioteer yelled for me to pick up a weapon and prepare to fight. This was altogether too real. I decided dream or not, I had a choice. I was not going to kill anyone, real or not. And, I wasn't going to let fear force me to act when the battle started. Holding on to the rail tightly with one hand, I began throwing the weapons off the chariot with the other. That done, I held on tight as we collided into a confused thunder of slapping wood, metal, and the screams of men and horses.

I woke staring at the weathered wood grain of a tabletop. My head was resting in my crossed arms. The day was bright and warm, and I marveled at the intricacy and beauty of the patterns in the wood. I found myself seated at a park picnic table, beneath a huge ancient oak tree. I was still on the battlefield, but it was much changed. Where a muddy field had been, was now a manicured park lawn with shade trees. The walls of the fortress on the hill were now stained with age, their sharp parapets worn with missing mortar and brick. It felt as if many centuries had passed. Whatever wars had been fought here happened long ago. I took a pathway to the fortress, passed open gates and empty courtyards, entered the main building. I found myself in a feasting hall, much like the great halls Vikings would gather in. At the head of a great rough-hewn table sat a huge man. He was eating with his fingers from a plate of food. He had long flowing hair and a thick unruly beard. He didn't bother to look up as I approached. "Who are you? Is there a reason I'm here?" I asked.

"Mara," he said, barely glancing up at me for an instant. He made a slight dismissive motion of his greasy hand to the wall in back of him. He clearly saw me as someone not worth spending any time talking to.

There was a great fireplace set into the wall, and on either side hung large triangular tapestries. Each had embroidered triangular sections filled with a flowing script. It reminded me of an artistic cross between Arabic and Sanskrit. I stared for a few moments, then, to my delight and surprise, I found I could actually read the words. I was reading an arcane language as easily as if I had been raised in it. It read like a hybrid of physics textbook and a religious myth. It was a technical set of instructions on the purpose and uses of the astral and mental bodies. It stated that each form is comprised of different energies that have separate, but related effects on the planes. It spoke of the energy fields that surround them, the auras. The text indicated the use of these forms results in either accelerated spiritual evolution, or becoming increasingly lost in personal illusion. The course depended on the choices made. As I read, I grew heavy, deeply fatigued. The dream was ending. Probably my brain was passing on to the next phase of the sleep cycle. As I strained to stay conscious, to read one last piece of information, I caught a piece of a phrase. "Tulpa."

Synchronistic Event

Back in my present time, my wife has just returned after being away at a convention for the weekend. At her convention, there was a vendor's area full of artists and crafts people. She has brought gifts. First, she presents me with a registered Native American artifact, a wolf-pipe. She said she hasn't seen one like it, and that she felt at the time that it was for my writing. She has not read the wolf story I wrote into this chapter a few hours ago. I thank her and just say I think it will be helpful. Next, she hands me a box, says to open it carefully, that it is very special. She explains that she would not have spent the money, but, again, she had never seen one like it before. It's a statue of the Norse God Thor: a huge man, with long flowing hair and a thick unruly beard. He is fighting the great world serpent, Jormungand, delivering the final blow with his mountain-crushing hammer. On his arms, this statue wears armored braces. Leather, with bronze plates riveted to them, disturbingly similar to the armor from the lucid dream I was just writing about.

I sit here, writing the end of this chapter, with three things on the desk to my right. There is the bowl with the remnants of the FSM, a beautiful wolf-pipe that seems to have appeared form the chapter's wolf story, and a warrior god that bears the trappings of the lucid dream I was retelling. It's an interesting gumbo of items. They seem to have appeared to flavor this chapter on mysticism and uncertainty. So, what does all of this really mean? Is this significant? It is as significant as you choose to make it.

You are the one that decides how you will react to SE, and ultimately, what it all means.

Ten

Tulpaware Party

CREATING YOUR REALITY

You are playing on the stage created by your thoughts. What objects are outside of yourself, and which are part of you, is largely a matter of choice. Your MN-bodies are part of you, as much a reality as your physical body. They exist here, now, as well as in an extended range of time, space, and probability. As you look out into the room, you are seeing a thin membrane, a surface impression of reality. You exist on the other side of that surface as much as you do on this one. The other side of that thin illusion has huge effects on how events happen on this side. In this chapter, you will learn that you can create objects in MN-Space that alter SEs here on this side. Much of what I am writing, although true, comes from the place of the trickster. Sometimes people need a good story, an

interesting myth, to allow them to see new possibilities. All stories sim-
plify reality and create their own limitations. Let's get rid of one part of
the story I have been telling you so far. Forget about the stage in your
brain's memory. Disregard knowing you create your own reality. Stop
taking any of this way-way-way off-Broadway show seriously. It's not a
stage production, it's a party. The point of the trickster is to show people where they take themselves too seriously. SEs aren't work, they are
not a post-industrial society trying to manufacture spirituality. There is
nothing you must become, nothing you have to evolve into. Don't worry
about being on stage and having to perform. We are all part of you, you
are amongst friends. SE exists for your entertainment. This is a party,
let your hair down. Put your fears and daily worries away. I'm going to
show you how to perform some party tricks. Use them to impress your
friends, or to amuse yourself. They are just party tricks. Anyone can do
them. Indeed, everyone already does them, they just aren't aware of what
they are already doing. I'm going to tell you how to create very specific
streaks of SEs by playing some simple games with your own thoughts.

Understanding Thoughtforms

Imagine for a moment that your thoughts are real things. Each time
you have a thought or emotion, objects are created from them in the
MN-fields around you body. These thoughtforms are actual objects on
their own dimensions. Some of them are as simple as a blob of color,
some as complex as the moving landscape of a lucid dream. They form,
change, and disperse around you as quickly as your stream of thought
flows. Auras are busy places. Most of your thoughts are brief. We tend to
think in associations; I wake up and reach for the iPod that I use as an
alarm, which reminds me I have to go to work, which gets me to thinking about getting gas on the way, which reminds me I should have done
the pots on the stove last night, that sends me wondering about what to
make for breakfast, which reminds me not to wake my wife with noise
from the kitchen because she will be home this morning and wants
to sleep, which reminds me my son should be dressed by the time she
wakes up. And on it goes for most of us throughout the day. All these

thoughts take form for brief periods in the MN-fields around you. These thoughtforms automatically cause changes in the direction you move in probability. What you think about becomes your navigational system through SE. Potentially, each thought can cause background SEs by changing your course through probability. Most never last long enough to have any significant effect. Think of most transient thoughts as tiny taps on your course. Many of our thoughts lead in opposite directions. We have many motivations and needs that our thoughts manifest. We are rarely just of one mind about anything.

Last time you went to visit family for the holidays, did you have mixed emotions and thoughts about it? These garden variety thoughts create a semi-chaotic, almost random gumbo of SEs around us that seem to have no matchable pattern. There are some tricks you can use to bring some of your thoughts out of this background, to make them more effective at creating SEs. Your mind is designed to follow your lead. If you decide a thought is more interesting or important, you pay more attention to it. Your attention imparts energy to the thoughts you choose. Neurologically, each thought is a pattern of electrical pulses passing across connected neurons. Think a thought once, the pathway soon disconnects. Neural pruning causes unused pathways to fade out over time, conserving resources for pathways used more often. Pay conscious attention to forming a thought; repeat that thought, and the pathway gets stronger. The activity draws connections from surrounding neurons. Put enough energy into any thought pattern, and it becomes a habit. Other thoughts begin organizing themselves around its pathways. This is the basis for learning. Engrain the pathway more, and it feels meaningful.

Thoughtforms operate on the same principles. If you choose to think any thought often enough, or put conscious attention into it, the thoughtform persists longer. Eventually, the thoughtform remains solid and coherent, even though you have turned your attention elsewhere. It remains in the MN-fields around you, automatically directing your course through probability. These persistent thoughtforms cause most of the SEs you experience. They organize events in probability around you and create the patterns of persistent SEs. Thoughtforms are created by all mental activity. The bulk of your thoughts are automated processes in the unconscious. These thoughts are the mental habits you have built through your thoughts and judgments about your life experiences. Most SEs are reflections of those processes, caused by the thoughtforms resulting from them. The more you understand about your own unconscious, the more familiar the patterns of SE become. Your party trick is you can create these thoughtforms consciously. You have the ability to choose to objectify chosen thoughts into persistent thoughtforms. So, what does "objective" mean? That seems to imply your thoughts become objects in the room around you. Yes. As improbable as it seems, mental objects made of MN-Space exist in the room around you right now. Think of them as ghosts, constructs, created by your thoughts. Thoughtforms.

Tulpa

In Vajrayana and Tibetan Buddhism, these thoughtforms are called *tulpa*. The term *thoughtform* was first used to describe tulpa by Evans-Wentz. The idea, pun intended, that thoughts create their own forms exists across many cultures, from Asian to native North American. The Yogacarna school even used tulpa as part of its training of adepts to teach the unitary nature of consciousness. The term seems to have first come to the west in the works of Alexandra David-Neel, who claimed that she had seen tulpa created on her travels in Tibet. A more low-brow use of the ability, she claims to have seen the creation of thoughtforms so coherent that they could be mistaken for real objects or people. She tells her own story of creating a tulpa, apparently out of boredom, loneliness, and curiosity. She created, through constant attention and expectation, a traveling companion. She created a thoughtform in the form of Friar Tuck. Seems to have been fun at first; he was a fat and jolly companion in a friars robe, mostly visible only to her. Unfortunately, travel in the Tibetan highlands was hard, and the good friar began to lose weight. Eventually he became not so jolly as well, more sullen, depressed, and anxious. She eventually became uncomfortable around him, felt vaguely threatened, and dispersed him.

Think of a tulpa as an android. It is a piece of natural technology. Thoughform, like a droid, can be programmed to respond as if they have individual consciousness, but they don't. They are thought machines.

MN-Space is literally emotional and mental energy. Build anything from it, and you have thoughtforms that have the computational, semi-intelligent, capacity to carry out sets of instructions. Just like your automated unconscious processes. David-Neel created her tulpa because she was lonely, and anxious. She was an intrepid young woman traveling closed areas of Tibet in the early 20th century. She was looking for companionship and positive emotional support. Friar Tuck represented what she thought she needed. He was jolly, good natured, sexually non-threatening. But this tulpa was created out of her real fears and frustrations. It was a surface presentation of what she needed, with a deep structure stemming from her fears. It eventually became how she actually felt and thought. Thoughtforms tend to evolve if you keep them around for a long time. Because they survive on the energy of the attention you give them, they become, over time, a reflection of all your internal states. They are associatively connected to the stream of thoughts they emerged from. Thoughtforms have no independent existence. Like a child's toy running on batteries, if you leave them running and don't pay attention to them, they eventually run down and stop. They simply fade away, like a neural pathway seldom used. But are they real, or just in the imagination?

THOUGHTFORMS AND OBJECTIVE REALITY

Thoughtforms are a way to focus attention. In lucid dreaming, your conscious awareness energizes the entire stage at once. The dream is one massive thoughtform. The SEs created are a scattered representation of all the thoughts and experiences of the dream. The statue of Thor on my right has characteristics of the armor I was wearing, the battle on the field, and the Viking at the table of the lucid dream. Interesting, but not particularly useful information by itself. Why were those particular facets of the dream turned into SEs? Those thoughtforms had the greatest emotional charge. Those were the things in the dream that caught my attention most. Knowing this allows me to recognize the emotions and experiences the unconscious is processing. SEs become a process of communication between different aspects of yourself. This form of "dream work" takes time and skill. It takes much less energy and time to just energize one object from the stage, rather than the entire dream. The lucid dream is a thoughtform. That's why it produces SEs. You have the ability to create single objects on that stage, instead of entire realities. It's easier, faster, much more specific, and you can do it in full waking consciousness. In fact, you already do it whenever you have a thought, automatically. But are they real? I'm mostly convinced they are. I've never seen one as a solid, physical object. I have tried to produce them, but either I don't have the "juice" to do it, or its not actually possible. I do believe some of my psychotic clients see their own thoughtforms. Still, it's an enticing fantasy; paying the mortgage in thoughtform money. I have some stories for you to consider.

I figured out the basics of constructing thoughtforms when I was in my mid-20s, about 30 years ago. Thoughtforms are pretty easy projects. You just picture what you want to build in your imagination, and hold that object in your attention for a while. If you assume it will stay coherent, thoughtforms seem to follow that intent and persist after you turn attention elsewhere. Thoughtforms also tend to behave as you expect them to after they are built. Pretty simple. My investigation of the various schools that teach thoughtforms found a pattern to the methods. All the breathing exercises, mantras, visualizations, and props are there to keep you reminded of what you are focusing on. There's no secret skill, no special exercise, no magic transmission of powers from teacher to student. Just think about what you're doing.

At first I built thoughtforms as an exercise in enhancing memory. I associated a thoughtform image with my car keys so it would remind me where I left them. I created them to remind me of something at a later date or time. I used them to wake me up in dream cycles. Later, I built my first thoughtform to test if they had any real independent existence. My wife and I were living in an apartment in the Bay Area. We worked opposite shifts, and the apartment often seemed lonely and empty without her. So, having read David-Neel's material on tulpa, I decided to make a thoughtform to keep me company. I thought about making an invisible cat, but decided the dog might sense it and have objections. I decided on a human figure. I didn't want to make anything that could be mistaken for having a personality of its own, I wanted more of a simple automated form that would randomly wander around and keep people company. For about an hour, I pictured a transparent human figure about five feet tall. It purposely had no sex, it was just a vague outline of a form, a shell. I stopped the meditation when it was time to leave for work. I returned home 10 hours later. My wife was home. She was pissed.

"Get rid of it!" She yelled.

"What…." I began, with my best innocent bystander look.

"Don't give me that innocent look, you made one of those things!"

"Oh, that." I tried to explain it was just a harmless thoughtform, a kind of pet to keep the place company. She wasn't calming down.

"Are you crazy? That thing woke me up. I got home and went to bed. I was asleep, and then it sat down on the bed next to me and woke me up! Get rid of it, right now!"

I tried to tell her it was harmless, but she would have none of it. I agreed to not put any more energy into it, and told her it would dissipate on its own in a few days. It did, and I had to come to some agreements with my wife. No more making thoughtforms in the apartment. It was her space too, and it was wrong of me subject her to my little experiments. A very good lesson. Don't create anything that will intrude on someone else's space without their permission. My wife now gives me permission to create whatever I want, but it has to stay in my den.

Keeping your thoughtforms to yourself

Even when you have permission, creating thoughtforms involving other people usually turns out to be a bad idea. Before I realized the thoughtforms were creating SEs in the environment, I was building them as objects of curiosity. I didn't understand they were natural bridges between the subjective and objective, and that they bore the complex mental patterns of the person who creates them.

Synchronistic Event

As part of my graduate studies I took courses in transpersonal psychology. One class was based on Native American shamanism, and centered on guided imagery journeys to the "underworld" and "skyworld." Part of the course was learning to conduct these rituals for others. The final exam was an overnight camping trip to the dunes at an area beach. We were to stay up that night and practice guiding these imaginary, trance-induced, journeys for each other. I wasn't really that interested by this point. I had been walking through alternate realities for years, and found drum-induced, light hypnotic, scripted shamanic journeys anti-climactic. I was, however, honored when another class member asked me to guide a journey for her. There are many standard shamanic journeys. She wanted to journey into the underworld to the World Tree, and meet her spirit animal. She went on her journey, and in her mind's eye, found an owl in the tree. My perception was that this was not some spirit animal or elemental; she was constructing a low-level thoughtform with the visualization. I couldn't resist. I asked her if she would like me to construct an artificial elemental, a thoughtform, a real spirit companion she could take away from the workshop with her. She thought that was a great idea.

I created the thoughtform, a grey owl, with her input about how it was to look and act. When I thought it was coherent, I pushed it out of my MN-field and into hers. Now, there's pretending, and then there is SE. As soon as she imagined she had the bird with her, we were suddenly shocked by being buzzed by a private aircraft flying low over the

beach. We all thought this was strange, and joked that it was her owl saying hello. Two days after returning from the camping trip, I had a strange lucid dream. I was in what appeared to be our apartment. The owl flew through an open window and perched on a chair. The thoughtform was in poor shape. It was missing pieces, disorganized; it looked like it had fought its way out of a bag of cats. I woke to the phone ringing. The woman I had made it for was on the phone, panicked. It seems that for the past two days her life had become a Twilight Zone of owl SEs. Everywhere she went, owls. She had been taking the shamanism course for fun, it wasn't supposed to be real. She was scared, understood the thoughtform I built was causing the effect, and, like my wife, wanted me to get rid of it immediately. I assured her that it had already returned, and wasn't going to bother her anymore. I didn't see much of her in class after that. Shame. It's just a party trick. People take these things much too seriously.

Making thoughtforms for other people never seems to work out. Each person needs to be at the center of their own creations. SEs generated by your energy are not perfectly matched to the energy and thought processes of others. You can create SEs for yourself by constructing your own thoughtforms, but don't bother creating SEs for others. If someone else in interested, and not going to take the whole thing too seriously, by all means do some party tricks for them. But teach them how to work the magic trick for themselves. Nowadays, I'm past the shamanic mythologies of creating spirit animals. I just build things that are fun. For example, I have haunted my den. Last time I saw *Jurassic Park* I decided to create a raptor. Mine is about three feet tall, wears a turned around baseball cap, has a lot of gold bling, and diamonds set in his teeth. He's a Veloci-rapper. It's programmed to hang out in the den and greet people. Of course, nobody sees him. Almost nobody. Last year my daughter's friend Rose went into my den to look for something, and came out rattled and upset. She's a little high strung anyway. She said there was a giant lizard in my room. It jumped up and greeted her like a puppy dog. She said it was some kind of dinosaur. Some things are only funny if you have a sense of humor.

Synchronistic Event

My daughter and her friend Rose are here for a visit. Rose has been reading one of the final versions of this book. She is here to tell me that she has been testing the model by making SEs about Australia appear around her. She says her mind is being blown because the universe appears to react to her thoughts. She is having a lot of SEs about Australia and Australians. She picked the subject because it was unlikely to appear much around her, until now. I remind her that the effect is produced by her own thoughtforms. If the SEs becomes annoying, I tell her to ignore them, letting the thoughtform fade away, and they will stop. She thanks me, and says she is going to use her blog to help promote the book. I thank her, and return to writing these lines. Sometimes I believe I have a touch of Attention Deficit Disorder. I had completely forgotten I had been writing about Rose and a thoughtform until I sat back down. I have the impression that some part of me was reminding the conscious part to tell you something important:

Attention reinforces thoughtforms, ignoring them dissipates them. A key point for controlling your SE.

BEWARE THE TRICKSTER

Let me tell you one more tulpa story. I did my post-doctoral internship at The Ann Martin Children's Center here in California. The center is based in a huge Victorian mansion in a residential neighborhood. Its living rooms and sitting parlors are now comfortable meeting areas. Its bedrooms have been divided and converted to therapy spaces where children and parents meet with interns being trained in the art of psychodynamic therapy. The staff would meet in the main living room for training and seminars several times a week. Usually there were about eight licensed PhD therapists, and about a dozen interns, most with doctorates in psychology. It was a wonderful place to learn. It had the feeling of a family, complete with parental conflicts, sibling rivalries, and much support. One morning, we were given an assignment as a group; bring in your favorite April fool's joke. Try to be creative. We will be psychoanalyzing your choice after you present. I'm a bit of a trickster, and I like a good challenge.

For my prank, I needed an accomplice. One of the interns was a young woman from India named Mira. She was one of those beautiful, bright, charming people everyone instantly trusted. She also had a playfully mischievous side as well. I asked her in private if she knew what a tulpa was, and she said she had some vague idea that it meant ghost. I showed her some material on the internet, and explained the basics of thoughtforms. Most of the staff had heard me talk about some aspect of it at some time, and she remembered a bit of it. I proposed that for my April fool's prank, I convince the staff that I have created an autonomous tulpa that would wander around the mansion. I was going to get them to believe I had haunted their house. I needed her to act upset in the group when she heard the news. She was to say she had heard of magicians doing this in her country, that it was very real, and very dangerous. She thought the idea was hilarious.

On the morning of the meeting, other interns told jokes, or brought in novelty store gags. After each gag, we speculated about the psychodynamics of their choices. When my turn came, I announced that my April fool's joke was not a joke at all. I explained that I had created a thoughtform that would gradually absorb the emotional energy released in the house's psychotherapy sessions, and convert that energy in SE and poltergeist activity. At the appropriate moment I used the word *tulpa*, Mira did an Oscar-level performance of being upset and scared. Soon more than a dozen PhDs were relating strange experiences they had had related to thoughtforms or ghosts. People talked about their own spiritual practices and similar myths they had heard. I answered many questions, and gave an explanation of my ghost similar to what I have given you in this chapter. Some people in the room were quite upset and frightened at the idea that the center was now haunted. They were even a little more concerned that anyone would know how to do such a thing. But, with Mira's star performance to lend credibility, and others pitching in their own anecdotal experiences, the majority of the room believed the story. Then I thanked Mira for her collaboration, and announced that this had been my April fool's joke. There were some laughs, and a few sighs of relief. I then said there was one small part of the prank left. I told them that everything I had told them about tulpa and thoughtforms was real, that I actually could have created one, and they would never be sure if I had done it or not. For the rest of that year, people wondered about the creaks and groans the house made at night.

Thoughtforms are a way of taking emotions and ideas you want to express as SEs, and turning them into internal objects. They place a representation of a part of yourself on your inner stage. Projected outward as SE, thoughtforms allow you to enter into a relationship with aspects of yourself that might not be reproducible in the world. They allow you to fully and consciously engage in processing your experiences in much the same way dreams do. SEs are a blend of the inner and outer worlds. Creating thoughtforms are one way to demonstrate to yourself that you are creating aspects of the reality you are living in. You are experiencing yourself. I invite you to create your own thoughtforms. Look for SE in the environment that bear its pattern. You will slowly see an increasing pattern of SE that follow the symbolic and emotional pattern you used to create it. If you continue to focus on the thoughtform and SE, it will become increasingly meaningful and important. They can seem to affect world-wide events, even events of literally astronomical importance.

This is sometimes mistaken by the creator of the thoughtforms for an indication they have some special power or destiny. The reason for the intensity of the experience is actually much more mundane. The more you focus on any thought, the more neural connections form around the pattern. The greater the neural pattern, the more the brain interprets it as meaningful. You can take any phrase or set of random sounds, and make a mantra. Even if its just nonsense syllables, say them often enough and it will eventually feel meaningful. Repetition becomes meaning. The brain has evolved to wire for faster recognition of whatever you pay the most attention to. This simple mechanism has been exploited to manipulate and enslave populations since before written history. Children are taught to repeat their rote prayers, memorize by repetition their holy books, pledge daily their allegiances. These become meaningful through repetition. This is how faith, and belief, are created. Such practices create stable coherent thoughtforms in the MN-fields, the emotional and thought fields around people. They engrain neural patterns into thought habits. That's what commercials are all about. The world then reflects the belief. What you have been taught to believe has been shaping the SEs around you all your life. What kind of world do you want to live in? Would you rather live in a world where you have to be scared of ghost stories, or where you have the ability to play with your reality, unafraid?

You have the power to determine much of the path your life will present to you.

You can choose what thoughts you wish to repeat and make meaningful.

You can even watch your thoughts to learn which ones you think often, determine who told you to think them, then choose to think for yourself. Make your own thoughtforms. Your life is your greatest art. Sculpt it with your thoughts, and then act on the opportunities SEs present. Be playful.

Eleven

Mystery
Tour

"Unless we prefer to be made fools of by our illusions, we shall, by carefully analyzing every fascination, extract from it a portion of our own personality, like a quintessence, and slowly come to recognize that we meet ourselves time and time again in a thousand disguises on the path of life. This, however, is a truth which only profits the man who is temperamentally convinced of the individual and irreducible reality of his fellow men."
—C.G. Jung

SE AND DELUSIONAL THINKING

Jung was right, it's a mirror. Everyone else is also looking at a mirror image of themselves. The people around you are as much at the center of the universe as you are. Everyone creates SEs. Jung was wrong; it doesn't matter if you care about others or not. Not as far as SEs are concerned. You can act as if you are the only real person in the world, the only person that matters. You will wind up alone. People don't like to be treated as objects. Having compassion and empathy for other will help you understand your own stories. It will also cause SEs that reflect a universal concern for your well-being. Come to think of it, Jung was right about that too.

Delusions can be positive or negative. A positive delusion is a thought you have which is held to despite significant evidence to the contrary. Positive delusions add something unnecessary to a person's interpretation of reality. A negative delusion keeps you from seeing something that is already apparent. You have a tremendous advantage over most people around you. If you understand SEs are a mirror, your view of others is about to change. You are going to realize that most of what the people around you believe is, well, delusional. You have been reading my explanations for how SEs emerge from emotional and mental energy. If you have a lick of sense, it all sounds nuts. It is. It's all completely delusional, and it all works quite well when applied. I believe most religion is craziness, most political views are out of touch with the complexity of actual situations, and most philosophy is just bizarre. Except, of course, the ones I see in my own mirror. In my better moments, I try to act on information I can verify, and treat others with kindness and respect no matter what they believe. It doesn't matter if what we believe is ultimately true. The pattern-matching programs in your brain just need to get you comfortably through your life, passing your genes on to the next generation if you are lucky and make that choice. People don't need to construct the starship. Your ancestors got along quite well with their bag of rocks. After all, you're here. So, I'm not advocating you run out and try to convince anyone they are running around in a cloud of SE. Please don't try to convince people their view of the world as separate objects in a ridged time structure is nuts. Most of all, don't disillusion people who need their delusions to function. It will just piss them off. I try to be therapeutic with people. Part of that is not intruding on someone's defenses and sense of reality unless they are asking me to. Even then, only very gently and with empathy and respect.

Your experience with SE is going to be different from mine. Consider me one of your primitive ancestors. Some of my ancestors spent three months on a miserable sailing ship to get to North America. Some of them walked 3,000 miles with a covered wagon next to them dragged by oxen to get to the west coast. Today you can hop a plane and cross the country in a few hours. While you're traveling at speeds inconceivable to our ancestors, have a drink of your choice, be entertained. Stay asleep if you like. I learned SE as a mirror the hard way. It was confusing, a long trip carrying lots of baggage. It took me a while of following the trail left behind by others. You can just take the plane and skip the Oregon Trail part. In this chapter, I'll be telling you about the trail, reading you parts of the map. People step on the SE trail from different personal spaces. Some of them get lost along the way. Some wander into dead ends. You're going to pass many people on this trail. Some are further along than others are. Some are lost. Study the map. Help them if you can, and if they are willing to listen. We are going on a road trip. More of a bus ride, actually. Going across country on a Greyhound bus isn't as comfortable or fast as flying. You have to stop at many small town destinations before you arrive where you're going. You also get to see those towns, and some roadside attractions along the way. I'm going to describe a developmental path. Think of it as the road our SE mystery tour is going to take. Let's get started. Here's a list of the towns of the SE bus route:

- ¤ Clueless
- ¤ Objective
- ¤ Subjective
- ¤ Projective
- ¤ Understanding

CLUELESS

You just got off the boat and are standing in the quaint little town of Clueless. It's a small town where nothing much is happening. At this stage of the journey people have no idea SEs exist. They have never seen an SE, don't believe in coincidence. In this town, all is exactly as it appears to be. Everything is linear, dependable, and explainable. It's also very dull; not a good place to keep your brain active. Time to get on the bus. Say hello to the other travelers, stow your luggage. By that, I mean put your skepticism in the overhead rack. Keep your sense of humor handy; it's a big comfort on a long trip.

OBJECTIVE

We arrive at the next stop on our journey, the little village of Objective. Objective SEs happen when a person who has been clueless starts noticing SEs. Clueless has nothing to do with its neighboring town, Intelligence. The passenger next to you may remain clueless about SEs because her frame of reference doesn't allow her to think in those terms. Objective SEs have no obvious personal connection to the person who observes them. They appear as just coincidences with no relationship to the person who experiences them. A person in Objective will often see an SE and ignore it. For example:

Imagine you are driving down the highway in the middle of the day. On the side of the road, you notice a billboard. It's an ad for White Owl whiskey. The ad features a large poster of a white owl. You look up and see a real white owl perched above the billboard directly over the picture in the ad. The real owl is sitting in the same position as the poster owl. You also realize that owls are nocturnal creatures that rarely show themselves during the day. Odd, but obviously just a coincidence. You believe anyone else could have driven by and seen the same thing and thought it unusual. You arrive at the pet store to buy some dog food. The store is offering a large white owl for sale. It watches you as you walk by. You get the feeling its trying to tell you something. Obviously, it watches everyone; just another coincidence. Getting back to the car, you step on something that sticks to your shoe. It's a wrapper from a White Owl cigar. Annoying litterbugs. What are the odds? Oh, well, dog needs feeding, better get going.

An extreme example of objective SE involves people who have watched for signs that the end of the world is near, in fulfillment of prophesy. The "signs" are SE, personal projections mistaken for causal messages. Many a person has looked for, and found, evidence that the end is near and waited past the appointed moment, only to find to their amazement and confusion life goes on as usual. They don't recognize that they have been chasing their own SEs. Such a delusional system requires a complex series of SEs to manifest the projected belief. The person believes that anyone who sees the external events would understand. Anyone who understood the revelations, from wherever or whoever the revelations were from, would come to the same, objective, conclusions. People in Objective often believe what they think.

By the way, be cautious of who you shake hands with here in Objective. There are some nasty viruses going around. SE viruses. Your supercomputing brain has vulnerability; it can be infected by other people's poorly written programming. Computer viruses are programs that infect your computer and take over areas of its functioning. Often harmless, sometimes malicious, they are instructions that make your mind produce the thoughtforms someone else needs. When I see a news report of some young man who has strapped on a bomb and blown up himself and others for his beliefs, I think viral infection. Someone taught him to see the world in terms of us/them SEs. Someone literally programmed him. People hand out many free books here in Objective, give away a lot of literature, and are always looking for receptive people. Don't take candy from strangers here.

Most people who live in Objective ignore SEs. So, it happens; big deal. Lots of strange stuff happens. It's somebody else's problem. People in Objective don't want to have to re-think the way reality works. SEs might threaten the stability of their view of the universe as a stable and ordered place. It would be like having to admit real magic exists in the world. Worse yet, you might find out magic is a technology and have to learn how to use it. This would cause anxiety. We wouldn't want to have people having to think unnecessarily. After all, thinking you have all the answers is so much more comfortable than having to look for them. Our bus lets some passengers off at this stop. Objective is home to lots of folks. Objective also has a local tourist attraction, which just so happens to be next to the bus stop. Let's walk over and check it out.

In what looks to be a dusty and shabbily refurbished abandoned gas station, is Joe Rassik's reptile emporium. A creaking spring slams the screen door behind us as we enter a room full of terrariums and poster-boarded newspaper articles, long since turned yellow from sun and time. The glass terrariums house various local snakes and lizards, but the star of the show is in what used to be the grease pit in the adjoining garage. Pay your $1.50 and follow the sign to see "The living dinosaur." This is where Joe keeps Bruce, his pet alligator. Bruce doesn't move much. As a reptile, he doesn't think much either. Calling him a pet is even a bit of a stretch. He doesn't have any real emotions, not in the human sense. His brain is similar to just the primitive inner core of your brain. The reptile brain can control basic body functions and drives, but there is no limbic system. The on-board computer has no ability to think about itself, or its relationship to anyone else. Everything is genetically pre-determined instinct. Bruce has very poor pattern-matching ability. He's not really looking for anything. In fact, unless something moves, he doesn't notice it. When something moves, it emerges from the background of his vision and becomes a separate object. He can locate objects in space, but has no personal relationship with them and no emotions about them. He makes no plans, and ignores anything that doesn't meet his immediate needs. Objective SE is similar to the way reptiles see the world. SEs emerge from the background of events for a moment, but there is no personal relationship or connection with them. Bruce hasn't so much as blinked while we watched him. Time for us to ride to the next town.

SUBJECTIVE

The town of Subjective has a small, often unnoticed sign on the road into town. It reads "Welcome to the *Twilight Zone*." They have a small TV station that shows a lot of re-runs. Just a coincidence. Subjective SEs are the ones aimed directly at you. No longer a general coincidence, you, specifically, are the center of the SEs. If you don't know you're looking in a mirror, the outskirts of Objective can be very disorienting. This town does require re-thinking reality. The following three events are typical objective SE:

Synchronistic Event

I had just finished an errand and was returning to my car. Synchronistic events were not on my mind, I just wanted to get home. I got into the car, put on the seat belt, and started the engine. In one swift motion, I reached to the dash and turned on the radio, then dropped my hand onto the manual shift and pulled it into reverse. As I pulled back on the shift, the first two words came from the car speakers were, "... shifting gears." These were the last two words of a sentence spoken by a politician being interviewed on the radio. He was discussing a change in his campaign strategy. I saw no personal meaning in the event, other than the feeling the event somehow occurred to get my attention.

The next event seemed to be a companion to the last, and occurred a few days later.

Synchronistic Event

As I drove away from work I turned on the radio to a local station. As I sat at the light waiting to turn onto the freeway the song "Radar Love" started to play. The light turned green and I put the car in first gear, as the singer said "...I'm shifting gears..." It was almost as if part of me was an observer somewhere commenting on my actions through the event.

This event follows the same pattern.

Synchronistic Event

My wife and I had just purchased a new set of steak knives. After years of cheap flatware, we decided on a fine set of Gerber knives resembling surgical instruments as much as eating utensils. One afternoon I was washing the dishes and listening to the news on the radio. As one report was ending, I was washing off one of our new knives. Admiring its shape, I turned it over and was looking at the Gerber name stamped into the steel handle. At that moment, the news report ended with the correspondent identifying herself, "...Nancy Gerber reporting...."

Our bus has just pulled into its stop in Subjective; time to get out for a bite to eat. They have a great little restaurant here, the Limbic Café. The staff here specialize in having a relationship with their customers. They take their cues from you about what kind of relationship that's going to be. Subjective SEs are all about the relationship and the emotional tonality the SEs elicit from you. Have a menu. The first thing you'll notice is the right half of the menu is black and printed in scary red ink. The left half is white and printed in peaceful gold lettering. The limbic system mid-brain is divided into two hemispheres that have different specializations. The right hemisphere looks for matches to overall global patterns. It spends a lot of time saying "no, that's not quite the same." The right limbic is looking for the lion hidden in the grass. The right side of the menu is where the "it's not good" emotions are processed. The left side of our brain specializes in fine detail pattern-matches. Its areas of the limbic system spends its time saying "yes, that matches, yes that works." It generates most of our positive emotions and sense of well-being. The two sides of your brain are constantly communicating with and regulating each other. Brain surgery is usually done while the paitent is awake. The brain itself feels no pain, so the patient needs only a local anesthetic. The medical team enlists the help of the conscious patient. The medical team asks the patient what they feel and how they are functioning during the procedures. In some rare procedures, it becomes necessary to shut down one hemisphere of the brain. Shut down the left hemisphere, leaving the right in charge, and people burst out crying in distress. Shut down the right, leaving the left in charge—bliss.

There's a piece of paper attached to the menu, it's the heaven or hell lunch special. Interpret SEs exclusively from one side of the menu or the other, and you get free admission to that custom designed, completely mirrored restroom, paranoia. Paranoid SEs come in two basic flavors, all good, and all bad. Left-hemisphere-dominant SEs can seem as if divinity itself is out to bring you into the light. Right-side-dominant-SE clients have told me demons are trying to steal their souls. When the brain is functioning normally, in most people, there is a preference for left hemispheric dominance. Day-to-day SEs tend to be on the positive side. Enjoying your life is neurologically normal.

Emotions are about relationships. Emotions are a way of thinking about what has met our needs in the past, and how events might affect us in the future. Your brain has the ability to represent people and events as internal objects, simulations of the real things, so it can arrange them to see how you "feel" about how things are going for you. We think in a kind of simplified internal cartoon version of reality. Often we artificially separate experiences into simpler categories. Who we are and what we experience at work is different than who we are at home. Pattern-matching means separating information into a pattern that is distinct from its surroundings. We think situationally. What we learn in school, we may not be able to apply in a real-world setting. The frames of reference we use change with our setting. If you know SEs are a mirror of your own thoughts, you know SEs are wherever you are. Most of the people riding the bus with you are looking for the source of SEs outside themselves. What they think becomes the SEs they see. Some of the other passengers have real small windows on this bus. The view of their frame of reference is very small.

Let's look at the menu again. There are some SE appetizers at the top. How about a side dish of lucky object? I hear the rabbit's foot and lucky charms are good. The holy relic is expensive, indulgent really, but sells well. Objects don't change SEs, but frames of reference do. Go to most large supermarkets, and you will find a section with candles. Many of them are in glass containers that help them burn for several days. These devotional seven-day candles often have religious icons, saints, or even good luck charms printed on them. I have even seen candles to burn to help resolve pending criminal charges. The objects remind us of what we want. Our thoughts create the SEs. Further down the menu, you will see blessed objects. Nice glass of holy water anyone? SEs do happen more often around objects that another person, one perceived as having special power or spiritual authority, have blessed. This is the bread and butter of priesthoods and shamans. Someone has a more direct line of power to the spirit world than you do. For a few bucks, they will share the mojo. As much as I'd like to make money waving my hand over inanimate objects, it's nonsense. Increased SEs around these objects happen because people expect it to, and, having the idea that a person is responsible for the magic, makes it easier for the brain to form a more complex personal relationship with it. People have killed each other for sacred relics, not realizing they themselves are the connection. Variations on these side dishes include sacred locations, holy lands, and most bloody and ridiculous of all, steaming piles of dogma. All of these are seasoned with dashes of fear.

Most of the main courses on the subjective SEs menu involve who is creating the SE you experience, and why are they doing it. Some of the most common choices for causal agents are various forms of divinity, Gods and saviors, demons and tempters, ancestral spirits, nature spirits of various types, persons endowed with magical powers, extra terrestrials, ghosts, and secret government agencies. The list is as endless as the person's imagination. All of it is interactive, and because we think by talking to ourselves, talking to SEs becomes fast food. Once you fall into the trap of assuming SE are from outside yourself; next stop: the *Twilight Zone*. A kind of inter-personal illusion of telepathy is set up. You can have a thought or ask a question, and the response comes in the form of SE. Have a thought, which causes a thoughtform, which causes patterns of SEs, complete with a personified frame of reference of your choice. The following is an example of an event that could be mistaken for a response from another being.

Synchronistic Event

It was a time of great change and turmoil in my life. I was only a few months out of my parent's home, working two jobs, and going to school full-time. There was also a social life, concerns over spiritual growth, and exploration of synchronistic phenomena to be balanced. One evening I was at home feeling swamped and sorry for myself. There was just too much to do and not enough time to get it all done.

The radio played a local rock station. I was aware of synchronistic events in general at the time, but not of any subjective connection to them. Exasperated at my situation and having a playful bent toward the dramatic, I raised my hands as if addressing heaven and called "Father, I'm tired of this. How about a break?" I must have said this exactly between songs, because the next words to boom out over the speakers were the first in a song by the group Kansas; "Carry on my wayward son, there will be peace when you are done. Lay your weary head to rest, don't you cry no more..." This seemingly intelligent response shocked me and left me in a state of wonder. The problems I was complaining about suddenly seemed unimportant.

Here's another example of when the conscious asks a question and the subconscious answers by way of a synchronistic event. The following event was so smooth in transition from question to SE, it was disorienting.

Synchronistic Event

While waiting for someone at the office, I was thinking about the space program. There had been a news story the previous night about yet another delay in a shuttle launch due to a solid rocket booster failure. As I wondered when the shuttle would fly again, a fellow worker walked up to me and said "The shuttle's going to be delayed, there's an accident somewhere."

"Huh?" I said, confused for a moment by the answer to my unasked question.

"The shuttle bus that goes to the lab and back is stuck on the road somewhere, they're being delayed by an accident on the freeway," he said.

The trip into the SE *Twilight Zone* can happen really fast. A personal mythological format may develop almost instantly, as in the case of people who immediately decide to format SE in the pattern of their own beliefs. The belief system can be quite complex, but is adopted quickly because it was developed to a high degree before its use as an SE format. If your beliefs and social support systems allow for god to work miracles in your life, wonderful. No need to think any further about it. Except for one tiny, little, nagging problem; you're talking to yourself and don't know it.

So how do I know when a client tells me that his SE are communication from god or other supernatural sources, that he is really talking to himself? I don't, really. Part of me wants to believe that divinity holds people's hands through life and guides them with signs and portents. I certainly have no counter for the proposition that we are seamlessly part of the transpersonal. But, personally, I tend to want to place my bets on the most likely outcome. I look for proof. I have done sessions with many psychotic clients, and some merely confused ones, who believed they were communicating with supernatural beings. I always give them the respect of the benefit of the doubt. I worked with a client who experienced SEs in the context of the songs he heard on the radio. Nowhere else, just on the radio, any radio, any station. His SE mythology was that his dead sister was speaking to him, asking him to find her killer, pleading for justice. Sounds like a Hollywood movie plot. Except his sister lives in Los Angeles and talks to him on the phone regularly. I have been privileged to peek in on the SEs of a few hundred people. Some SEs main courses are more popular than others are, but people are definitely choosing off the menu themselves. I hear the bus driver honking. Time to move on to the next town. Many people are comfortable here in Subjective. Not many people left on the bus now, but we are moving on to our next destination. As we pass out of town, take note of the small sign on the border: "Thank you for visiting Subjective. You are now leaving the *Twilight Zone.*"

PROJECTIVE

Projective is a city. It is complex, organically integrated, well-structured, and thought-driven. This is the miracle of your cortex, the latest and greatest addition to that amazing brain of yours. In Projective you bring all that computing power, particularly the frontal lobes, on-line. This is the place where you start directing SEs consciously. The task during the projective stage of SE is to separate yourself from the illusions of unconscious formats. This is the mental plane folks, N-Space, and the big time of spiritual magic. This is where people discover they have been creating their own reality for a long time. This is where you claim ownership of your ability to create SEs. The following SE helped me understand I was projecting my own patterns of SEs:

Synchronistic Event

That summer I had been living in a small valley with cliffs on either side. The floor of the valley was mostly wooded, except for an open field in front of the owner's home. He was a friend, and I was renting a cottage on another part of the property. We both had used archery as a pastime on occasion, and one afternoon were practicing outside the house in the field. We decided to see if either of us could reach the cliff face, about 100 yards away. We both fired an arrow, both of which disappeared into the woods toward the cliff. There was no way to tell if they had reached the target or not. The event stuck out in my mind because my bowstring snapped during the shot and wrapped itself neatly around and into the bow's arrow holder, as if tucked in deliberately for carrying.

A few months later, I had just finished a several hour meditation and decided to go for a walk in the woods. I had been doing a yoga meditation that included a posture based on the image of an archer with bent bow at the base of a tree, shooting up the tree toward the sky. The image represents the rising of kundalini, up the spinal column, tree, towards the transpersonal sky. The goal of the meditation was to produce unity with the higher self. I was disappointed with the results; felt they had fallen short of my desires. Pondering this on my walk through the woods, I stopped. I looked down. There at my feet was the arrow I'd fired months before. It had fallen short of its goal. There was a moment of realization where the external and internal seemed to reflect each other. The archer was a symbol for the self I sought. I was already the archer. My understanding, the arrow, had fallen short.

The following is a more direct demonstration of the way SEs can mirror thoughts:

Synchronistic Event

The housework had been neglected for the week, so arriving home after work, I spent several hours doing chores. After cleaning the kitchen, living area, picking up laundry, and vacuuming, I sat down to relax in front of the TV. A detective show was on and about half over. Looking around the living room, I started to say to myself "I did a really good job of cleaning up around here." As the thought started with the word "I...," the main character on the show said "Somebody did a really good job of cleaning up around here." The segment, "did a really good job of cleaning up around here" occurred at the exact moment the thought did. The match was so exact it seemed as if one thought was being expressed through two mediums at the same time.

How you get to Projective matters. I wandered around in subjective SEs for years. It was a crazy-making experience. Every myth I made up for how SEs worked manifested before my eyes, in spectacular detail and scope. I was as delusional as any of the clients I now work with. Except for one important detail; I refuse to believe in things that just don't make any sense. I want proof—real, physical, cause and effect proof. After experiencing my own mythologies for a while, I came to realize I was seeing my own internal processes. When you have doubts about what is causing SEs, they respond by giving messages that no longer make any rational sense, that fit no pattern. The stories we tell ourselves begin to unravel. There are many characters in the city of Projective. One is the street mime. One of the most annoying things you can do to another person is mime their actions, postures, and words as they say them.

Children do this to each other, and the one being imitated usually ends up screaming, "stop it!" In Projective, the mime greets you at the bus stop. You can clearly see the SEs reflect your thoughts and emotions. You may be carrying the baggage. You may be thinking the SEs are caused by some external influence. But, you know for sure you're being imitated.

In this city, there are some crazy people walking around the streets. They are yelling and arguing with people we just don't see. Listen closely. They are arguing with their own unseen mime.

"Why are you doing this to me?"

"Stop reading my thoughts!"

"Why, God, why me?"

"Stop doing that!"

Mimes are annoying, especially when you have no sense of humor. That's why you need to take humor with you on the SE bus. The big city can be dangerous. Here in Projective you can get hurt if you don't pay attention to where you're going. Many of the delusional clients experiencing SEs get caught in a pattern of fear and paranoia. Imagine believing SEs flow from a force that can read your mind and shape events around you. What happens when you get annoyed at the mime? The mime reflects your anger back to you. You experience angry and fearful SEs. I don't take what I think all that seriously. That is a blessing and a saving grace where SEs are concerned. My own SE myths never turned very dark, they were more like being disappointed with promises the SEs could never keep. Some people believe SEs are whichever god they believe is communicating with them. When they get pissed off with SEs, they think they are offending God. Guilt, apprehension, and fear follow close behind. SEs that appear threatening and demanding follow as surely as the mime will be imitating your annoyance.

There is no boogieman. Scare yourself silly if you like, ain't nobody else in the house but you.

It's a letdown if you believe you were talking to god, and realize you were talking to yourself. Some passengers just ride the bus back to Subjective at this realization. People can tend to mistake their thoughts for themselves. If their belief turns out to be wrong, it's as if someone is killing them. Challenge a dearly held belief, and people feel as though you are stealing from them. There are people in the world who kill each other over cartoons that make fun of their beliefs. They feel attacked, so they attack back. Best to just let these folks ride the bus back.

SE can mirror your fears and insecurities as well as your more positive aspects. It's just a mirror. Nothing ever jumps out from the glass to bite you. The mime is just a performer there to amuse. If SEs ever seem scary, break out your sense of humor and laugh at yourself. Here's an example:

Synchronistic Event

I had been working as a social worker for my county and had formed a friendship with S, a co-worker with the same position. One of our jobs was to go to homes and interview relatives seeking to have children placed in their home under foster care. People have different things that give them the creeps. For S it was clowns. It was late October, close to Halloween. S had been making small comments whenever she saw someone with clown paraphernalia for the past few days. That day she asked me to go with her to evaluate a home in a neighborhood she did not feel comfortable going to alone. Along the way, we saw someone walking in a clown costume. This set off a conversation about how much S really, really, did not like clowns. She didn't like them at birthday parties, in circuses, and especially not at Halloween. She considered them a way to frighten children, and felt traumatized by them. She didn't think my description of the bad sci-fi spoof *Killer Clowns From Outer Space* was very funny.

We arrived at the housing complex, and were soon at the door of the apartment where S was to interview a grandmother seeking placement of her grandchild with her. We rang the bell, and a few moments later, a middle-aged woman in a robe and slippers answered the door. She apologized for not having her make-up on yet. She invited us into the hallway of the apartment, and excused herself to go upstairs and get dressed. We were told to make ourselves at home. On the way up the stairs, she called over her shoulder "You understand this is a clown house, right?"

S was staring down the hall with a deer-in-the-headlights kind of look. Slowly, I began to register the obvious. There were clown paintings and portraits on the walls of the hallway, and in the adjacent kitchen, and covering the walls of the living room. There were statues of clowns floating from bunches of balloons on tabletops, clown posters, furniture in basic bright clown colors. The refrigerator was completely covered with clown magnets. The wall clocks were made of clown faces. The wallpaper and carpet had circus and clown patterns on them, there were clown mobiles hanging from the ceilings. We made our way to the table in the dining room, also covered wall-to-wall in clown decorations of various kinds, and sat down. One wall of the room had been made into a giant rack containing dozens of pairs of over-sized circus clown shoes. Trays of bright make-up and a bowl of large red clown noses covered the table where we sat. The grandmother soon returned, in full clown make-up and in costume. She said she hated people seeing her without her make-up on. While S was staring I slipped on one of the red clown noses, and she jumped about a foot when she turned around. She snatched the nose off my face and declared, "Don't do that!"

The woman explained that after she retired from nursing she took up entertaining children as her clown persona, and there was actually a substantial clown sub-culture. She even showed us her driver's license. Her official picture is taken in full clown make-up. She said the apartment doubled as a school where she taught the art of clowning to adults and children. She wanted to show us the clown train, but it was in storage.

I had the chance to see one of S's fears manifested in SEs. It wasn't funny…well, actually, yeah, it was. As far as I can tell this set of SE was all hers. I have no emotional investment in clowns one way or the other, although I was highly entertained by the experience. Time for us to get back on the bus and head out to the last stop.

UNDERSTANDING

It's just damn fun to create synchronistic events by choice. You can set a theme or story, and then selectively forget you did it. You can play with SEs the way a child does when they suspend disbelief to become absorbed in the drama they enact. Once you understand SEs are projections of your thoughts, you can select what you look for and expect. Look for the story you want to live. Choose wisely. Be careful what you consume here. The brain takes sensory data and experiences and processes them into memory. Some memories take literally years before the data crunching is complete. All the while, you're generating low-intensity thoughtforms that are affecting the SEs around you. What you choose to fill your mind with becomes the pattern of the SEs you create. A lot of popular culture and entertainment is junk food for the mind. I don't feed my mind violence, intolerance, anger, or fear if I can help it. Our culture does a good enough job of selling these without any help. There are health foods for the mind. Kindness is probably the best of them all. Do unto others as you would have them do unto you, because they, are you.

Eventually you will understand how truly one you are. The SEs of personal myths and fantasies tend to fade with understanding. For me, SEs are a constant background reflection. I live in the kind of SEs I have been describing every day. They tell me about what I'm feeling and thinking beneath the surface. I indulge myself in a story from time to time; create themes in SEs just to make sure it works. Mostly SEs remind me of what I believe, and what I want to believe. Your understanding will be different from mine. It will be yours. All the homes in Understanding are custom built by the people who live here. Thanks for taking the tour. Please do keep the map as a memento.

Twelve

Altered States of Consciousness

"This is an absolute necessity for anybody today. You must have a room, or a certain hour or so in a day, where you don't know what was in the newspapers that morning, you don't know who your friends are, you don't know what you owe anybody....This is a place where you can simply experience and bring forth what you are and what you might be. This is the place of creative incubation. At first you may find that nothing happens there. But if you have a sacred place and use it, something will eventually happen."—Joseph Campbell

People experience SEs within particular contexts. Four of these contexts are prayer, drug use and abuse, meditation, and mental illness. Each of these sets up a different set of conditions for SEs. Each of them tends to lend its own aspects and limitations to it. These categories are extremely general and there may be a lot of overlap for some people. I'm going to look briefly at each and try to point out one or two characteristics of the SEs they can produce. Your ability to produce SEs is part of your hard-wired nature. But developing a sense of what you're already doing can take some practice. There are pre-made frames of reference you can use that make the learning curve gentler. Consider this chapter about using training wheels on your SE bicycle. They help you keep your balance while you learn to travel in SEs. They also limit your mobility. Eventually you should out grow the need for them.

PRAYER

Let's begin with prayer. We will be dealing with only those aspects of prayer that can be useful in the development of SEs. What one prays to, and why, is a matter of personal preference. Those choices are more the story you are creating with SEs than the reason it works. Some aspects of prayer both help and limit your ability to create SEs.

Prayer is the most widespread spiritual practice. More people pray than meditate. The names of what they pray to vary, but the general pattern of trying to communicate with a greater, more powerful force, is universal. Supernatural beings are, well, supernatural. We assume they are outside of our limitations and can do things for us we can't do for ourselves. Prayer implies the unusual may occur as a response. SEs respond readily to prayer. Generally, prayer is practiced within the context of some spiritual belief system. People pray in patterns taught by their belief systems. These systems are very diverse and have developed to meet many needs, economic, cultural, political, and spiritual. Some were founded to commemorate a great teacher and his philosophy, some as outgrowths of cultural development, some as means of social and economic control over populations. Their definitions of divinity vary from incarnate beings to gods who remain forever outside manifestation. The relationships between follower and divinity range from total submission and subservience, to each as an inseparable part of their god, each worthy of the same respect. Regardless of what conditions the belief system sets, the response the individual receives to personal prayer is basic for its continued existence. If people did not receive some kind of actual reinforcement of their beliefs, the system would die out. People generally don't put up with praying to ineffective or uncommunicative gods for very long. Because there are so many systems flourishing, systems that, although diverse from each other have many sincere, intelligent, and faithful believers, it seems either all are partial expressions of a greater whole that encompasses all, or each individual is experiencing some kind of perception based on the projection of their own beliefs. Both are probably true.

Prayer is almost an ideal way to set up an SE format. Two aspects of most systems of prayer contribute to this. The first having to do with effects on the person's focus of attention, the second with the mythologies that surround prayer. Prayer should be a regular activity, done each day at specific times, and should follow certain general patterns set up by the belief system. These can include prayers already constructed and used as standards, different numbers of repetitions, or different prayers arranged as a ritual. The best prayers are conversations, a heart-to-heart. Regular focus is good for creating SEs. It sets regular patterns in your thoughts and emotions. This causes the same patterns of neurons to fire and wire together in your brain. The more you think a thought, the easier it is to think it again. This sets the patterns and energy of your emotional and mental bodies into better defined thoughtforms. That in turn causes SEs in the pattern of prayers you repeat. It causes a regular transmission of energy, confined to specific frequency ranges, producing more noticeable SEs because of the steady focus for a longer period. Prayer is powerfully effective at creating SEs. It's also a trap. All pattern recognition carries a sense of meaning with it. When our hunter ancestor recognized the pattern of a lion hiding in the grass nearby, believe me, it was meaningful! Individual blades of grass on the savanna, not so much. The core of your emotional limbic system is the amygdale. These structures determine how meaningful an experience is by attaching valiance, emotional importance, to the data. This gives priority to wiring neurons to transmit that data quickly. Wide deeply connected pathways can be created very quickly with fear-threat responses. Many religions and political strategies thrive on getting the fear response active. People react and hardwire before the slower cortex based rational thought process comes on line. The targets feel the message is highly meaningful because the brain has been tricked into giving it valence.

The other way to create a feeling of deep meaning is repetition. When we recognize a pattern repeatedly, that set of neural pathways wires together for faster recognition next time. We experience the pattern as having deeper meaning. Even completely meaningless phrases, repeated often enough, become highly meaningful. Prayer strengthens faith. It allows you to believe in greater depth what you think. It increases SEs because it allows you to focus more of your thought, your sense of meaning, on chosen patterns. Those patterns have the potential of becoming as habit forming as any drug. Please understand, I'm not taking another pot shot at religion. I'm warning you about becoming addicted to SEs you create that limit your choices.

Belief systems create frames of reference, which will determine the relationship of the person to the deity, and the way responses are expected to occur. Most prayer implies a communication with an entity, a personified other on a cosmic scale. This allows the person to look for responses that have intelligent meaning behind them. Believers expect responses made through SEs. How many times have you heard someone say an event answered his or her prayers? How many people you know have said an event seemed to be the universe giving them a message? Many religions actually encourage practitioners to look for the answers to their prayers in the patterns of events around them. The continued focus on possible response makes noticeable SEs more likely. The specialized context of divine response gives the believer permission to perceive SE patterns. The person may not allow themselves to experience SEs outside of the format their belief system. Few believers would allow anyone but a god to have the ability to use events as a language. Some cultures pray to their ancestors or nature spirits. They talk to their image in the SE mirror too. It only sounds strange if you're looking through a different frame of reference. If a person says to a conservative psychiatrist, "I communicate telepathically to a supernatural being who changes events for me on occasion. His name is Larry," they may find themselves diagnosed as schizophrenic, prescribed psychotropic chemicals, or admitted to an institution for observation. If the same person says, "I am a religious person and feel that occasionally my silent prayer has been answered by (fill in the blank)," it probably would not even be given a footnote in their file. The inner process is the same, but one expression is part of a social norm and one is not. SEs often come in the context of a belief system. Sometimes it is the only form the person will allow.

Praying to supernatural beings implies there is someone on the other side of the conversation talking back. This is the problem with talking to yourself in the SE mirror. Talk to a loving parental divinity that accepts all its children as created, you get nice, warm, and fuzzy SEs. Praying to the "god is love" personality is a wonderful and positive way to start creating SEs. Pray to the wrathful, angry, and demanding figures, the responding SE reflections become dark and order obedience. This negative emotional valence has been used by religious leaders from the beginning to keep the believers in line. Here's an idea for you: Create an SE viral thoughtform that helps people understand their own connectedness and creative power. You're reading it right now.

DRUGS

Drug use and abuse is another context in which SEs occur. It is the least dependable, but there are more people abusing drugs in our society than there are meditating, so drug use deserves consideration. SEs in the context of intoxication is not nearly as rare as one might expect. Every society has powerful mind-altering substances. The shamans and priests of all cultures have traditionally had some substance, considered a sacrament, under the influence of which unusual events were more likely to occur. Our ancestors used plant-based drugs for divining the future. Shamans use them for seeking communication with whatever supernatural forces their beliefs espouse. The mystery schools of Greece and Rome depended on ergot-based hallucinogens for their initiation rites. Descriptions of which mushrooms to take to dance with the gods are encoded into the iconographic Tanka paintings of eastern religions. Even the early Christians believed alcohol causes intoxication because the Holy Spirit resided in it. Drinking it caused the power of the deity to emerge in the believer partaking of the sacrament. This is not an endorsement to mix SEs with intoxicants. Quite the opposite. My dissertation was

on the effects of drugs on personality. Overall, the news isn't very en-
couraging. Even our ancestors had a lot of respect and trepidation about
intoxicants. Dionysian rituals were more than getting drunk on wine
laced with other plants and ecstatically communicating with the gods.
They were often bloody and dangerous rites in which revelers' frontal
lobes were off-line.

In the modern world, substance abuse has become more prevalent
with the easy availability of very powerful chemicals that can cause a
wide variety of distortions in neurological function. What was once confined to the sacred use of the shamanic elite is now the amusement of
recreational use. Enthogenic psychonaughts report SEs that were personally powerful, and linked to the altered state of consciousness produced by the substance used. I heard this story from someone I knew
during college:

Synchronistic Event

B. was an intellectually oriental person who was
aware of synchronistic events. He followed them in his
life and had a clear understanding of what was, and
was not synchronistic. B. and a friend were in Brook-
lyn and had just tried a drug called M.D.A. He said
it made them feel kind of "creepy," that something
was definitely dangerous about it. As they walked the
streets, the neighborhood got worse, until they were
in an area with many abandoned buildings. B. turned to
his companion and said "M.D.A." in a sentence. At that
moment, a wolf appeared from behind a nearby corner,
gaunt and mangy, but definitely a wolf, in the city. It
seemed their fear of the predators and poverty of the
area appeared as an SE.

They left the area feeling the mention of the
drug's name and the appearance of the wolf were

connected. They went back across town to the friend's middle class brownstone home. They were talking about the event when one of them said "M.D.A." again. There was a sudden huge crash from the next room that shook the house. Rushing to the room, they found the entire ceiling had collapsed. They both took these events as meaning the drug was dangerous, and the events seemed to be a kind of warning.

All thoughts and emotions are chemical interactions within the brain that follow definite laws of biochemistry. Our thoughts may be linked to other planes and have effects on them, but we are primarily physically focused beings and are bound by the laws of our chemistry. We are dependent on our chemical states for the perception and processing of all sensory input, memory, and pattern-matching. Mess with your brain chemistry, and you change your ability to process information. Terence McKenna claimed that hallucinogenic plants were seeded on the earth by alien intelligences to hasten human spiritual evolution. He was a brilliant man, he did a lot of drugs. He died of a brain tumor. Probably no direct connection, not a provable one anyway. I endorse a more practical explanation for plant intoxicants. Some plants evolved natural insecticides to keep from being eaten. If most animals eat something that make them stagger around and see patterns that aren't there, they don't go back for a second bite.

Rhine showed drinking caffeine increases SE ability in laboratory subjects. Alcohol lowers it. I believe the reason is very straightforward. Stimulants increase brain activity. More neurons are active, thought-forms are stronger, pattern processing is better. If you want to look for SEs, have a cup of coffee. Most of the delusional and hallucinating clients I treat who have SEs got that way doing stimulant drugs. Most were abusing methamphetamines, PCP, or cocaine. Usually clients were using more than one. Psychosis from hallucinogens and stimulants via dopamine and serotonin pathways, are uncommon, but real. They allow you to pretend to change your frame of reference. You are already creating the SEs around you. Timothy Leary advised his students to use LSD to, "Turn on, tune in, and drop out." He already had a job. The casualty list of people who wound up on psych wards from this advice is substantial. My advice, as far as SEs, is to just "tune in."

Messing with your brain chemistry is messing with your ability to think and interpret information. The disturbed processing that results may cause distorted and inaccurate pattern-matching. It is possible under these disturbed conditions to become confused about what events are internal, which are external, and how they are related. People may perceive SEs resulting from their own altered chemical balance and have no environmental reality. Most drugs work by selectively altering brain activity. Some make areas of brain sensitive to dopamine more active, some make areas sensitive to serotonin more active. Either way, the brain gets "out of sync" with itself. Inevitably, some computational processes are not going to run smoothly if you intoxicate the computer. You may assign meaning to synchronistic events that grossly misinterpret them, even if the SE are real.

Drugs are commonly used in psychiatry to tune activity in selected areas of the brain up or down. When substance abusers introduce chemicals into their bodies, there is no way to determine what aspects of their personalities may be affected. Defenses may be chemically defeated, or artificially destroyed because the chemical balance maintaining them is complex and delicate. The effect of the drug is general and extreme. When defenses are artificially weakened, repressed content may be released powerfully before the ego is capable of coping with it. Large-scale subconscious disturbances may result as the surfacing content becomes mis-associated with processes it was never meant to be involved with. New neuron-pathways are formed in the brain that do not have their origin in actual experience. Established personality patterns may be disrupted. The results could be beneficial growth experiences, or a psychotic break. Shamans understood that each time they took a plant-based drug they were dealing with matters of life and death; they saw the risks as real. Using drugs while creating SEs is just stupid.

MEDITATION

The safest and most stable SEs are created using meditation. I'm not going to recommend you sit in an uncomfortable posture and do arcane breathing exercises. This isn't a secret practice handed down from master to student. You don't have to take off your shoes, light incense, or candles. You don't need a quiet space or a clean room. You don't even have to clear your mind. You are already deep in meditation at this very moment. Have you noticed your underwear in the last few seconds? Seriously. Have you? The cloth is producing sensory signals from the nerve endings in your skin. There is a constant signal from this sensation going to your brain. If you take a moment to tune in to the sensation, you can feel what you're wearing. The interesting question is, why didn't you notice this until your attention was directed there? You are in deep meditation all the time. You meditate whenever you make a choice about where to focus your attention. At the top of this paragraph I said your were already meditating. You have chosen to focus your attention on reading these words. That ability to direct attention is the essence of all meditation practices. Even trying not to focus on anything is an attempt to direct attention. We can't be consciously aware of everything we are experiencing all at the same time. You can't be aware of a fraction of the complex data processing, the thoughts your brain creates. It's too much data. Being aware of the sensations of your clothing, the way your big toe feels, and what your last meal tasted like, leaves you without the computational power to make decisions. Focusing your attention on reading gives a lower priority to the rest of the information. The information is still there. Thought and sensation never stop. You are selecting what information gets your attention. That's meditation.

Understanding how the brain allows you to focus allows you to understand how you create patterns of SEs. It also explains why so few people are consciously aware of SEs. You don't remember things that don't matter to you. Processing experiences from the senses into memory can't be done unless emotion is added to the mix. Your sensory processing passes forward to you on massive neural data highways. The main highway passes directly through your emotional mind.

The limbic system, your mid-brain emotional system, alerts you to the general importance of your experiences. You can experience your senses without any emotion attached to them, but you won't remember any of it. Memory depends on emotional valence. Popular psychologies of the past have artificially separated the emotions from the intellect. So have many spiritual and religious philosophies. Separation is an illusion. Emotion is a form of thought. We are back at thoughtforms and the emotional body again, in case it didn't cross your mind. Those emotions tell your memory systems what to keep, and what to forget. No feeling to an experience; not worth remembering. Emotion gets your attention, makes things worth focusing your precious frontal lobe processing power on. Emotion helps regulate attention; emotion directs much of your meditations. If someone doesn't know SEs exists, they have no emotional valence attached to SE. There is no instruction to match for that pattern. Even if an SE happens in front of them, no memories are created.

There is a logic, stretched or not, to saying SEs are direct reflections of your thoughts. You might even buy into the claim that emotional energy creates the overall theme of your SE. Why, then, do SE show up when your not thinking about them or having an emotional reaction? You are creating reality, in a sense. You never experience the physical world without the brain creating it for you from sensory data. You also never experience it in real-time. The representation of reality you are now experiencing is happening in areas of your memory. Memory is the internal stage on which all experience plays out. You have no direct experience. You do have different types of memory. Some memory areas specialize in skills already learned. Some tell you who you are. Some tell you what's happening now, a few minutes ago, or years in the past. Some are faster than others. Long-term experiences, emotions, complex data, can take the brain years to process and file away. The hippocampus, a large structure in your limbic system, seems to be the computer's main switching and processing station for turning short-term experiences into long-term memories. If a surgeon stimulates this area with a pin-point electrical signal, patients have reported suddenly experiencing memories from decades earlier. Not just "oh yeah I remember that" experiences.

They are completely real, lucid emersions in brain re-created realities. Even though the person experienced the event years before, the brain is still crunching the data for long-term memory storage. The more powerful and complex the experience, the more vivid and lasting the memories. Long-term patterns of SEs happen because you are still thinking about what is being processed in memory. Thinking and not being aware you're thinking? This sounds like a self-serving explanation. In a sense, it is.

Your brain is serving you, even when you need to move on and turn your attention elsewhere. Meditation isn't hard; you do it even when you're not aware of it. Forgot about the sensation of the clothing you're wearing again, didn't you? What about your big toe? You turned your attention elsewhere, began contemplating what you are reading. You gave an instruction to your emotional brain not to attach any importance to those sensations. They happened, but no memory was formed. Very deliberate and complex tasks can be automated by your brain, freeing you to do more interesting things.

One day, I was driving the highway to work. I have been down this route hundreds of times. For a few months I had been commuting from San Francisco to Sacramento daily. A 90-minute drive without traffic gave me lots of time to think. After a few months, I chose a closer workplace along the same highway, only half the distance. One morning, I began the usual drive and hit a long stretch of the road where nothing much was needed from my attention. I began to think of other things, such as what this book was going to say to you. Suddenly, I didn't recognize where I was. I was in pre-dawn darkness, and unable to figure out where on the route I was. When the next exit came up, I found I had over-shot my exit by 20 miles!

At first, I was scared by this. Had I fallen asleep at the wheel? No, my brain had done exactly what I instructed. Driving a car is a massively complex computational task. In real-life conditions, the complex variables that have to be figured out are beyond current technology. Falling asleep would have meant drifting off the road, not following it, and obeying traffic laws for 20 miles. What happened? I told my brain that there was no importance to the task, no emotional valence. I entered a state of meditation in which my thoughts became more important than the routine task I was doing. My brain still did as instructed, drove down the highway, but no memory resulted because there was no emotional energy attached. The frontal lobe told the limbic system there was nothing interesting happening. Induced amnesia is common. Many people have had a traumatic injury and needed emergency surgery. Some have had amnesia chemically induced by their treating doctor without knowing it. In some circumstances, procedures have to be done while the patient is awake. It might be risky to use an anesthetic that might lower brain activity, respiration, or heart rate. Doctors also don't want to traumatize the person with memories of the pain that might last a lifetime. So, they save the person's life, and then administer an amnesiac drug that prevents the memory from being processed from short-term to long-term memory. Typically, these drugs interfere in the limbic system's ability to create emotional valence. The person was fully awake, but no memory data is processed.

To create SEs using meditation, you take advantage of your brain's ability to continue to process information after your attention turned elsewhere. There are just a few tricks. In contemplative meditations, you choose an external object or internal thought, and direct your attention there. You contemplate your chosen thoughtform. As a spiritual practice, this often is done with a picture of a deity, a guru, or something that reminds the mediator of an internal experience he wants to have. To create SEs, just direct your attention to a pattern you want to see manifested as SEs. Hold your attention there during your meditation. When you inevitably wander away from the thought, just bring attention back to it. That's all there is to it. Your brain will continue to process this request into memory long after you move on to other activities. The neuroscience of memory and learning gives some useful tips. First, don't bother doing this for more than 20 minutes a day. Forcing yourself into hours of meditation is counter-productive. Neurons are living things. They get tired. Fire them in the same pattern for more than 20 minutes; they use up their glucose and transmitter reserves. They stop making those extra connections with other neurons. Memory consolidation seems to happen better when you take yourself out of the way and stop forcing yourself to focus. You will learn more if you study for an hour, and then sleep for an hour, than if you studied the same material for two hours straight. You will get better results creating SEs if you focus attention on the pattern you want for 20 minutes, then stop. Your mind will automatically continue working for you, looking for the pattern of the SEs in the data stream from your senses.

Give some emotional valence to the pattern you want to create in SE.

Make it something juicy and important. Make it something that has meaning for you. This causes emotional energy in the thoughtforms you create. M-Space gets curvier, paths in probability get faster, the limbic system tells memory to keep consolidating, and pattern recognition comes on-line. Listen very carefully to what I'm going to tell you now. Focus all the attention you can on the next words: "With great power comes great responsibility."

Yeah, I stole the line from a *Spiderman* comic book. Shout-out to Stan Lee. It's also very important. Not because you owe anybody else, but because you have a responsibility to take care of yourself. Choose the emotional valence carefully, Grasshopper. I stole that from old episodes of Kung-Fu. You will experience SEs based on the emotional tonality of the valence you put your attention on. The more intense the emotion, the less mental processing you will be able to do. That is the evolutionary survival mechanism of the brain. You can think fast with the emotions, but they are less accurate and detailed. If you focus on emotionally intense SEs, no matter what the emotion, you will tend to forget you set them up to begin with. You may get lost in the story you tell yourself. You may believe what you think. This is how some of the clients I have treated came to believe they were the one and only god. Boosting the emotion of love feels good. Seeing transpersonal love displayed as SE is absolutely intoxicating. Fear works the same way.

Don't create SE around dark patterns and emotions.

We all have enough of them already. Don't scare yourself into paranoia. Always keep your sense of humor and wonder close by. SEs have an amazing sense of humor. It can seem as though the entire universe, the entire script of your life, has been set up to deliver a single-moment SE punch line. It's only funny if you have a sense of humor.

You have to create an internal object if you want to elicit the emotional energy you need. Your brain creates emotions, but not on conscious demand. The limbic system creates emotion based on the way it interprets sensory data. You, up in the frontal lobes, tell the emotional brain what data it has created that you are finding of use. You then choose thoughts to illicit more or less of the emotions created. You direct your super-computer to run simulations, drawn from memory, in your internal representation of the world. You need a "handle," an internal object on stage that you associate with the emotional pattern you want to turn into SEs. If you want to create SEs that mime talking to whatever you believe god is, contemplate an image of your chosen deity. The object has emotions associated with it. Those emotions drive the SE patterns created from contemplating the object. When you meditate on an object that has emotional significance to you, your brain constructs an internal representation of the object in memory. That object held in memory is a thoughtform. There, see? You are already creating M-space objects that alter the structure of reality. Not so difficult. In fact, it's automatic. You do have to be careful about what other emotions and patterns are associated with the thoughtform you create. Most symbols, most objects are connected in memory with vast cascades of data. The back-stories of the thoughtforms you create become important. Echoes of them are turned into SEs as well. Suppose you want to have an SE conversation with Hercules. He was widely worshiped as a god in the ancient world. Strength was seen as having been favored by the gods, so naturally there was a god of strength. You may be seeking the emotional comfort of a strong male protector figure; maybe you just liked the Disney movie. Either way, creating SEs in a Hercules pattern is easy enough. The problem is there was more to his story, and yours, than just the strong hero part. Hercules was (how do I put this delicately?), a tragically flawed hero. Hercules had been abandoned by his father, at war with his mother, and prone to murderous rages. He was very much the classical world's model of a bipolar adult. Somewhere in your brain's vast associations are pieces of the story that contain the emotions associated with the entire myth. You might not want manifest SEs using thoughtforms that have a lot of emotional baggage.

USING YOUR MEMORY

The next trick uses your working memory structures. Working memory is a temporary scratch-pad area you use for very short-term tasks. It can hold about seven objects at a time, like a short shopping list. Complex patterns are difficult to maintain in your working memory. It is even more difficult to get complex patterns into long-term memory. When you consciously create thoughtforms, you do it in working memory. Holding your attention on the object you create for 20 minutes ensures that it passes from consciously controlled short-term working memory, into unconsciously automated long-term memory. This creates the thoughtforms that pattern-match for SEs after you have turned your attention back to the world around you. Simple patterns are easier to manifest than complex patterns. Complex patterns are less likely to survive the transition to long-term SEs. Here's a practical example:

Synchronistic Event

I decided to test how far my ability to create complex SE patterns could be pushed. I am an occasional chess player. Deciding to create SEs based on a chess game, I set up a board in my mind, set the intention with a short meditation, and soon had many SEs based on chess symbols. Getting SEs to respond was easy. Within a few days, I had met a series of people named King and Bishop. There were SEs about knights, castles, and pawns. There was even an associated sub-plot about the meaning of the black and white squares on the board. Having the basic pattern

set, I tried to play the game. I meditated on the first
move, Pawn to D4. There was an SE a few hours later
that gave an appropriate opponent's opening move. I
moved again, and SE responded with a move. There are
some gifted people that can play a chess game in their
minds without a board. I'm not one of them. After the
third SE move, the SE pattern fell apart into random
chess SEs.

The pattern was just too complex to maintain. I had tried the chess pattern because it was emotionally simple. I don't get very excited about chess. However, the thought needed exceeded my working memory's ability. Looking at a static chessboard in your mind isn't that complex if you have played a while. But, when I tried to figure out individual moves, my internal attention wandered from piece to piece, over and over. Which pawn was that? The result was a jumbled pattern of SEs. If you are going to create your own patterns of SEs consciously, start with simple patterns, associated with positive emotions.

Once you become good at creating SEs with meditation, you will gradually find you don't need the context of the meditation at all. SEs become automatic, based on your moment-to-moment thoughts. If you create patterns consciously, it's a good idea to change patterns every few weeks. Neurons that fire together wire together. SEs of single patterns tend to get more frequent and intense the more you use them. They feel more meaningful because stronger neural pathways have been formed. Their thoughtforms become more energetic and easier to create. They can even become habit-forming. Your on-board starship computer learns the tasks you direct it to repeat. It takes over the burden of you having to give it directions for those tasks, and automates them. Pattern matches you make often with conscious effort automatically are moved to faster, unconscious, procedural memory. You can consciously forget what thoughtforms you have created. You may leave the SE faucet running without realizing it. The SEs in your environment may then reinforce your belief in the pattern you have created. You can come to believe what you were thinking when you set up the pattern for the SEs. The antidote for this is to set a new pattern, remind yourself of your powers, and re-confirm that you are the one creating the SEs.

Your bio-computer is so advanced, it can even learn without your conscious awareness. It can also condition your responses automatically if you leave the autopilot on. People alter their state of consciousness in many ways. Ultimately, it's all changes in brain chemistry and neurological pathways. I have no moral or ethical objections to anyone altering their state of consciousness by conscious choice. I do get a little preachy about people infringing on their own free will by making silly choices that limit them later. You can control SEs. You can make it seem as if you are the center of time and space and events dance around you for your entertainment. If that's all you want from SEs, go for it. The best way to do this is by cultivating stability in your consciousness. The patterns you make consciously become difficult to spot if your consciousness is bouncing all over the place. You already have all the on-board technology and energy you need to make SEs. You don't have to "do" anything. You don't have to be "altered" in any way. Just tell the computer what you want it to do.

Thirteen

Illusions
and
Anomalies

"Time present and time past are both perhaps present in time future. And time future contained in time past."—T.S.Eliot

THINKING OUTSIDE OF TIME

In this chapter, we are going to take a trip deep into the rabbit hole of SEs. In previous chapters, we have been building a model of the details of your inner technology. If the model of SE-as-mirror is correct, you exist over areas of time and probability. Through your brain structure and activity, you should be able to see some very strange distortions in time. Einstein predicted that light would bend around curves in space-time. This effect was then observed happening near the sun. His model predicted time moves at different rates relative to motion and mass. Again, verified by experimentation and observation. If a part of you exists outside time and space, you should be able to see SEs created by those parts of you in the past and in the future. You should live in the effects caused by adjacent probable versions of yourself on different branes. This sounds a little scary at first. Probable other selves? Relax. You are a unified being; it's all you. You are always at the center of your own consciousness. You can still experience SEs in the physical now that have been created in the probabilities of the past and future, by you. You are living through very complex patterns of SEs all the time. Some of those patterns formed from emotional processing and pattern-matching strategies you have created in the past. The thoughtforms you created then appear as SEs now. Some SEs happening now are the result of thoughtforms you will create in the future. We live in constant reverberating echoes of SEs across areas of time.

Using your SE abilities means learning to think outside the box of space-time.

It means thinking about reality as data processing. Thoughtforms include their own internalized dimensions of time. De-coupling the idea that time was a constant made relativity work. Giving individual particles their own dimensions in time made String Theory work. Realizing your thoughtforms are not dependent on linear time gives you the ability to play with SEs. Once you start playing with the structure of time itself, the fun really starts. I am going to describe several kinds of SEs caused by the reverberations your thoughts create in your other dimensions. Remember, I am a storyteller giving you a good excuse to use abilities you already have. The SE story can be told as physics, as neuropsychology, or philosophy. None individually explains all SEs, so I like to mix them up a bit. It's a story, but it works in practice.

The essence of SE is meaning. We find meaningful connection in events, and call them SEs. That sense of meaning stems more from feelings of familiarity than from reasoned connections. Your brain has no verbatim memory. Your billions of sensory nerves provide far too much data to store exactly as received. Your brain abstracts them. Your experiences are not stored according to when they happened. Each brain has a slightly different set of associative structures, but most try to store experiences by emotional relevance. Confusions about when a memory happened are common. Confusions in meaning are as well. Here is an example some people find enlightening, others irritating:

Break out your sense of humor again; I'm going to play another little trick on you. Metaphors can often help us make sense of situations where we otherwise would remain at a loss. A good example of this comes from religious philosophy. Think about the problem of the Trinity. Trinity deities occur in many religions and mythologies (mythology being other people's religion). In Christian philosophy the Father, Son, and Holy Ghost are said to be separate, yet one and indivisible. How is this possible? How can one understand this relationship? Visualize a square cardboard box. The box has three dimensions, height, length, and width. The three dimensions are separate, but inseparable, without any one of them, the box itself has no real existence. As with the Trinity, the reality of the one is dependent on the existence of the three, which are inseparable, yet different aspects of the one. At this point, most people nod their heads, understanding the meaning fostered by the metaphor. You now perceive a meaningful relationship where none existed before. The problem is, there is no relationship. There is no connection between the dimensions of a cardboard box and the Trinity whatsoever. I made the example up to make sure there was no actual relationship. This is where I hope you had your sense of humor handy. The example produces the illusion of a meaningful relationship, a kind of artificial SEs. Here is how it's done: the mind is trying to match patterns. First, state the pattern of the Trinity, then the cardboard box analogy. Proximity to each other causes working memory to hold both at the same time. Both have a similar pattern in that there are three "somethings," related to one "something." One has three aspects or persons, the other three dimensions in space. Both assume that there is an inclusive unity. The mind recognizes the common patterns between the two, and that feels like meaning. The brain generalizes the feeling of meaning and mistakes one as an explanation for the other. This is how most advertising and political speeches are constructed. It is also how many SEs share meaning between events. One event sets the pattern of associated meaning for other events that occur in close proximity.

We do what we were evolved to do, find a pattern match and jump to conclusions that enable us to act as if certain. Our logic is fuzzy and wonderfully creative. The tendency to believe our own fuzzy logic causes many delusions, and many SEs as well.

REFLECTION SE

Reflection SEs allow you to experience your own thoughts as SEs. Time anomalies are more complex. Your thoughtforms have a range in time that includes parts of the past and future. SEs sometimes originate from the past, future, or other probability timelines. They are confusing because the SEs reflect emotional and mental activity, from more than just your present thoughts. To understand these SEs, it helps to think about both the psychology, and the time mechanics. You project your psychological processes on SE, and bend the events of space-time. The way the brain processes information provides an explanation for some SEs. The brain can generate any reality imaginable. I work with some clients who literally live in a different world from the rest of us. In their world, the creative power of the brain manufactures realities from within itself. Hallucinations are completely real to those who experience them. Similarly, the brain can mis-file the order of events. It can create meaning where there is none. It can give vivid memories of things that never happened. Your computer is fully capable of creating the illusion of SEs by re-arranging data in memory. I do not believe what I think because my training and experience has taught me thought and memory are unreliable. The meanings SEs present are equally unreliable. Rational explanations for SEs are comforting. Usually they are insufficient. Some SEs present as so outlandish that coincidence is just not a rational explanation. You are more than your physical brain processes. Nevertheless, you are dependent on them to experience physical reality. The brain can tell you virtually anything. Your supercomputer is the master storyteller. It adapts the story to the reactions of you, the listener. The story it tells reflects your attention, both in the way it processes information, and in SEs. If time is a variable in the story you tell yourself, so shall it be.

Time-delayed SE

Delayed SEs seem to be coming from some time in the past, but happen in the present. This gives the impression the past is happening at the same time as the present. Picture yourself creating a pattern of SEs. You consciously choose a pattern and focus on it, but after several weeks of trying, there is no sign of SEs. Not having a chosen pattern of SEs appear is very unusual. Once you ask the brain to look for an SE pattern, you should experience at least traces of it around you. If nothing at all happens, something is up. So, you give up on the pattern you were trying to manifest. You place your attention on a new pattern, which soon begins creating SEs around you the way it's supposed to. Soon you forget about the pattern that did not manifest. Five years later, you are working with SE patterns you know well. Suddenly the failed and forgotten pattern of SEs start to emerge. You recognize what seem to be references to psychological and emotional states you experienced years before. Current SEs appear, mirroring who you were five years ago. It seems a past pattern has moved directly into the future, now your present. The format lasts for the same number of weeks you had originally tried to project it, and then disappears. Your current pattern of SEs returns where it left off, with the addition of patterns of confusion and concerns over what has just happened. This "blast from the past" might be triggered by many different psychodynamic processes. Perhaps delayed SEs happen because there is some unconscious objection to thoughts and emotions associated with the chosen pattern-match. They also might be exactly what they appear to be; you becoming aware of aspects of yourself not restricted to the present moment.

Historically referenced SE

Historically referenced SEs give the illusion the SEs you create are changing events in the past. Changing the past sounds truly crazy. SEs depend on meaning, not time. Time is a box. Your thoughts are already outside the box. Imagine you have set up an SE pattern about owls. The birds appear in the context of SE as expected. You start to notice the symbol of the owl is appearing in your memory of past events.

You notice an abstract painting at work is actually an artistic rendition of an owl. The painting has been there for years without you noticing it. You find an old picture of yourself and a friend on a camping trip. For the first time, you notice the owl in a tree in the background. Next you are talking to one of your parents when they mention a stuffed owl toy someone gave you as an infant. You had not remembered that toy for years. Owl SEs are manifesting in the past instead of just the present.

What is occurring is a form of memory sorting. Your ability to search and process patterns in memory is truly amazing. Memory searches don't even have to be conscious. Most of us have had the experience of having trouble retrieving some piece of information from memory, then having the missing piece of information pop into awareness hours or days later. Once the conscious mind requests the information, it can turn its attention elsewhere. The unconscious will continue to sort patterns and memories, presenting its findings later. The unconscious is thinking. That creates thoughtforms, which in turn cause SEs. In the case of the re-appearing owl, the subconscious can do you a favor by carrying out a comprehensive search of all memory. Your computer sorts out all memories of events with an owl. This memory sort creates an internal memory structure of specific experiences of owl associated together. This new associated memory pattern/structure makes it appear as if all the events with that symbol are somehow centrally connected. Memories being associated together create a sense of meaning. An association links the pattern you match for and the actual past events. The pattern of "owl," is mistaken for having caused SEs in the past. You can experience SEs in patterns from memory, and actual current SEs in the present at the same time. For SEs, it all happens in the present. That present, the present of your whole self, encompasses areas of the past and future. Look into the past, and you will find SEs created by your present.

HERALDING SE

Heralding SEs seem to be generated by future thoughts and emotions. That's right, effects in the present caused by the future. The physical universe operates on a strictly cause and effect basis. That cause and effect reality depends on the forward flow of events through time. I broke my leg once in a climbing accident. As I healed, I often really, really wished I could have turned back time. Unfortunately, physical time has no do-overs. I would have loved to warn myself. Fortunately, SEs don't have the same limitations. Part of you exists over areas of time that do allow for this. The impression I get is that our other dimensions experience time not in moments, but as objects. We experience time as thoughtforms. No longer arranged by the limitations of linear time, thoughtforms appear to be associative. Here's an example of a heralding pattern I experienced:

Synchronistic Event

I had set up a chess pattern in SE using a simple mindfulness meditation. The SEs soon responded as intended. Attempting SE as complicated as a chess game is very challenging for me. Trying to sort all the chess-related SE events into an intelligent response pushes the envelope. After a few weeks of being hyper vigilant for the chess pattern, an entirely different pattern of SEs started to appear. It began with a few complicated coincidences that made me feel worried and uneasy. I did not understand the pattern, and could not see them as reflections. They seemed outside the game I was playing. These rogue SEs usually involved almost having something bad happen, narrow avoidances of accidents, or events beyond my control. There were near misses by other drivers, strings of radio songs with cautionary messages, which referenced things I was looking at that moment. There were worrisome, non-specific warnings about losses. These SEs became more and more frequent over a period of about 10 days. I was becoming increasingly edgy and insecure. The chess format faded away. A series of SE messages about loss, self-reproach, and concern replaced it. I felt caught in a negative feedback loop. The more concerned I became about the tone of the SEs, the more of them appeared. The self-fulfilling prophesy aspect of the situation was not lost on me. It was like someone telling you not to think about elephants; it makes you think about them obsessively. Worse yet, some of the messages seemed to be implying that some huge event was approaching, and the messages were getting more frequent and insistent.

Paranoia will destroy ya, as the saying goes. Fortunately, I don't believe in reacting to SE as actual instructions or prophesies. At about the two-week mark, I was distracted and in a funk. I was visiting a woman I was dating at the time, and my distracted, self-focused, and self-indulgent state of mind sparked an argument. That progressed to core issues of the relationship and a passionate shouting match. It was one of those arguments that clears the air, but feels like it puts the entire relationship on the line while it's happening. It reached an emotional peak in about 20 minutes. After it was over, I had a disturbing realization. This argument created the SEs of the last few weeks. The emotions of the argument were like ripples in time. The ripples of SEs spread out backward in time, becoming more intense as the event approached. After the argument, I noticed a similar pattern of synchronistic events, growing less frequent and intense during the next week. These SEs seemed like the dispersing ripples on the other side of the event. The chess format appeared again, as if it had been interrupted and was picking up where it left off.

The subconscious won't always faithfully follow the SE pattern you set. Other parts of yourself are always trying to communicate with you. Demanding SE to always follow just the patterns you set is like saying to a partner "When I want your opinion, I'll give it to you." The goal is communication, and that rarely happens unless the "other" has the chance to speak. The unconscious communicates through dreams, or SEs. It uses the patterns that it needs to work with, not just patterns ego thinks it wants. I chose to focus on a pattern so restrictive, it had become useless. My unconscious may have been saying, "Let's get real and work on something meaningful, like real self-esteem and relationship issues. And while we're at it, let's throw in the time anomaly to teach you something new about SEs." The unconscious is smarter than we are. It often knows what we are going to do, how our actions may affect others, before we do. The real meaning of the SE in the previous example was my own self-concern and neglect of my relationship with my friend. The unconscious knew it would lead to the very argument that took place. That argument also created the powerful emotions that generated the SEs. SEs generated by the unconscious had been giving me a heads-up. Of course, if I had been paying attention to my actual relationships instead of SEs, I would not have needed this tap on the shoulder.

Don't become obsessed with SE; the people around you are much more important.

Think about our hunting ancestor in the grasslands for a moment. While hunting for dinner, he would have been reading the SEs in the motions of the grass. He would look up at the clouds and see pictures sent by the spirits of what path he should take. Every motion, every event, could be read for the SEs that gave him that slight edge of information needed for survival. Had our hunter become obsessed with the SEs, he would forget his purpose, become lost in the reverie, missed the real opportunities he was seeking. Your ability to create SEs evolved to enhance your life, not to distract you from it.

SEs will provide you with at least the illusion of whatever you are looking for. Would you like to rule the world? How about control the weather? Want to be God's special someone on earth and have the right to say what He wants? How about driving the stock market up and down according to your mood? Want to win the lottery? If it were possible, I'd be rich by now and you would probably never have seen the book you are reading. I have worked with clients who believed they could do all of this. We all have favorite fantasies. They comfort us, and activate emotions that make the present moment tolerable in times of stress. They may even motivate us to act toward long-term goals. Fantasy is healthy. Fantasy is also thought. Fantasies create thoughtforms, which in turn create SEs. You can create any pattern of SE, play out any fantasy. The key is to do so with intent, knowing the SEs you create are local, centered on you. Everyone else does the same; you are only responsible for your own SEs.

Some people believe SEs are the granddaddy of psychic phenomena. I'm not a big believer in psychic phenomena, at least not in the ability to accurately predict events or get information from out there in the ethers somewhere. Impressions would have to come through experiences and memories in storage, then reconstituted into some kind of personal experience. The possibilities for distortion and misinterpretation based on personal psychological processes are great. Add to this the complicated matter of interpreting meanings in the context of SEs, and one gets mostly predictions that do not manifest, and assumptions about reality that turn out to be personal fantasy. Still, some interesting SEs that seem to be related to various ESP phenomena do happen.

SE and telekenisis

Telekinesis is the moving of objects by non-physical means. Telekinetic SE happen when a person wants an object to move, and the object is displaced by some natural physical event. The house pushed over by the bulldozer in the introduction is one example. Here's another:

Synchronistic Event

It was a warm summer afternoon. I was sitting on the deck, a glass of iced tea on the chair arm next to me. Once again, the thought of what it would be like to move objects came to mind. The night before, I had seen a *Star Trek* episode in which a character levitated a cup across a room. As I thought about this, I glanced down at the glass next to me. I thought about what it would be like to retrieve the cup without touching it. At that moment the neighbor's cat jumped out from somewhere into the table, knocking the glass off the arm of the chair into my lap.

The glass, the overturned house, the way dice fell in Rhine's experiments, none involves objects being moved by a psychic force. The order of events, changes in probability based on thoughts and meaning, is responsible. In a way, all SEs are telekinetic. Events are objects, thought-forms, in mental and emotional space. When you choose your thoughts, you move these thoughtforms around, patterns of SE change around you. Just don't bet the rent on a roulette wheel—odds are still in the house's favor.

SE and clairvoyance

Clairvoyance is getting information from somewhere outside the range of the physical senses. When this happens through SEs and is accurate, which is rare, it is difficult to explain. I have known many clients who have had SEs tell them about events that have not yet happened. Generally, the predictions are wrong. Usually, the SEs reflect what the person has been thinking about, worrying might happen, or wishing would happen. Sometimes SEs do seem to provide information the conscious mind probably doesn't have access to. I try to be conservative when analyzing SEs. I look for more conventional psychological explanations before I jump to conclusions, such as SEs reflect our own natural ESP. I just don't have any other explanation for the following SE:

Synchronistic Event

It was fall and I had been living in the Catskill Mountains of New York. One evening I had busied myself with various small household chores that occasionally brought me past the radio in the kitchen. It provided a background that I was only conscious of when my tasks took me close to the kitchen. After an hour or so, I became aware that the radio was playing the song "Woodstock." Somehow, it seemed significant, as if the song stood out from the usual play list. It didn't seem important or clear, just an impression of something different. A short time later, I noticed two station DJs talking; both of them were named Bob. They were using this as semi-comic patter between song sets. I thought it interesting two Bobs would be on the air at the same time; this also seemed to stand out somehow. I started to think about a friend of mine named Bob who lived in Woodstock. I hadn't seen him for a few months and was wondering if I should get in touch with him to say hello. I thought about him as I continued listening to the radio. The next set of songs all seemed to stand out. There was nothing unusual about them separately, but taken together they seemed to have a message. The set included "Leaving on a Jet Plane," "Monday, Monday," "Copa Cabana," and some song about one person wanting to see another. I knew it sounded crazy, but I got the impression that I should go see Bob, that he was leaving for some tropical location. He lived in the hills and didn't

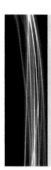

have a phone, so the next day, Monday, I drove over to see him. When I arrived, he was already packed. His plane would leave in a few hours. He accepted a job in Puerto Rico that had opened up suddenly and had to leave almost immediately. The contract was for a year. If I hadn't gone to see him when I did, chances are I wouldn't have seen him again.

SE and telepathy

Telepathy is becoming aware of the thoughts and/or feelings of another person without using the physical senses. The SE version happens when you seem to read the SEs caused by the thoughts of someone else. Here is a simple example:

Synchronistic Event

One evening, my wife and I were watching TV together at home. As we sat, we were discussing our relationship. We came to a minor impasse, she saying, "You don't understand me," me repeating, "Yes, I do" in response. This went on several times. Suddenly an actor on the television yelled; "You don't understand me" as part of the plot. Both of us picked up on the event immediately, she laughed and said, "You see, the TV agrees with me; you don't understand me!"

In this situation, the two sets of thoughts are simple, intensely charged and diametrically opposed to each other. The likelihood we both were having the same thought was small because of the opposite focuses. It appeared her thoughts became an SE, I perceived them, and was able to discriminate the source as not within me.

Testing models of SE becomes difficult because they reflect your thoughts about them. Even seemingly carefully constructed SE experiments give uncertain results. The mind can think about itself, but what if its own estimations are flawed? We experience time because we have thoughts about time. Ultimately, we are thinking about our own thoughts.

I have one more piece of theoretical SE weirdness to leave you. You can create SEs in locations other than where you are. You can create SEs for other people, you can create SEs centered on chosen locations. To your multi-dimensional self, space as well as time is relatively meaningless. Not believing it, not including this ability in your frame of reference, is the only thing that prevents you from creating SE at a distance. Please allow me to tweak your frame for a few moments. I wish I could claim that thoughtforms were my idea. The concept is very, very old. It appears in the oldest mystical traditions throughout Asia, North Africa, and Europe. Look carefully at even the shamanic traditions of cultures without written language. Thoughtform construction and utilization is the advanced natural technology at the core of all magical beliefs. If you understand thoughtforms are objects constructed from your emotional and mental energy, you become able to manipulate them as objects. You can build them. You can instill functionality and complex processes in them. You can detach them from your M- and N-Space bodies. You can send them places to perform tasks and gather information. You can create automated, semi-autonomous, thoughtforms. R2D2 anyone? Western mystical mumbo-jumbo calls these thoughtforms artificial elementals. Whether you believe this or not, the idea does give you one of those metaphorical ways to think about how you can use your SE abilities. All you have to do is create the thought and feeling you want in your mind. Then just imagine you left that object where you want the effect to happen. Look for SEs that indicates your thoughtform is doing its job, and you will eventually find them.

CREATING YOUR OWN ILLUSIONS

SEs are a mirror. You can create any illusion that amuses you. If you like, bend straight linear timelines into paper clips. Just be aware you're molding the sacred substance of your own being while you're doing it. It's all you, it's all alive. Be kind to yourself. If you find yourself caught in this fun house of SE illusions, there is a ready exit. You are always in the present moment. No matter how time-twisted SEs appear, you remain in the one and only present moment. Your thoughts determine what SE means. You decide what is happening. These stories should serve you, not the other way around. Illusions happen when we believe what our mind tells us without question. No one that lives in a desert believes the mirages they see. Don't believe what you think. I'm going to end this chapter with another SE story that seemed a fitting comment for a chapter on illusions:

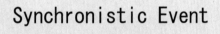

Synchronistic Event

I was nearing the end of the draft for the chapter you are now reading and was feeling I had missed something. I wanted to convey what a series of SE illusions feels like, and how to find a way out when needed.

It was Sunday, and the plan for the day was to take the family to the county fair. The kids' main interest was the mid-way, with its rides, games, and attractions. Having caved-in to their pleas, we were soon being pulled and directed to various attractions. As I walked along, enjoying the crowd and the kids' excitement, I couldn't keep the problem of how to explain to the average person what living with SEs as a constant frame of reference is like out of my mind. I found myself standing on line with my daughter for a funhouse attraction. It was a house of mirrors. Strange as it seems now, I had never been in a true house of mirrors. I experienced halls with mirrors, which create distorted reflections, but had never been in an actual house of mirrors before. I thought I knew what they were like from movies where a hero and villain wind up chasing each other inside one. The inevitable problem is which of the images was the real person, and which were merely reflections. I thought I was going to have mildly interesting but predictable experience. I was unprepared for the reality.

The experience of the real house of mirrors was very disorienting. It's a very closely confined maze of sharp turns and dead ends. Instead of an entertaining walk through a predictable path, the maze becomes almost instantly disorienting. I was soon lost and directionless. The task becomes not to figure out what reflection comes from where, but to just be able to find your way out. I was lost within moments. My daughter had raced on ahead, I didn't even have a reflection of her anywhere to orient by. There was barely enough room to move in this maze of mirrors. My own reflection was everywhere, making it impossible to tell if what was in front of me was a solid mirror a foot away, or an open pathway with my image reflected on the next mirror four feet away. To make the experience even more disorienting, not all of the mirrors are real. Some of the walls are actually clear glass. You look through them at other distant reflections and think they are mirrors. Several times, I thought I had figured out the pattern of the mirror's placement, and knew what direction the path was, only to walk directly into one of the clear glass walls. After a while of bouncing off my own reflections and becoming frustrated at my inability to predict the pattern of the maze, I was getting anxious and ir- ritated instead of amused. I could not figure out what to do and wanted out.

Then I had a revelation of sorts. Relax. This wasn't a personal challenge. It's not a test. It's a funhouse. Since there were no lost souls crowded in the corners begging for food and water, obviously nobody was getting forever lost in the place. There was a pattern of choices that would take me without error to the exit, but I didn't have to know what they were. All I had to do was keep moving. Eventually, by pure random chance, by persistently making choices, correct or not, I found my way out of the maze. The solution to the puzzle was just to be amused and keep moving. I met up with my family on the mid-way outside the funhouse. My daughter cleared the maze some time ago by just running around gleefully inside without a plan until she stumbled on the exit. That experi- ence over, my thoughts picked up where they had left off: How do I explain what it feels like to be caught in a pattern of SE that reflects aspects of yourself back to you?

Fourteen

Practical Magic

"Don't be satisfied with stories, how things have gone with others. Unfold your own myth."—Rumi

CAUTION

I have been trying to keep the tone of this book light, even a bit comical. The model of SE you have been presented with has been an explanatory fiction, a best guess of how SE works. Explanatory fictions are where most science starts. A dreamer has an idea that fills in the blank spots between the known and the obscured with a flash of imagination. All in good fun, but eventually someone finds a way to test the fiction, to test in practical terms if an idea is real. The time has come for you to decide if you want to claim your extraordinary powers. This has been a difficult chapter for me to write. I originally intended to title it "Fun and Games." It was to be a series of exercises that teach you how to create SEs for yourself as a light-hearted and playful demonstration of how easy it is for you to alter the rules of reality around you. It had to be light in presentation so that readers would not scare themselves with the faces they made in the mirror of SEs. At this stage in the book's production, in my present moment, many people are reading the draft material, and an interesting pattern is developing. Reading the book is causing explosions of SEs around the readers, as intended. My editor is raising an issue with this chapter. This chapter presents a real safety concern for the reader. She says I should be up front about this, and place a direct warning to the reader about the effects of doing the exercises. Please read on, you are about to be warned, and this is no joke or flight of fancy, though I will try to make it amusing.

Synchronistic Event

As I wondered exactly how to present this, SE once again came to the rescue in the form of a family outing to the Disney Museum here in San Francisco. As I wandered the exibits, playing cat-hearder to the kids while obsessing over this chapter, I literally walked into the example I needed. It was an exhibit on the movie *Fantasia*. In perfect SE timing I was suddenly face-to-face with a screening of Mickey Mouse in "The Sorcerer's Apprentice." In this segment of the film, our famous rodent is a lowly apprentice to a powerful sorcerer. When the wizard leaves the room, the apprentice puts on the magic hat left behind and tries his hand at spell casting. Soon lost in the intoxication of magical power the hat gives him, Mickey animates brooms to do his work, plays with the primal elements, and soon loses control of the magic he has called forth. All is soon lost in chaos. The hapless apprentice finds himself unable to shut down the magic he has brought forth. The master returns, and with a wave of his arms, sets all to right, and the apprentice back to his chores.

You have the magic hat in your hands at this moment. It is the book you are reading. This chapter has the incantations and thoughtforms you can use to put on the hat, and make the universe dance to your command. Tune in to the eternal present moment, the one in which I am here with you now, talking directly to you through these pages. This is your warning. SEs become very difficult to turn off once you know you create them. The excitement and novelty of finding out how connected and powerful you actually are can drive the SEs around you to a difficult to imagine intensity. SEs react to you. They are a mirror of your conscious and unconscious mind. I'm very comfortable in my unconscious, so SEs are old friends for me. How ready are you to become a real life sorcerer's apprentice? People can create real dangers for themselves by how they interpret their reality, by what patterns they choose to look for.

HOW TO MAKE YOURSELF REALLY PARANOID

Do you remember Bobby Fischer? He was perhaps the greatest chess player in the last 300 years. A brilliant, unparalleled genius, his 1972 world championship matches with Russian grandmaster Boris Spassky was perhaps the most watched international contest of all time. What ever happened to Bobby Fischer? The short version is, like many great chess masters throughout history, he went completely mad. He became gradually more paranoid as he got older, became obsessed with conspiracy theories about Jews taking over the world, and the government creating nuclear power plants so that they could use radiation to monitor his thoughts. Spassky was no model of mental health either. During the 1972 match he refused to play at one point because he thought magnetic rays were being beamed through his chair to disrupt his concentration. Great chess minds through the centuries seem to have fallen to remarkably similar symptoms of fear and paranoia. How is it that men of such genius could fall to such insanity? Because they see what they have been looking for.

People can be driven mad by SEs for the same reasons that some great chess masters are driven to paranoid delusions by the game. Imagine what the brain is doing during a chess game. The brain is a pattern-matching computational system. It's evolutionary niche is to look at a situation, then make guesses about what might happen next. Chess is a cosmically complex game: 20 possible first moves, times 20 each move after that. For a game that lasts 40 moves, there are about 1×20 to the 40th possible variations. The chess master is typically trying to look seven moves ahead. That could mean accounting for millions of possible variations. Now, this is not actually all that impressive in some ways. The pattern of the chess game is actually fairly simple. An 8×8 board of black and white squares, 6 kinds of pieces. Your brain does much more complex calculations when you drive a car or argue with your significant other. Human relationships are much more complex than chess. What can drive the chess master mad is not the complexity; it's the context that underlies the game, and the power we have to direct the brain's activity unintentionally.

Picture Bobby Fischer and Boris Spassky at a chess board. Each man lives a life totally obsessed with chess. They consciously pattern-match chess problems 16 hours a day. Its an obsession. You command much of your brain's functioning. You decide much of what your biological super computer deems important. You decide with your attention what is deleted and enhanced before it reaches your conscious awareness. And, very importantly, you decide what is real. That's your job as the prefrontal executive.

You tell the brain how to filter.

When you turn your attention to other tasks, the brain continues on autopilot, filtering and constructing according to your last instructions. Many of our instructions are given without being fully conscious. This is where our chess masters put themselves in danger. Chess is a game of war.

Your opponent is trying to destroy you. Bobby spends 16 hours a day not just matching the patterns of chess moves, he spends *16 hours a day* at war with invisible opponents; he defends himself from constant attack; he faces opponents who try to read his thoughts, outsmart him, trick him into making a mistake; he tries to figure out the conspiracy on the board seven moves ahead. He spent his life uncovering his opponent's brilliant conspiracy to trick him, to figure out what his own secret plan against his opponent was going to be. Chess is an innately paranoid game. Paranoia and conspiracy permeate the structure of the game itself. To play chess at a competitive level for 16 hours a day is to be instructing the brain to do more than pattern-match for patterns of movement on the board. It is to tell the brain to look for threat and hidden conspiracy in every pattern.

ATTENTION AND UNCONSCIOUS PROCESSING

Sometimes when I watch a baseball game for a few hours I get a baseball hangover. I go to bed and close my eyes, and there in my mind's eye are scenes from the game, running like a faded movie in the background. The brain is still processing the experience of the game in the unconscious. I have paid attention to the game, the brain has assumed it must have therefore been important, and I can see the computer processing the experience. Even in sleep, our brains are data processing. Sometimes when I dream, I realize I have been formulating case conceptualizations and treatment plans for clients I have seen during the day. Sometimes I dream of worlds constructed by alternative laws of physics and philosophy. Your brain is always running data based on experiences you have had and the instructions you have given it. Bobby Fisher's brain continued to run the paranoia, confrontation, and conspiracy patterns built into the game's emotional context even when he was not playing chess. The pattern-matching rules of chess were still running when he looked out into the world. His world became thick with paranoid conspiracies of opponents out to read his mind and plot against him. The SEs of his world became a mirror of the game of chess he was obsessed with. Bobby became the sorcerer's apprentice, he just didn't remember putting the magic hat on.

CREATING THE RULES OF THE GAME

Creating SE is a game. When you play this game you have to be aware that you create the rules. Sadly, in this culture steeped in the ignorance of separation and competition, games that foster joy and cooperation are rare. I went to Toys "R" Us to find a board game to play with the kids. In virtually every game the goal is to win. Even our legal systems are not based on the good or the true. It's an adversarial system, a thin veil for trial by combat. This notion of fighting against, or for, a win or loss for our efforts, is played out for most of us automatically. We pattern-match for it without knowing because we know no other way. We create SEs that bear these patterns, and they are deadly. If you are going to sit down to this game, think carefully about the board and rules you are creating. Create no gods you cannot dismiss. You can live in a universe of your own creation. Live in one that you actually want to live in. This vast universe is just energy. You choose how you experience it. You decide what it all means.

I was told again by a reviewer that my view that you can create SEs is a "maverick" perspective. It's not supported by the general scientific community. An understatement at the least. Really, the idea that you, and I do mean you, have so much power over the nature of your reality, sounds absurd to an orthodox scientific perspective. Arthur C. Clarke, British scientist and writer, created three rules of prediction for determining what is possible. They are:

1. "When a distinguished but elderly scientist states that something is possible, he is almost certainly right. When he states that something is impossible, he is very probably wrong."

    Don't assume you don't already exercise these abilities because anyone else says it's not possible. If you have to ask a question, ask why it's not possible.

2. "The only way of discovering the limits of the possible is to venture a little way past them into the impossible."

Don't believe you have the god-like power inherent in the tiny fraction of the unified field that you are? Try it. Do the exercises for a few weeks and see if the nature of reality shifts for you. Don't accept that the world is flat because others say it is. Sail your own ship past the boundaries of the known. Find your own truth from your own experience.

3. "Any sufficiently advanced technology is indistinguishable from magic."

SE is magic. Real magic.

The book in your hands is the most powerful magic tome ever created. (I love saying that, sounds so dramatic and over the top.) This natural ability, now at your command, is just that. Natural. Nature is the most advanced technology. We discover very little, we just catch up a little at a time with the technology of nature all around us. Magic (SE for lack of a better term) is complex. You are complex. Bask in your complexity; revel in the unknowable details of creation. Play with your abilities freely with rules you consciously create. You never have to be sure. Play without goal or care. Create and be overjoyed in the process.

In my present moment, as I write this chapter, I am teaching my son to play chess. As a therapist, I have worked with children with self-esteem problems. Sometimes I teach them chess to show them how smart they really are. Children often see chess the way adults see creating their own SEs. They think it's not for them because only smart people play chess. You have to have a special gift. They feel like losing a game is a failure. It's only a game. Games are supposed to be fun. My son is becoming a teenager. He is hell-bent on beating me at chess, it comes with the age. My goal: teach him to play. In our games, I let him make the rules. I tell him what I'm planning, why I make each move. He can take back as many moves as he likes. If he gets too far behind, I give him back his queen. We play to the last few pieces. We spend time together, he learns the game, and we both win. The outcome of the game doesn't matter.

Synchronistic Event

I have a list of guidelines on my computer screen now. I have been trying to decide which of them you will find the most valuable. My daughter came into my home office a few moments ago with a question: "Can you drive us to Alpha and Omega?" "Huh? What?" was my brilliant response. The second guideline on my list was telling you never to forget you are the source of SE, their beginning and end. Never assume SE comes from any other source. She was asking me to drive them to the just released movie *Alpha and Omega*. Alpha and Omega represents the beginning and the end. That pretty much moved that choice to the top of the guidelines list.

Here are a few brief guidelines you will need before trying the exercises. I am talking in my present moment to you, in your present moment. SE operates in a present moment that includes both. The commonality is that we each experience ourselves in the present moment. You may read meaning into events that indicate that influences occurring in the past or future are in play, but we live here, now.

Never assume SEs are involved in cause and effect based reality.

All SEs happen in real time. Our time-based physical minds are slow, computationally driven, data processors. Our sense of time depends on how our bio-computers crunch and tag the data. One of my favorite *Star Trek* lines came from an engineer trying to explain a plot twist involving time loops. He said, "I hate temporal mechanics." It was a running joke in the series. Instead of explaining the unexplainable, a character would just say they failed time travel theory at the academy. The audience understood it was an inside joke, to just forget the reasoning, and move on with the story. SE reflects the story you are telling. Be here now. If you chase SE causes in time, you will soon be bumping off the funhouse mirrors.

Don't believe the game you create.

The next general guideline is the "be here" of "be here now." The default position for all SEs has to be you at the center of the SE. It's easy to get caught up in thinking something outside you is the source of SEs. Whatever you want to believe, that's the way SE will be. If you want to believe a Flying Spaghetti Monster is creating SEs, SEs will tell you he's out there somewhere. There are enough con artists and delusional folks in the world trying to get you to believe they represent the source of SEs. Don't help them out by fooling yourself. The only possible vantage point for experiencing SEs is yours. You are always at the center of what you are experiencing. Think for yourself. Make your own decisions about what SEs mean. If someone starts talking about God, spirits, or other forms of paranoia, smile and politely back away.

RESPECTING THE EXPERIENCE OF OTHERS

My final guideline is actually a thoughtform I'd like to give you. Keep it in a mental pocket somewhere and use it often. Visualize a "do not disturb sign," the kind people put on hotel room doors so that people will let them sleep undisturbed. Imagine this sign as a thoughtform that you can hang around people's necks. You should always have copies of this one around. Not for them, for you. Knowing you create your own SEs, and that existing as a separate being is an illusion, is not for everyone. Most people have no pressing need for this knowledge in their lives. When you start creating your own SEs, you might have a tendency to want to share more of your experience than others want to hear. I certainly do. Please don't go knocking on the doors of sleeping people. You are going to see some amazing SEs involving the people around you. For the most part, the people around you will have no clue about their part in these SEs. The SEs belong to you. Other people have their own. People generally have their own personal myths already in place.

Their self-created SE patterns are already up and running. Most people have no idea what they are already doing. They are asleep as far as SEs are concerned. They are dreaming a dream in which they have separate existences. People rarely experience being woken up prematurely as a kindness. Sometimes, you may need to take out your mental "do not disturb" sign and hang it around a person's neck. This is to remind you to be courteous to others.

The exercises that follow can alter the nature of your reality significantly. For some, creating SEs seems to come naturally. Some people have difficulty adjusting to a reality in which they are the central creative force. Each exercise creates its own chessboard, each with a different set of assumptions. I designed these exercises to demonstrate your power to you, and to orient you to a new way of seeing reality. Each may require significant adjustments, or abandonments, of cherished philosophies. The direction is toward demonstrating your freedom, self-determination, and above all, choice about what you believe

GAME ONE: JUMPSTART

Your attention causes SE.

If your SEs seem few and far between, start putting some attention into the SEs when they happen. Write them down. Consider keeping an SE logbook. Jung said many SEs are dismissed as mere coincidence. You experience a coincidence, and then forget the details. The memory soon fades. The SE, based on one of your thoughtforms, will happen again, clothed in different events. If you don't remember the first, no connection forms to the second. Both eventually fade unreinforced from memory. I find if I try to trust my memory about SEs, I tend to forget details. I also find that when I write events down, and read them again months or years later, I sometimes have not been remembering them the way they actually happened. Memory is a variable, and changes over time. Keeping a record of each event helps solve these problems. SE meanings require the context of what you were thinking or feeling at that moment. If the SE is not written down, the context it occurred in may be lost, along with the underlying pattern it expresses. Your first game is going to be solitaire. You are going to create order from the deck of your perceptions. Fill out a record sheet as follows:

DATE: The date the SE happened.

TIME: When it happened, and its duration.

PLACE: Where it happened, and who you were with. These place the event in a context, both in your life, and with other events. More complex meanings often emerge from comparing sequences of events, not just single occurrences. The individual events may only make sense as part of a larger pattern if you can compare where in the larger sequence they occurred.

THOUGHTS AND FEELINGS BEFORE THE EVENT: Many SE are reflections of thoughts and feelings you had just prior to the event. These thoughts may be conscious, or just below the surface of awareness. SE requires that some part of your inner process be running parallel to outside events. Record your psychological state prior to the event.

DESCRIPTION OF EVENTS: Write down the actual event. Put down why it seemed to be a SE. What was coincidental about it? Write down your thoughts and feelings during the event, and any meanings, insights, or associations that seemed connected to it.

THOUGHTS, FEELINGS, AND ASSOCIATION AFTER EVENT: The real meaning of an event is usually our reaction to it. The SE is literally a manifested thoughtform. In this section, record your reactions to the event. Record anything the event reminded you of, a person, event, perhaps an emotion you are now having. This is likely to become the beginning thoughtform for the next SE.

Some people don't keep track of these events; they just experience them without trying to analyze the experience. Please feel free to do whatever seems best for you. I have found larger patterns appear in groups of events. These larger patterns may have the same base meaning as a single event, but reveal more detail. The more you look, the richer the experience becomes. The more you pay attention, the more frequent, and obvious SEs become. The attention you give them when writing them down jumpstarts SEs. One common reaction is to feel as if you have just picked up on a faint trail of SEs that becomes wider and clearer over time. Keeping records helps keep you from wandering in circles.

GAME TWO: JOIN THE PARTY

Let's start small, with a popular computer game, Bejeweled. This game presents you with an 8×8 grid of colored jewels. Each of six jewel shapes has its own specific color, mixed randomly on the grid. Your task is to match patterns, lining up jewels of the same shape and color. The game, like SE, is free to try. As you stare at the grid, you can demonstrate to yourself how you can direct your pattern recognition skills. If you stare at the entire grid at once, not looking at individual jewels, you can verbally direct your brain to match for specific patterns. For example, tell yourself, "See red." All the red jewels appear highlighted in your visual field. Say, "See green." The green jewels seem to pop out more. If you systematically do this one color at a time, you get to see every possible combination. Doing this uses both sides of your brain. The right side looks for the wide overall pattern; the left sees the particular pattern, the color, you have requested. To do this trick you have to work as a unified mind. Your right-brain communicates across the corpus callosum with your left-brain. You experience a consciousness bases on the two brains operating together as one data processing system. Now we are going to take this skill off the screen and into the real world.

If you go to any major sports event in a stadium, you have probably seen the wave. Fans at one end of the stands raise their arms together. Then they lower them as the next section picks up the motion, and then passes it on to the next. The effect is a wave of motion that passes through the crowd across the stadium. A pattern emerges using the thousands of individuals; it makes them seem like one interconnected mass. The pattern is not SE. It was created by someone initiating it causally. In this game you are going to pattern-match a crowd of people using SE. Picture your hunting ancestor scanning the grasslands for patterns. The savannah fills his vision. He looks not for individual blades of grass, he pattern-matches for the mass movement of thousands of blades of grass at once. He sees the wind causing waves across vast planes. The movement of the grass reveals the otherwise invisible wind. You are going to find patterns of SEs in the movements of a mass of people. To do this, you will have to find a gathering. Any gathering of more than a few dozen will do. You can use an audience, the crowds in a shopping mall, people seated at a meeting, or even pedestrians strolling by on any street. Position yourself so that you can comfortably see the group without having to look around. Look at the entire scene at once, without scanning from person to person. When you are able to do this without habitually having to pick out individuals, you are in a right-brain dominant mode.

Now, we are going to change your basic assumptions about what you're looking at. You are going to ask your computer for a specific kindof pattern-match. Instead of believing you are looking at many individual people moving randomly, tell your mind it is seeing only one being. One consciousness moving many forms. Everything you are seeing, all motions, are coordinated by a single force that generates patterns across all the individuals you see. Open your eyes and stare wide at the entire scene at once. Now, tell your mind "See patterns." You are now bringing the detail-oriented left-brain online with the right-brain still active. Very quickly, you will notice common movements between people. A person on one side of your vision may move in the same way at the same time as another person in a different area. If the crowd is large enough, soon you will see common motions passing through the crowd like ripples on the surface of a lake. Patterns of movement emerge for a moment, melt back into the scene, arise between different people, and pass to others. You are seeing SE patterns reverberating through the people you are watching.

When you see this, two important things are happening. First, you are skirting the outer edges of enlightenment. You are seeing the world as you, and as one outside unifying awareness moving everyone else. You could extend your inclusive frame of reference to include the entire world around you. You could extend the SE patterns to the movement of the leaves and clouds, the traffic nearby, passing birds, everything as one being. When you see this, you have established a duality. You and the universe. We won't be taking the last step into unity just yet. Do you remember the story earlier in the book about seeing auras? I had fooled myself into seeing traces of activity in visual memory projected onto the outside world. That is what this game does. You are seeing your own brain activity, your pattern-matching processes, in the SEs of the movement around you. Is this just a trick, a kind of mental illusion? Part of it is. Some of what you are seeing is actual SEs you created. It's not one or the other, its both. Both sides of your brain, both subjective and objective, both individual and unified. This game dissolves the false sense that time, space, and individuality are fixed and separate.

GAME THREE: GAMES PEOPLE PLAY

SEs act as a feedback system. You see your thoughts in the stream of events around you. For that to happen, there have to be events. When Rhine did his dice toss experiments, he could see people were affecting the events. Die tosses aren't very complicated. You can't project the plot from *Star Wars* into the pattern of a dice toss. The more complex and varied the events you look for SE in, the closer you will be able to come to seeing the patterns you look for. Zen rock gardens; not the best place to look for events. So, where do you suppose you could find a set of hugely complex events pre-designed to match your emotional and mental processes in real-time? People. We are the most complex and interactive systems in the known universe. We evolved to communicate with and respond to each other. We are our own best mirrors. What we believe we see in others, how we assume they feel, happens in ourselves. In our last game, we looked for just patterns. In this game, you are going to look for awareness. This game assumes that each of us has several levels of awareness operating simultaneously. You are going to look for SEs in your interactions with another person that seem to indicate you are speaking with more than one being in a single body. You are going to pretend to be in telepathic communication directly with another person's unconscious.

This is a covert game.

You can play any games you like in your own mind. The key is understanding it's your game. Other people don't have to participate while you're playing.

The pattern-matching set-up for this game is a set of assumptions. First, the person you play the game with has an unconscious that is as present and communicative as their conscious self is. Behind the personality driving the body is a vastly more intelligent and aware entity. If you like, consider it a soul, that is as "in" on SEs as you are. In fact, this inner self knows about the universal connection and is part of the one being. It speaks to you through the other person in the context of your normal interactions. The surface personality has no awareness of this deeper level of communication. Just keep in mind that there is a larger, more aware "person" behind the actions of the person you're talking to. In Sanskrit, you are talking to Soham (meaning, I myself); the aspect of god incarnated within the individual. The game is simple. Talk to someone, and during the conversation think toward them "hello." Then look for acknowledging SEs in their responses. Most often, you get back a kind of delighted SE response from the person's unconscious. It feels like a "Wow, hi, nice to meet you, don't get to talk with many awake people," kind of response. If you're fast enough, or practiced enough, you can carry on two conversations at once. One conversation with the personality, one with the unconscious.

Are you talking to a piece of the unitary consciousness, someone else's unconscious, or your own mirror neurons? Most likely, it's all three. These SEs games are with yourself, no matter how loosely you want to frame yourself. Once you get this game up and running there is a test. Change the frame you created just a little. Instead of speaking to the inner self of each individual, start communicating with the single collective being that is each individual. This is the kind of paranoid fantasy, albeit with a positive twist, that sci-fi movies and religions are made of. Treat your private conversation as if one conscious being animates all the people you meet—one running conversation manifested in the SEs of every person in existence. Happy trails. One last note for this game; other people are as real as you are. You may just meet someone talking to your inner self.

GAME FOUR: CO-OCCURRENCE

Let's assume you have had some success at the previous game. You can effectively say "hello" to SE and have them respond. In this game, we are going to dis-embody your imaginary friend. No longer confined to people, your SE companion now uses the entire physical universe as a body. Let's completely mix-up myth and metaphor this time. Some branches of Christianity see the mystical meaning of the Eucharist as Christ's body being the whole world. I'm going to borrow that piece, truly respectfully, for this game. So, your frame is now you are communicating with the most positive force in creation. In Hinduism, the god Krishna incarnates as a series of world saviors. In the *Bhagavad Gita*, Krishna incarnate befriends prince Arjuna. Here, I am borrowing the idea of universal consciousness not as judge, creator, or dictator, but as a true and devoted friend. Your true and beloved friend. Your friend incarnated as the universe. Your friend who frolics in the fields of SEs with you. That appealing frame of reference is the pattern you are going to create.

I was watching an episode of those same two brothers on television again. You remember, writing come to life. They had just drunk a magic potion. Feeling nothing, one asks "So what do we do now? Sync-up *The Wizard of Oz* and *Dark Side of the Moon*?" There's an urban legend that some college students get stoned, put *The Wizard of Oz* on television with the sound off, and play the Pink Floyd album *Dark Side of the Moon* as the movie soundtrack. Supposedly, the two synchronize, become matching sources of SEs. Supposedly, it's hysterically funny. For this game you are going to take two event sources, such as a video and unrelated audio track, and treat them as a single co-occurring, coordinated event. For arguments sake, let's suppose you repeated the urban legend. Your frame of reference is that your dear friend, collective consciousness, is in the room with you, has control over the SEs, and is trying to make you laugh. Why? Because that's what friends do when they get together. They enjoy each other.

Humor is an evolved social response. It signals other people that an unusual situation, especially socially awkward ones, are not a true threat. We learn to laugh at each other and ourselves as a reassurance that things are actually all right.

Let SE make you laugh. You are supposed to be enjoying yourself.

Nobody out here but aspects of yourself. All well and good, you might say. But are SEs really being coordinated between the two sources for my amusement? Or is it another illusion? Much more than an illusion, this SE requires coordination of three sources of events. Your thoughts and emotions become the third stream of events. Your sacred play-pal is reading your thoughts and weaving them into events for your amusement. In this game, the frame of reference gradually expands to include all events in the universe. Gods have cosmic senses of humor. You have friends in high places.

GAME FIVE: CREATION OF A SIMPLE PATTERN

In this game, you stop giving away your control to imaginary forces. The previous games train you to look passively for patterns. In this game, you are going to start creating the pattern of the SEs yourself. This game has a simple, but wide frame of reference. You are going to look for SEs happening in any and every place you turn your attention. There are no "others" in this game. Just you and the effect you have on the SEs around you. First, choose a pattern that is easily recognizable and has some interest for you. You are going to build a thoughtform based on your chosen pattern. Might I suggest a power animal? No, I'm not suggesting you try to align yourself with an animal spirit the way our ancestors did. You create your "animal" from your own thoughts and emotions just by thinking about it for 20 minutes a day. If you like, look up power animals on the internet. You will find lists of the various qualities different cultures have ascribed to animals. Pick one you want to see. There are African, Native American, European, and Eskimo power animals. You are going to build your own pet thoughtform. I have a few basic suggestions. Pick something you are likely to find in your normal event stream. I like to make owls. The symbol is represented in the culture commonly enough, but is not so common that it is commonplace. If you choose a rare animal, there is less chance the pattern will be available to pattern match. Duck-billed platypuses are harder to pattern-match than wolves, horses, or bears.

Your brain stores memories and thinks in associative patterns. Some things remind you of similar things immediately because they share the same storage areas in the brain. Creating patterns of SE always follows your brain function. Aiming at one pattern often produces closely associated SEs, just as one thought often triggers similar ones. If you try to create a pattern of owl SEs, you typically also get series of generalized bird SEs as well. The stronger you make your owl thoughtform, the more specifically "owl" your SEs become. It is possible Jung saw universalized archetypal patterns in SE because we store and process data in such generalized associations. Studying the fish archetype, triggers whole categories in memory of fish-like things. Jung may have been studying the technology of human biological information storage. He may have been the first person systematically exploring genetic neuropsychology. Our ancestors survived to reproduce because we specialized in flexible thinking.

The more mentally flexible you are around your patterns of association, the easier it is to create and read SE. By the way, the more fun you have doing this, the better the results become.

GAME SIX: THE INSIDE JOKE

The secret is, there is no secret.

I struggled to come up with a good introduction for this game. Sometimes when I write I have the feeling there is something I would like to say, but making the thought clear eludes me. SE often provides clarity to murky thoughts. Each of these games helps you avoid different limitations in thinking. There are common traps people who stare into mirrors fall into. One often-exploited pattern is the need to feel we belong to something special, or have some special understanding. I was trying to think of a way to express this without offending anyone, when the following SE appeared:

Synchronistic Event

I was standing at a urinal in the office restroom, not a glamorous start to a story, but, that's where I was. Another doctor who had never spoken to me before was standing at the sink. He started a conversation by commenting that I had lost some weight. Then, went on to explain how I probably really needed a sense of inner fulfillment in my life. Without really cuing into my responses, he followed me into the hallway and continued the conversation.

"I have one word for you," he said with a dramatic pause.

"Plastics?" I thought, remembering the scene from *The Graduate*.

"Yoga," he said, clearly believing me completely ignorant and needing instruction. He started to explain the idea in the simplest language.

"Its more than just body positions, you know." He stated simply enough for even me to understand.

"Dude," I responded. "I know what *to yoke* means. I was reading Pantanjali when I was 16."

He continued undisturbed by my having responded. "There is this great teacher, Yogananda. He wrote this amazing book..."

"Yeah, *Autobiography of a Yogi*. Read it, been to the center in Los Angeles, read all the associated first wave of Hindu-based Guru, devotional Sixth ray type teachers. Been through a lot of the Upanishads, collective works of Vivekananda..." I said, starting to wonder who he was talking to.

He began telling me I should read the book again.
I considered telling him I was writing a book that
actually quoted from Yogananda. I just listened politely. This was clearly a sales pitch. Sure enough,
a few days later, a free copy of some of Yogananda's
writing appeared in my office mailbox. Shortly after
that, I was invited to a retreat.

When I was 19 one of my best friends was indoctrinated and brain-washed by a cult. They took everything he had, eventually burned him out, and left him in debt. Cults are often very astute in knowing how to hook people's need for belonging and being a part of something special. From Freemasonry to Moonies, they all promise the secret keys to creation to true believers. Magical rites, secret meditations passed on from Gurus, tests of devotion, and secret handshakes have been the stock of this trade for thousands of years. Don't pay anyone for such snake oil. All of the information you want on any spiritual secret is openly available, for free, somewhere on the internet. There is no magical energy transmission from special teachers.

There is no better state of grace than the one you have always had. You are the "insider" already.

Rather than take any kind of secret doctrine, sacred knowledge, or mystical achievement seriously, this game creates a frame in which connection to the powers that be becomes an "inside joke." Here are the background assumptions of the frame:

Shakespeare said all the world is a stage, and this is literally true. Reality, every event, no matter how insignificant, or vast in scale, is intentionally created. We are the on-stage actors, incarnated onto the physical stage for this reality show called life. We have become so absorbed in our parts that we have forgotten we are on stage. You have just awakened, here, now, to the awareness that you are on stage. The other actors around you are still proceeding through their lives in their semi-trancelike state. Use your "do not disturb sign." You have awakened in a highly engineered reality, similar to the holodecks of *Star Trek* or the computer-generated realities of *The Matrix*.

This is where the standard conflict-driven science fiction theme ends, because unlike the literary fantasy worlds, the reality you have awakened in is not driven by any dark conspiracy or hidden purpose. This world has been constructed to meet the needs of the actors who inhabit it. There is no innate evolutionary direction, no spiritual goal or moral philosophy, anymore than an ordinary stage has a plot built into the floors and lighting. You are free to act as you please. And, lucky you, you are not alone on stage trying to direct, produce, and star in your production all by yourself. There is a stage crew, people working behind the scenes on the technical matters that keep the play going smoothly. This crew, living and working in the surrounding N- and M-Space dimensions of our world, is hard at work arranging all the events and circumstances of moment-to-moment life. You are like an actor on a flatland stage. Your production crew uses the extra dimensions you can't see to arrange the SEs that give meaning to your production. Now, most of the other actors never come out of character and notice the stage crew. They take matters unfolding in their plays very seriously, and are unaware of the support they receive in arranging the dramas of their reality. You on the other hand, are now conscious, and know the stage crew is there, ready to arrange events for you to help in your chosen plot. Who are these crew members? Just folks like yourself, with a creative bent, good intentions, highly intelligent, and with a wicked sense of humor. They hang out in the control booth of reality waiting to lend a hand. Now that you know they are there, you are "in on the joke," and can converse with them through the SEs they create. They can communicate through events, and through the other actors on stage, who remain consciously unaware of the stage crew.

So here you are, in the present moment, having just dropped the script you were reading your life from, knowing you exist in an artificial reality maintained by a technical crew waiting to hear from you. In this new frame of reference, your first task is to establish communication with the stage crew. Look for SEs that indicate signals from the stage crew welcoming you as an actor now "in on the joke." Look at everything, its all connected and coordinated at deeper levels. Expect SEs to happen, the crew will welcome you and begin the game. One quick way of establishing this rapport is to just listen to a radio and compare what you are thinking to what people on the radio are saying or singing. SE means someone in the control booth is signaling back. Once you are in contact, where you go with the game is up to you.

I have given this game to many people over the years. Inevitably, some come back all excited, telling me how amazing it is that it's all true, the behind-the-scenes crew is talking to them. The crew says they are really what people have meant through the ages by angels, or spirits, guides, gods, technologically advanced multidimensional aliens, part of the evolutionary spiritual hierarchy of the planet, and how wonderful it is to be one of the people who are now "in on it." This arouses my sense of responsibility, and I have to burst the bubble of their enthusiasm by pointing out SEs are responding exactly as they set them up. If they had asked SEs to respond as if the world were being run by retired cartoon characters, they would probably be awed by being in communication with Betty Boop and Steam Boat Willy.

Don't believe what other people think.

GAME SEVEN: TALKING TO GOD

You can't not cast a reflection in a mirror, but you can refuse to believe it's your reflection. This next exercise upsets people. It challenges cherished religious and spiritual beliefs that give comfort and a sense of order and purpose to the world. We are going to set up a synchronistic format in which you are going to talk to God, and God is going to respond directly to you. The uncomfortable implication here is that the billions of people who talk to God through prayer and ritual have in fact been talking to themselves. As I said, this game upsets people.

In this game, we are going to return to some of the assumptions of the "Inside joke" game. You have just become aware that you exist in an engineered reality. All events great and small are created by forces not limited to the dimensions of the physical world. You can communicate with those behind-the-scene movers and shakers through the SEs they arrange around you. In this game though, we are going to assume there is a single directive force creating all of it, and call that force God. God is here, now, at this very moment, in this very place, all around you, within you, all-knowing, all-seeing, all-powerful. The language God speaks is the alteration of events all around you. You have merely to look out into your environment, and expect God will speak directly to you using everything and everyone to carry his word. Seek and ye shall find, ask and ye shall receive.

If you start making faces in the mirror of synchronicity, the reflections you get back can be amusing, repulsive, or fascinating. All bear the image of the face you presented, and the relationship you put into it. In the "Talking to God" game, the face reflected back is the face you make when you pretend to be God in the conversations you have with yourself. Does this mean that God doesn't talk to people through SEs? Does it mean that the billions of people who see God in the events around them are delusional or engaged in a massive self-deception? We use frames unconsciously.

SE show us assumptions operating outside our conscious awareness.

So, let's suppose I am running an SE-based on the "Talking to God" exercise, and am getting a good number of responses from the environment. What is talking to God like? If synchronistic events were truly talking to God, I would expect different people would be getting the same kind of responses to this game, find God giving the same kind of messages and presentation to everyone, which is decidedly not the case. When I engage in this game, my personal SEs give consistent messages that reflect my experiences and philosophical beliefs. If I ask God in this format "Who are you?" SEs respond "I'm you." If I say back "That's obviously not true, I need a better explanation," I start to get a familiar sequence of meanings. SEs state there is a continuum between the singular personal, and the all-inclusive transpersonal. It's all one being, so the distinction isn't that important. If I push the point, I get messages that point out I'm talking to the unconscious. I'm getting back whatever answer I'm most invested in getting back. These meanings come from my understanding and frame. I believe I'm talking to myself. Other people doing this exercise report being firmly convinced they are communicating with God.

Beyond all this unconscious projection, do people talk to God in the guise of SE? I don't know. I have worked with many psychotic clients who either talk to God, or think God has chosen them for some special purpose. Many of them report synchronistic events they take as proof of this special status. Perhaps they are having legitimate spiritual experiences displayed through the SE their thoughts create. I'm trying to keep an open mind, but personally, I don't believe every face I make in the mirror. I can tell you this: real magic is always unifying.

Last Words

Ending a book is hard. There are always loose ends, more that needed to be said, material left out that might have been useful, but didn't quite fit. I hope you have many questions and misgivings about the stories of SE I have been telling you. I have been trying to tell you a story about yourself, as true a story as I can estimate it to be. But, I'm not you, not in the sense that I am aware of your unique vantage point in the universe. I do believe that you have the ability to shape SEs, regardless of what stories you choose to attach to their causes. If you are going to put your SE abilities to good use, what you think about them does matter.

SE behaves in the patterns you expect. More than that, they respond in the pattern of relationship you ask them to.

How you start relating to them often determines the pattern for many years. First impressions are hard to change. This book largely resulted from a personal delusion. Many years ago, an SE turned over and crushed a house at my request, or so it seemed. I had no idea SEs were a mirror at the time. In amazement and exasperation, I asked a loaded question with a hidden frame of reference. "I can't possibly figure this out on my own, please teach me how synchronicity works." SE became a conversation, a relationship with a nameless omnipresent teacher because that's how I asked the question. In the end though, I have come to believe in us, our ability to sort information and act on it as best we can in uncertain situations.

Ending this story has been difficult. I wanted to leave you with a mystery more than an explanation. I wanted you to believe more in yourself and your own abilities than in anything I have to say. There will always be people claiming to represent secret doctrines and spiritual truths. Likewise, scientific theories and fads will come and go. Cold fusion had many scientists excited, until they tried to repeat the experiment. We see what we desire to see. I desired an SE that could give me an ending for this book that would point you to your own thoughts and abilities.

Synchronistic Event

Just as I was going to give up, a few moments ago in my time, my daughter came in to ask a question, again.

"Can you take us to the *Guardians*?"

"You have to be kidding." I said out-loud to myself.

She was asking me to drive her and her brother to the movies again. *Legend of the Guardians*, another 3D animated movie had just been released. I started to explain to her the SEs of typing an ending to a book that was saying there are no "guardians" out there creating SEs, and having her come in and ask to be taken to them. She gave me a patient look.

"Ven, last Sunday I was sitting right here writing when you asked me to take you and George to see *Alpha and Omega*. It created an SE around what I was writing, just like now," I said.

"Dad," she said, "The show is starting soon, you coming?"

Notes

Foreword

1. Allan Combs, *The Radiance of being: Understanding the grand integral vision; Living the integral life*. St. Paul, Minn: Paragon House; 2002.

2. Arthur Koestler, *The Case of the Midwife Toad*. New York: Random House; 1972.

3. Emile Deschamps, *Oeuvres completes : Tomes I–VI*, Reimpr. de l'ed. de Paris 1872–74

4. Carl G. Jung, *Synchronicity: An Acausal Connecting Principle*, 2nd ed. Princeton, N.J.: Princeton University Press, 1973.

5. See, for example, my own work with Mark Holland, *Synchronicity: Through the Eyes of Science, Myth, and the Trickster*. Da Capo Press; 3rd edition; 2000. And David Peat's *Synchronicity, the Bridge Between Matter and Mind*. Bantam Doubleday Dell Publications; 1987.

Bibliography

Abraham, Ben and Kent Robertson. *Extraterrestrial Physics 101: Gravity is the 4th Dimension*. San Francisco: 20th Century Lunar Society Press, 1975.

Assagioli, Roberto, M.D., *Psychosynthesis*. New York: Penguin Books Ltd., 1976.

Baars, Bernard J. *In the Theater of Consciousness*. New York: Oxford University Press, 1997.

Bailey, Alice A., *A Treatise on Cosmic Fire*. New York: Lucis Publishing Co., 1925.

———. *A Treatise on White Magic*. New York: Lucis Publishing Co., 1934.

———. *The Light of the Soul: The Yoga Sutras of Patanjali*. NewYork: Lucis Publishing Co., 1934.

Barnett, Lincoln. *The Universe and Dr. Einstein*. New York: Bantam, 1968.

Beck,Charlotte Joko. *Everyday Zen*. San Francisco: Harper and Row, 1989.

Beloff, John. "Psi Phenomena: Causal Verses Accausal Interpretations." *Journal of the Society for Psychical Research*, 49 (773): 573–82, 1977.

Bendit, Lawrence and Phoebe Bendit. *The Etheric Body of Man: The Bridge of Consciousness*. Wheaton, Ill.: Quest, 1977.

Besant, Annie. *Man and His Bodies*. Wheaton, Ill.: Theosophical Publishing House, 1912.

Blavatsky, H.P. *The Secret Doctrine: Vol 1-5*. Madras, India: Vasanta Press, 1978.

———. *The Theosophical Glossary*. London: The Theosophical Publishing Society, 1892.

Bolen, Jean, M.D. Shinoda. *The Tau of Psychology, Synchronicity and the Self*. San Francisco: Harper and Row. 1979.

Braud, William. "Towards the qualitative assessment of 'Meaningful co-incidences.'" *Parapsychology Review*. 1983.

Chopra, Deepak. *The Spontaneous Fulfillment of Desire: Harnessing the Infinite Power of Coincidence*. New York: Harmony Books, 2003.

Combs, Allen, and Holland,Mark, *Synchronicity, Science, Myth and the Trickster*. New York: Paragon, 1990.

Cox, David. *Modern Psychology: The Teachings of Carl Gustav Jung*. New York: Barnes & Noble, 1968.

DePurucker, G. *Fundamentals of Esoteric Philosophy*. Pasadena, Calif.: Theosophical University Press, 1947.

Dumolilin Hienrich. *Zen Buddhism: A History, India and China*. New York: Macmillan, 1988.

———. *Zen Buddhism: A History, Japan*. New York: Macmillan, 1990.

Einstein, Albert. *Ideas and Opinions*. New York: Crown Publishing, 1954.

Fiedd, Rebecca. "The Return of the Goddess: The Return of the Female Principle in Theosophic Thought and Transpersonal Psychology." *Dissertation Abstracts International*: 42(9): 3911-A, 1982.

Freud, Sigmund. *An Outline of Psycho-Analysis*. New York: W. W. Norton & Co., Inc. 1949.

————. *On Dreams*. New York: W. W. Norton & Co., Inc. 1952.

Frick, Willard, B. "The Symbolic Growth Experience." *Journal of Humanistic Psychology*: Vol. 23(1) 108–125, 1983.

Garfield, David A. "The use of primary process in psychotherapy: II. Transformational categories and the precipitating event." *Worcester Psychotherapy*, Vol 23(4): 548-555, 1986.

Gatlin, Lila. "L. Meaningful Information Creation: An Alternative Interpretation of the PSI Phenomena." *Journal of the Society for Psychical Research*, 71(1):1–18,1977.

Grattan-Guinness, I. "What Are Coincidences?" *Journal of the Society for Psychical Research*, 49 (778): 949-955, 1978.

Greenberg & Mitchell. *Object Relations in Psychoanalytic Theory*. Boston: Harvard University Press, 1983.

Henschin, Thomas. "Causality, synchronicity, and biofeedback." *American Journal of Biofeedback*, Vol 6(2): 103–110, 1983.

Holder, Robert J. "Synchronicity: a key aspect of opportunity discovery." *Organization Development Journal*, Vol 6(4): 53–57, 1988.

Hopcke, Robert H. "Synchronicity in analysis: various types and their various roles for patient and analyst." *Quadrant*, Vol 21(1): 55-64, 1988.

Iyengar, B.K.S. *Light on Pranayama*. New York: Crossroad, 1981.

Jacobi, Jolande. *The Psychology of C.G. Jung*. London: Yale University Press, 1942.

Jung, C.G. *Analytical Psychology: Its Theory & Practice*. New York: Vintage, 1968.

————. "On synchronicity." *Collective works of C.G.Jung*, Vol 8, p. 520–531. 1972.

————. *Psyche & Symbol*. New York: Doubleday Anchor, 1958.

————. *Psychology and the Occult*. New Jersey: Princeton University Press, 1977.

————. "The structure and dynamics of the psyche. Letters on synchronicity: to Michael Fordham." *Collective Works of C.G.Jung*, Vol 18, p. 508-509. 1976.

————. "The structure and dynamics of the psyche. Letters on synchronicity: To Markus Fierz." *Collective Works of C.G.Jung*, Vol 18, p. 502-507. 1976.

————. *Synchronicity*. New Jersey: Princeton University Press, 1973.

————. "Synchronicity: An accausal connecting principal.1. Exposition." *Collective works of C.G.Jung*, Vol 8, p. 421-458. 1972.

————. "Synchronicity: An accausal connecting principal.3. Forerunners of the idea of synchronicity." *Collective works of C.G.Jung*, Vol 8, p. 485-504. 1972.

————. "Synchronicity: An accausal connecting principal. Part 4. Conclusion." *Collective works of C.G.Jung*, Vol 8, p. 505-519. 1972.

Jung C. G. and Roderick Main. *Jung on Synchronicity and the Paranormal*. New Jersey: Princeton University Press: 1998.

Jung, Sinling. "Psychotherapeutic implications of consulting the Yi Jing (I Ching): A phenomenological approach." *Dissertation abstracts international*, Vol.46/08-b, pg.2812, 1985.

Kaha, C.W. "The creative mind: Form and process." *Journal of Creative Behavior*, Vol 17(2): 84-94, 1983.

Kapleau,Philip. *The Three Pillars of Zen*. New York: Harper and Row, 1966.

Keen, Sam. *Your Mythic Journey*. Los Angeles: Jeremy P. Tarcher Inc., 1973.

Keutzer,Carolin S. "Archetypes, synchronicity and the theory of formative causation." *Journal of Analytical Psychology*, Vol 27(3) 255-262, 1982.

————. "The Power of Meaning: From Quantum Mechanics to Synchronicity." *Journal of Humanistic Psychology*, Vol 24:1 80-94, 1984.

————. "Synchronicity in psychotherapy." *Journal of Analytical Psychology*, Vol 29(4): 373-381, 1984.

Kilner, Waiter J. *The Human Aura*. New Jersey: Citadel, 1980.

Kul, Djwal. *Intermediate Studies of the Human Aura*. Los Angeles: Summit University Press, 1980.

Langiulli, Nino. *The Existentialist Tradition*. New Jersey: Grove, 1971.

Larsen, Stephen. *The Mythic Imagination*. New York: Bantam, 1990.

————. *The Shaman's Doorway*. New York: Harper, 1976.

Ledoux, Joseph. *The emotional brain: the mysterious underpinnings of emotional life*. New York: Simon & Schuster, 1998.

————. *Synaptic Self: How Our Brains Become Who We Are*. New York: Penguin, 2003.

Luria, Aleksander R. *The Working Brain: An Introduction to Neuropsychology*. New York: Penguin, 1973.

Marshall, Ronald Clemens. "A journey through non-causal dimensions: A Heuristic study of synchronicity." *Dissertation Abstracts International*, Vol.48/07-b, pg. 2125, 1987.

Meyer, Martin Barry. "Role of personality and cognitive variables in the reporting of experienced meaningful coincidences or 'synchronicity.'" *Dissertation Abstracts International*, Vol.50/04-b, pg.1678, 1988.

Mindell, Arnold. "An investigation of the unitary background patterning synchronous phenomena (A psychoid approach to the unconscious)." Dissertation Abstracts International, Vol.37/02-b, pg.957, 1972.

————. "The Golem: an image governing synchronicity." *Quadrant*, 8(2):107-114, 1975.

Mlodinow, Leonard. *The Drunkard's Walk: How Randomness Rules OurLives*. New York: Vintage, 2009.

Monroe, Robert. *Journeys Out of the Body*. New York: Anchor Press, 1971.

Muldoon, Syvan & Carrington. Hereward: *The Phenomena of Astral Projection*. New York: Weiser, 1974.

Peat, David F., *Synchronicity: The Bridge Between Mind and Matter*. New York: Bantam, 1987.

Perkins, James. *A Geometry of Space-Consciousness*. Adyar, India: Theosophical Publishing House, 1978.

Pinker, Steven. *How the Mind Works*. New York: W. W. Norton & Company; 2009.

Plummer, Gordon. *The Mathematics of the Cosmic Mind.* Wheaton, Ill.: The Theosophical Publishing House, 1970.

Powell, A.E. *The Astral Body.* Wheaton, Ill: Quest, 1978)

———. *The Causal Body and the Ego.* London: Theosophical Publishing House, 1967.

———. *The Etheric Double.* Wheaton, Ill.: Quest, 1979.

———. *The Mental Body.* London: Theosophical Publishing House, 1967.

Progroff, Ira. *Jung Synchronicity and Human Destiny.* New York: Julian, 1973.

Rhine, Louisa. *Mind Over Matter.* New York: Collier, 1972.

Reich, Wilhelm. *The Function of the Orgasm.* New York: Pocket, 1975.

Roehlke, Helen J. "Critical incidents in counselor development: Examples of Jung's concept of synchronicity." *Journal of Counseling and Development,* Vol 67(2): 133-134, 1988.

Rosengarten, Arthur E. "Assessing the unconscious: A comparative study of dreams, the TAT, and Tarot." *Dissertation Abstracts International,* Vol.46/08-b, pg. 2822, 1985.

Rucker, Rudy. Infinity and the Mind. New York: Bantam, 1982.

Schacter, Daniel L, Searching for Memory. New York: Basic Books, 1996.

Sannella, Lee. *Kundalini-Psychosis or Transcendence?* San Francisco: H.S. Dakin, 1981.

Schwartz, Berthold E. "Synchronicity and telepathy." *Psychoanalitic Review,* 56(1): 44-56, 1969.

Schwarz, Jack. *Human Energy Systems.* New York: E.P. Dutton, 1980.

Sekida, Katsuki. *Zen Training.* New York: Weatherhill, 1975.

Stein, Murray. *Jungian Analysis.* Boston: Shambhala, 1984.

Stern, Mark, E. "A case of possible PSI phenomena in psychotherapy: intrusion and/or synchronicity and/or convergence." *Voices,* 8(2): 51-53, 1975.

Suzuki,D,T. *Essays in Zen Buddhism.* New York: Grove, 1949.

Tworkov, Helen. *Zen in America.* San Francisco: North Point, 1989.

Van Nuys, David Whitman. "An Experience of Precognition, A String of Skulls." *Voices* 13(3): 57-61, 1977.

Vaughan, Alan. *Incredible Coincidence*. New York: Signet, 1979.

Vaughan, Allen. "Part 3: The synchronicity of synchronicity." *Psychic*, 6(4): 56-61, 1975.

Vaughan, Allen. "Synchronicity: curious coincidences or cosmic causes?" *Psychic Magazine*, 6(2):56-61, 1975.

Von Franz, Marie-Louise. *On Divination and Synchronicity*. Toronto: Inner City Books, 1980.

Watts, Allen. *The Way of Zen*. New York: Vintage, 1989.

Weinberg, Steven. *The First Three Minutes*. New York: Bantam, 1977.

Wharton, Barbara. "Deintegration and two synchronistic events." *Journal of Analytical Psychology*, Vol 31(3): 281-285, 1986.

Whitmont, Edward. *The Symbolic Quest*. New Jersey: Princeton University Press, 1969.

Wilber, Ken. *The Atman Project*. Wheaton, Ill.: The Theosophical Publishing House, 1982.

Yogananda, Paramahansa. *Autobiography of a Yogi*. Los Angeles: Self-Realization Fellowship, 1987.

Index

F

faith, margin of error and, 62-63
feedback, psychological, 44-45
fiction, explanatory, 117-118
Fischer, Bobby, 241-243
fish archetype, 36-37
Flatlanders, 120-125
Flying Spaghetti Monster, the, 151-153
fMRI, 103
forces, supernatural, 95-96
forms, other, 133-134

G

Galileo, 61-62
God, talking to, 260-262

H

hallucinations, 137-139
historical references, 225-226

I

I Ching, 33-36
illusion, inter-personal, 192
illusions and anomalies, 221-237
illusions, creating your own, 235-237
inducing satori, 104-107
inter-personal illusion, 192
interpretation, accidents of, 21
irrational beliefs, 53-57

J

Jung, Carl, 26-27, 30-35
    contradiction of theory, 38
    coincidence and, 248
    delusional thinking and, 183

K

Key of Solomon, The, 53-57

L

limitations, practical, 155-156
logic, utilitarian, 91

M

magic, 16, 53-57
    practical, 239-262
Matrix, The Real, 29-30
Matrix, The, 259
meaning vs. causation, 23
meaning, experience of, 63-66
meditation, 211-217
memory, 212
    using your, 217-219
mental body, 139-141
mid-brain emotional system, 212
minds, time-based physical, 246-247
mirror,
    recognizing yourself in the, 77-78
    synchronicity as a, 45-50
misinterpretation, pattern, 72

About the Author

Yes, Surprise is his real given name. Dr. Surprise received his Doctorate in Counseling Psychology in 2007 from the Institute for Integral Studies in San Francisco and his Masters in advanced psychodynamic and transpersonal studies from John F. Kennedy University. He worked for 14 years as a social worker in impoverished areas before returning to graduate school. He did his pre and post doctoral studies in the psychodynamic treatment of children and families. Dr. Surprise received his license as a psychologist in 2009, and currently works in an advanced outpatient program for the state of California. The inspiration for his writing comes from a lifelong interest in psychology, metaphysics, philosophy, history, science, and his work with his clients. His interest in Synchronicity stemmed from experiencing frequent and surprising SE, and needing a working understanding of the phenomena. He has lectured and given workshops on synchronicity, and currently runs weekly psycho-educational groups for the state of California.

He grew up in Bethpage, New York, with his parents Gladys and Alfred, and his older brother Tom. Dr. Surprise met his wife Patricia while in college in New York. They have been married for 29 years and have two children, Vencenza and George.